GLADSTONE

Gladstone is one of the most important political figures in modern British history. He held the office of prime minister four times over, at a turbulent and changing time in Britain's history, during which he and his great rival, Disraeli, dominated the political world.

Michael Partridge provides a new assessment of Gladstone's life and career, placing him firmly in the context of nineteenth-century Britain, and covering both his intriguing private life and his public career. Surveying a broad range of source material, Partridge begins by looking at Gladstone's early life, education and entry into Parliament, before looking at his marriage, and his service with Peel. He then goes on to consider in detail Gladstone's terms as prime minister, concluding with his fourth ministry, when, by now in his eighties, he returned to power. For the last time Gladstone tried and failed to resolve the problems of Ireland, which had become his great obsession, and eventually retired from politics in 1894. He died four years later.

This biography provides a deep and thorough study of Gladstone's life and his political significance, and is an ideal starting point for all those interested in one of the most prominent and complex characters of Victorian Britain.

Michael Partridge is Reader in History at St Mary's College, Strawberry Hill, London and researches largely in nineteenth-century Britain. His publications include *The Duke of Wellington: A Bibliography* (1990), and *Lord Palmerston: A Bibliography* (1994) with K.E. Partridge.

ROUTLEDGE HISTORICAL BIOGRAPHIES

Series Editor: Robert Pearce

Routledge Historical Biographies provide engaging, readable and academically credible biographies written from an explicitly historical perspective. These concise and accessible accounts will bring important historical figures to life for students and general readers alike.

In the same series:

Bismarck by Edgar Feuchtwanger
Churchill by Robert Pearce
Gandhi by Crispin Bates
Gladstone by Michael Partridge
Henry VII by Sean Cunningham
Hitler by Martyn Housden
Jinnah by Sikander Hayat
Martin Luther King Jr. by Peter J. Ling
Lenin by Christopher Read
Martin Luther by Michael Mullet
Mao by Michael Lynch
Mary Queen of Scots by Reitha Warnicke
Mussolini by Peter Neville
Nehru by Ben Zachariah
Emmeline Pankhurst by Paula Bartley
Franklin D.Roosevelt by Stuart Kidd
Stalin by Geoffrey Roberts
Trotsky by Ian Thatcher

GLADSTONE

Michael Partridge

LONDON AND NEW YORK

First published 2003
by Routledge
11 New Fetter Lane, London EC4P 4EE

Simultaneously published in the USA and Canada
by Routledge
29 West 35th Street, New York, NY 10001

Routledge is an imprint of the Taylor & Francis Group

Typeset in Garamond and Scala Sans by Taylor & Francis Ltd
Printed and bound in Great Britain by TJ International Ltd, Padstow, Cornwall

British Library Cataloguing in Publication Data
A catalogue record for this book is available from the British Library

Library of Congress Cataloging in Publication Data
Partridge, Michael Stephen.
Gladstone / Michael Partridge.
Includes bibliographical references and index.
(alk. Paper)
1. Gladstone, W. E. (William Ewart), 1809–1898. 2. Great Britain—Politics and government—1837–1901. 3. Prime ministers—Great Britain—Biography. I. Title.

DA563.4 .P29 2002
941.081'092—dc21

2002015223

ISBN 0–415–21626–5 (hbk)
ISBN 0–415–21627–3 (pbk)

Contents

Plates

Preface

This book is by no means the first to be written about William Gladstone. Its intention is to provide readers with a clear text which will serve as a survey of the life and career of one of Britain's best-remembered political figures, placing him in the context of developments in nineteenth-century Britain.

Many scholars have studied Gladstone. Some of those whose work have been particularly relied on are acknowledged in the Bibliography, but others have also contributed their share and I would like to thank them all. I should also like to express my gratitude to my colleagues and students, past and present, in the History Programme at St Mary's College, Strawberry Hill, and particularly to Dr Mark Donnelly. They have no doubt heard enough of the Grand Old Man for the time being. The Series editor, Dr Bob Pearce, has been a most valuable and friendly critic and commentator. The supervisor of my doctoral research, the late Professor Kenneth Bourne, has inspired much of my work. Finally, I would like to thank my wife, Karen, who has typed this manuscript, made many helpful suggestions for improvements and amendments and, in short, done as she always does: made the book possible.

Chronology

Date	*Personal events*	*Political events*	*National/ International events*
1809 29 December	Birth in Liverpool		
1829 19 February	Death of sister Anne		
1832 June			Passage of the first Parliamentary Reform Act (Great Reform Act)
1832 13 December		Election for Newark	
1833 3 June		Speech against abolition of slavery	
1834 26 December		Appointment as junior Lord of the Treasury in Peel's first ministry, necessitating re-election	
1835 3 January		Returned unopposed for Newark	
1835 27 January		Appointment as Under-Secretary for War and Colonies	
1835 April		Out of office on fall of Peel's government	
1835 23 September	Death of mother, Anne Gladstone		
1837 24 April		Return unopposed for Newark	

Date	*Personal events*	*Political events*	*National/ International events*
1838 August	Visit to Italy; meeting and proposal to Catherine Glynne		
1838 December	Publication of *The State in its Relations with the Church*		
1839 6 May			First Chartist petition presented to Parliament
1839 25 July	Marriage at Hawarden		
1840 3 June	Birth of eldest son, William Henry (Willy)		
1841 29 July		Re-election for Newark	
1841 3 September		Appointment as Vice-President of Board of Trade in Peel's second ministry	
1841 14 September		Re-election for Newark	
1842 18 October	Birth of eldest daughter, Agnes		
1843 15 May		Promotion to Presidency of Board of Trade, with a seat in the cabinet	

Date	*Personal events*	*Political events*	*National/ International events*
1844 4 April	Birth of son, Stephen Edward		
1845 28 January		Resignation from cabinet	
1845 27 July	Birth of daughter, Catherine Jessy		
1845 23 December		Return to office as Colonial Secretary, retirement from Newark East	
1846 25 June		Fall of Peel's government following Corn Law Repeal	
1847 3 August		Election for one of two seats at Oxford University	
1847 November	Birth of daughter, Mary		
1849 28 August	Birth of daughter, Helen		
1850 9 April	Death of daughter, Catherine Jessy		
1850 27 June		Attack on Palmerston in Dom Pacifico debate	
1851 7 December	Death of Sir John Gladstone		
1852 20 February		Defeat of Lord John Russell's Whig ministry; succession of Lord Derby	
1852 2 April	Birth of son, Henry Neville		

Date	*Personal events*	*Political events*	*National/ International events*
1852 14 July		Re-election for Oxford University	
1852 2 December			Louis Napoleon Bonaparte becomes Emperor Napoleon III
1852 16–17 December		Attack on Disraeli's budget; resignation of Derby ministry; formation of Aberdeen coalition ministry; appointed Chancellor of the Exchequer	
1853 20 January		Re-election for Oxford University	
1853 18 April		Introduction of first budget	
1854 7 January	Birth of son, Herbert John		
1854 31 March			Anglo-French declaration of war on Russia
1855 3 February		Fall of Aberdeen government; succession of Lord Palmerston	
1855 22 February		Resignation of Gladstone, Herbert and Graham from Palmerston ministry	
1856 30 March			Treaty of Paris; end of Crimean War
1857 27 March		Returned unopposed for Oxford University	

Date	*Personal events*	*Political events*	*National/ International events*
1858 19 February		Opposes Conspiracy to Murder Bill, helps defeat Palmerston's government; succession of Lord Derby	
1858 12 November		Leaves Britain as High Commissioner Extraordinary to the Ionian Islands for Derby's government	
1859 12 February		Returned unopposed for Oxford University	
1859 12 March	Returns to London		
1859 26 April			French declaration of war on Austria
1859 6 June		Willis's Rooms meeting; formation of the 'Liberal Party'	
1859 20 June		Joins Palmerston's government as Chancellor of the Exchequer	
1860 9 March		Defends Cobden Free Trade Treaty with France	
1860 July		Passage of the Fortifications Loans Act	
1861 April			Start of American Civil War
1862 7 October		Newcastle speech supporting Confederacy in the American Civil War	
1864 11 May		Speech asserting more popular right to vote	
1864 May	First contact with Laura Thistlethwayte		

Date	*Personal events*	*Political events*	*National/ International events*
1865 May			End of American Civil War
1865 22 July		Election for South Lancashire	
1865 October		Death of Palmerston; succession of Russell as prime minister	
1866 March		Attempted passage of Reform Bill begins	
1866 26 June		Resignation of Russell ministry; succession of Lord Derby	
1867 March–July		Passage of Second Reform Act	
1868 23 March		Gives notice of three Resolutions for the disestablishment of the Church of Ireland	
1868 17 November		Election for Greenwich	
1868 9 December		Becomes Prime Minister	
1868 23 December		Returned unopposed for Greenwich	
1869 1 March		Introduction of Bill for the disestablishment of the Church of Ireland	
1869 22 July		Disestablishment Bill finally passed, with amendments	
1870 February–May		Passage of Irish Land Act	
1870 June		Passage of Forster's Education Act	

Date	*Personal events*	*Political events*	*National/ International events*
1870 June		Passage of Forster's Education Act	
1870 19 July			French declaration of war on Prussia
1871 1 January			Creation of German Reich
1871 10 May			Treaty of Frankfurt; cession of Alsace-Lorraine by France to Germany
1871 20 July		Issue of Royal Warrant abolishing the purchase of army commissions, following failure of Bill	
1871 23 October		Speech at Blackheath on the policy of the government	
1872 18 July		Passage of the Parliamentary and Municipal Bill, adopting the secret ballot	
1873 February		Introduction of Irish Universities Bill	
1873 12 March		Defeat of government, resignation next day; Disraeli's refusal to take office	
1873 16 March		Return to office	
1873 9 August		Succeeds Robert Lowe as chancellor of the Exchequer	
1874 January		Dissolution of Parliament	

Date	Personal events	Political events	National/ International events
1874 4 February		Re-election for Greenwich, Liberals defeated overall; resignation as prime minister, succession of Disraeli	
1875 September	Death of brother, Robertson		
1875 December		Drafts letter formally resigning Liberal Party leadership (announced publicly, 13 January 1879)	
1876 6 September		Publishes *Bulgarian Horrors and the question of the East*	
1878 June–July			Congress of Berlin
1878 December– 1880 January			Wars in Afghanistan
1879 January		Acceptance of nomination for Midlothian	Defeat of British forces in Zululand
1879 25November– 8 December		First Midlothian campaign	
1880 16 January	Death of sister, Helen Gladstone		
1880 8 March		Beaconsfield dissolves Parliament	
1880 5 April		Election for Midlothian	
1880 2 April		Becomes Prime Minister and Chancellor of the Exchequer	

Date	*Personal events*	*Political events*	*National/ International events*
1880 8 May		Returned unopposed for Midlothian	
1880 December			Boers in South Africa begin attack on British forces
1881 23 February	Injured in fall in Downing Street		
1881 27 February			British forces defeated at Majuba Hill
1881 April–August		Passage of Land Law (Ireland) Bill, granting 'Three Fs' (fair rent, free sale, fixity of tenure)	
1881 3 August			Convention of Pretoria agreed with Boers
1882 6 May		Phoenix Park murders; death of Lord Frederick Cavendish	
1882 7 May		'Kilmainham Treaty'; Parnell released	
1882 May–August		Passage of Arrears of Rent (Ireland) Bill and Prevention of Crimes (Ireland) Bill	
1882 11 July		Bombardment of Alexandria by British fleet	
1882 September		Occupation of Egypt by British troops	
1882 December		Resignation of Chancellorship to Childers	

Date	*Personal events*	*Political events*	*National/ International events*
1884 18 January		Despatch of General Charles Gordon to oversee withdrawal from Sudan	
1884 March		Introduction of Land Law (Ireland) Bill	
1884 8 July		Rejection by Lords of Representation of the People Bill	
1884 24 October		Reintroduction of Representation of the People Bill	
1884 November		Liberal–Tory talks on franchise and redistribution of Parliamentary seats; agreement to discuss separately	Opening of Berlin West Africa Conference (to March 1885)
1884 5 December		Approval by Commons of franchise reform	
1884 10 December		Approval by Lords of franchise reform	
1885 23 January		Fall of Khartoum; death of Gordon	
1885 5 February		News of Gordon's death received in London	
1885 27 February		Ministry survives vote of confidence	
1885 April		Pendjeh crisis over Afghanistan with Russia	
1885 9 June		Defeat of government on Budget; resignation and replacement by Marquess of Salisbury's Conservatives	
1885 25 June		Approval of Redistribution Bill	

Date	*Personal events*	*Political events*	*National/ International events*
1885 27 November		Re-election for Midlothian	
1885 17 December		Herbert flies the 'Hawarden Kite'	
1886 3 February		Becomes Prime Minister and Lord Privy Seal	
1886 8 April		First reading of the Irish Home Rule Bill	
1886 June		Defeat of the Home Rule Bill in the Commons; split in the Liberal Party; resignation of the government	
1886 2 July		Returned unopposed for Midlothian	
1889 2 March	Willy Gladstone suffers stroke		
1889 March	Death of brother, Sir Thomas Gladstone		
1889 26 August	Celebration of Golden Wedding		
1890 March			Bismarck dismissed by Kaiser Wilhelm II
1891 4 July	Death of Willy Gladstone		
1891 October		Adoption of the 'Newcastle Programme' by the Liberal Party conference	

Date	*Personal events*	*Political events*	*National/ International events*
1892 13 July		Re-election for Midlothian	
1892 15 August		Becomes Prime Minister and Lord Privy Seal	
1892 September		Crisis over possible withdrawal from Uganda	
1893 January			Formation of the Independent Labour Party
1893 13 February		Passage of second Government of Ireland Bill by the Commons	
1893 8 September		Rejection of Government of Ireland by the Lords	
1893 November		Start of the 'Navy scare'	
1894 January–February	In Biarritz, discussing future		
1894 3 March		Final cabinet and resignation as prime minister; succession of Lord Rosebery	
1894 24 May	Cataract operation on right eye		
1894 30 May	Death of Laura Thistlethwayte		
1894 19 June		Uganda declared a British protectorate	
1895 21 June		Defeat of Rosebery's government	
1896 26 September		Speech on Armenian question	

Date	*Personal events*	*Political events*	*National/ International events*
1897 November and 1898 February	Visits France		
1898 22 March	Return to Hawarden		
1898 19 May	Death at Hawarden		
1898 26–27 May	Lies in State at Westminster Hall		
1898 28 May	Burial in Westminster Abbey		
1900	Death of Catherine Gladstone; burial in Westminster Abbey		

INTRODUCTION

William Ewart Gladstone was one of the longest-serving members of the British House of Commons, having sat as an MP for over sixty years. He first took his seat, for Newark, in December 1832 and, having represented five different constituencies, he last attended the House on 1 March 1894. He retired from it in July 1895 at the time of the next General Election. He began his career as a backbencher in Sir Robert Peel's 'Conservative' Party and he ended it as the personification of Victorian Liberalism. During this time he participated in nearly all of the major political crises of nineteenth-century Britain, and always aimed to support what he believed to be the cause of right. He remained throughout a devout and practising Christian and he struggled to carry this belief into his politics.

Gladstone was certainly a larger-than-life character to his contemporaries, some of whom admired him and some of whom did not: 'he is a dangerous man: keep him in Oxford, and he is practically muzzled: but send him elsewhere, and he will run wild.'[1] These words about Gladstone were spoken in 1864, by one of the leading Liberal politicians of the nineteenth century, Henry, Lord Palmerston. From them it is possible to conclude that not all Liberals had a particular love for Gladstone. Some of his outright political opponents, of course, went even further, among them Gathorne Hardy, Viscount Cranbrook, who was Conservative Home Secretary in 1868 and Secretary of State for War (1874) and India (1878–80). According to Hardy, Gladstone

> Has left a history which no right thinker could consistently follow, that his fullest statements are uniformly obscure, if not studiedly so; that his weapon has been the axe, with which he has felled stately trees which can never be replaced, and that he has laid down principles upon which no righteous treatment of man could be founded.[2]

This was at least written after Gladstone's death, and for private consumption, but needless to say Gathorne Hardy was not Gladstone's only Conservative opponent. Another was Richard Assheton Cross, who was Home Secretary from 1874 to 1880 and from 1885 to 1886. He told the House of Commons in 1886 that 'the Right Honourable gentleman has a power which I envy greatly, that of persuading others: but he also has a power which, I thank God, I never had, that of persuading himself.'[3] The charge of hypocrisy was one which Gladstone frequently faced, as will become apparent, and it is not difficult to see why.

The most well-known of his Conservative enemies, in part because he was to Gladstone the most flamboyant and vexatious one, was Benjamin Disraeli, Earl of Beaconsfield, the party leader from 1868 until his death in 1881. It was Disraeli, as much as anything or anyone, who stood between Gladstone and his rejoining the 'Conservatives' in the 1850s. In response to Gladstone's celebrated pamphlet and speeches attacking the Turks for their massacres of Bulgarians in 1875, he denounced Gladstone to the electors of Aylesbury. His activities, declared Disraeli, were 'worse than any of those Bulgarian atrocities which now occupy attention'.[4] He informed his Foreign Secretary, the Earl of Derby in October 1876 that 'Posterity will do justice to that unprincipled maniac, Gladstone – extraordinary mixture of envy, vindictiveness, hypocrisy, and superstition, and with one commanding characteristic – whether preaching, praying, speechifying, or scribbling – never a gentleman.[5] It is easy to understand, then, why these two men, despite occasional moments of personal reconciliation, such as that following the death of Disraeli's wife in 1873, should have been both mortal political enemies, and, unusually for Gladstone, personal ones as well.

Queen Victoria, who as Head of State should have remained politically neutral, found it more and more difficult as time went by to get on with Gladstone. When he took office for the last time in 1892, she wrote to the Conservative Marquess of Lansdowne that 'the danger to her country, to Europe, to her vast empire, which is involved in having all these interests entrusted to the shaking hand of an old, wild, and incomprehensible man of 82, is very great!'[6] She thought he addressed her as if she was a public meeting, and found it harder and harder to understand his motives.

The Queen's political sympathies were generally Conservative, however, and her disillusionment with Gladstone, which began to become apparent after the death of her husband, Prince Albert, in 1863, was therefore not surprising. The reservations of some of those who formed the coalition making up the mid-Victorian Liberal Party are, perhaps, rather more unexpected. Palmerston was not the only Liberal with his doubts about him. One outsider, the Marquess of Salisbury, who was later to become Conservative Party leader, observed about one group of them in 1867, 'it is doubtful if the Whigs will back up Gladstone … the policy is very perilous, but their hatred of Gladstone almost exceeds, if that be possible, their hatred of Dizzy'.[7]

One more Liberal individual, William Vernon Harcourt, who later became a firm supporter of Gladstone, perhaps because he hoped to succeed him as Liberal leader, had grave uncertainties about him in the 1870s. He told one of his allies 'Gladstone's will-o'-the wisp genius has been fatal to a party to which he has never really belonged and whose principles he does not now understand',[8] and he explained to another

> If Gladstone will stick to the principles of Liberal Party I am ready to act with him under him. But I will not undertake to support any wild proposal which his flighty nature may at any time think fit to go in for![9]

These doubts did not prevent him acting as Gladstone's Home Secretary in 1880–5 and Chancellor of the Exchequer in 1886 and 1892–5. Sir Charles Dilke, a more radical figure than Harcourt, also had reservations, though for different reasons. Unlike Harcourt, he did not think Gladstone was a spent force in the 1870s, and at the end of the decade noted in his diary: 'Gladstone still a great power, and but for his Scotch deference to the aristocracy, which is a sad drawback, I could admire him with little check.'[10] Dilke nevertheless found it possible to work with Gladstone, joining his second government in 1880 as Under-Secretary of State at the Foreign Office. But for an unfortunate personal scandal, he might well have succeeded the 'Grand Old Man' as Liberal leader.

If Gladstone had both enemies and lukewarm friends, however, he also had plenty of allies who were outspoken in their admiration and respect for him. Earl Granville, three times Gladstone's Foreign Secretary and one of his closest friends, told readers of the less-than-Liberal *Pall Mall Gazette*

> I have served under several Prime Ministers, men for whom I had high respect and to whom I had the greatest attachment, but I can say that I never knew one who showed a finer temper, a greater patience, or more consideration for his colleagues than Mr. Gladstone in all deliberations on any important subject.[11]

John Morley, later author of the official biography of Gladstone, felt equally certain of his greatness. He was, he thought, 'a titanic figure subduing the tumultuous elements of life by force of character'.[12]

While some political journals had their doubts about Gladstone, others did not. The *Spectator* in October 1864 explained to its readers that he was the man of the future:

> All his speeches point to the inauguration of a new activity in all internal affairs, to a steady determination to improve, if possible, both the constitution and the condition of the millions who have to live under it. Most ministers have that idea in their heads, but Mr. Gladstone has more than the idea, he has plans, and the courage to propose and maintain them. He ... does not hesitate to apply the full power of the state to ameliorate social anomalies ... He of all men alive could most easily reduce our anarchical system into something like order; he, perhaps, alone among statesmen would have the art and the energy to try as a deliberate plan to effect the final conciliation of Ireland.[13]

At much the same time as this editorial was published, Gladstone received a letter from one unnamed individual who wanted to tell him what he, and he believed, countless others, felt for him, namely,

> sentiments of warm aspiration, deep sympathy, fervent hopes, longing expectation of lasting national blessing from your certain elevation to high responsibility ... In the moral power you wield, go on to

> elevate and purify public life, and we shall all bless you, dear sir, as a regenerator of England. Keep the hearts of the people. *They* will never envy you and never forsake you.[14]

Gladstone was a political figure of almost unequalled importance in Victorian Britain, and he generated feelings of hatred and adulation on a grand scale. The underlying question to be determined is why this was so, to find out what it was that he did that made him have this effect on so many of his contemporaries. How was it that this one man, born into a middle-class family in a provincial town, became such a towering figure in Britain, and a source of inspiration and at the same time loathing for many in the British Isles and beyond?

GLADSTONE AND THE HISTORIANS

A political career the length and importance of Gladstone's has attracted no lack of attention from later writers. The most significant early biography of Gladstone, though not the first, was that produced in three large volumes in 1904 by John Morley. Morley was given access to Gladstone's papers by his family, but was also set a specific task by them: he was to write a biography of the Liberal statesman, but he was not (mainly because he himself was an atheist) to deal with his religious beliefs or make too much mention of his family (the births of his daughters are not mentioned in the book, though his sons at least receive a mention in the chronology). Morley, however, gave it as his opinion that

> Not for two centuries ... had our island produced a ruler in whom the religious motive was paramount in the like degree. He was not only a political force but a moral force ... Nevertheless his mission in all its forms was action ... The track in which he moved, the instruments that he employed, were the track and the instruments, the sword and the trowel, of political action; and what is called the Gladstonian era was distinctively a political era.[15]

The result of Morley's labours is a detailed political life of the great man, quoting freely from his papers and creating a largely secular image of Gladstone as a committed Liberal reformer that later writers have found difficult to challenge. There is really no room in Morley's work for much comment on Gladstone's personal life, even if he had wished to include it. D.C. Lathbury's two volumes on Gladstone's religion, once again commissioned by the family and published in 1910, have had much less of an impact than Morley's magisterial work.

Works about Gladstone himself were somewhat few and far between during the years to 1945, though he continued to figure in most books to appear on Victorian Britain. An interesting contribution was that by his son, Herbert Gladstone. Published in 1928, *After Thirty Years* acted as a strident defence of his father's reputation at a time when 'Victorian values' were coming under increasing pressure, and many 'great' Victorians were being strongly attacked.

One of the first significant biographies of Gladstone was that published in 1954 by Philip Magnus. Much of its importance derives from the fact that, unlike most of the earlier biographers, Magnus was given full access to all of Gladstone's papers, not merely the 200,000 or so letters at the British Library, but also the 50,000 'personal and intimate papers' at Hawarden Castle. Magnus believed in Gladstone as the 'Great Liberal', the head of a Liberal Party which 'owed its unity and enthusiasm almost entirely to him'. He felt Gladstone's political life had three phases: the first being when he 'graduated' from theology to financial management, helped by Peel. The second phase was his fight against 'tyranny and oppression', of which 'the crowning moment was the Midlothian campaign of 1879. Gladstone's efforts in that cause made him the foremost statesman in Great Britain and a moral force in Europe.' The third phase ended with the failure to secure Irish Home Rule in 1886 and 1893. The failures, declared Magnus, 'were due in part to temperamental defects in Gladstone himself, in part to accident, but mainly to the fact that Gladstone's principal opponents and colleagues were more worldly, and ultimately less far-sighted and high-minded, than he was.' Even so, Magnus informed his readers, 'Gladstone was undaunted in the face of humiliation and defeat. He towered in moral grandeur over his contemporaries and stood before the world as the inspired prophet of the nineteenth-century Liberal experiment.'[16] There can be no doubt where Magnus's sympathies lay.

In a brief lecture, first broadcast in 1960, A.J.P. Taylor, another leading historian, made it very clear why he had chosen to talk about

Gladstone: 'William Ewart Gladstone was the greatest political figure of the nineteenth century. I do not mean by that he was necessarily the greatest statesman, certainly not the most successful. What I mean is that he dominated the scene.'[17] For Taylor, Gladstone had created and directed Victorian Liberalism, usually for his own purposes, the last of which was the policy of Home Rule for Ireland. The Liberal party became more devoted to policies of social reform later, but this development, as far as Taylor was concerned, had nothing to do with Gladstone.

Almost exactly twenty years after Magnus's biography was published another, by E.J. Feuchtwanger, appeared. The emphasis of this work, as the author openly states, is 'fairly and squarely on Gladstone's political life: his private life and his manifold activities as scholar, theologian and in other fields has been comparatively neglected'. A lengthy introduction to the second edition, published in 1989, allowed further reflections on Gladstone's private life to be included. This lays emphasis on the strains Gladstone faced in the years 1850 and 1851, with his daughter Jessy's death and the 'loss' of his friends Manning and Hope and his sister, Helen, to the Church of Rome. It shows Gladstone trying to adapt to the new style of mass politics, something his own Midlothian campaigns in 1879 and 1880 had helped to bring about, but it suggested 'one cannot avoid feeling that Gladstone was increasingly out of tune with the times after 1880'. We are told

> He became more alienated from the contemporary world, from its materialism, and from the harsher climate between the nations abroad and the classes at home. The age of which he was so quintessential if exceptional a representative, with its deep religious feeling, moral earnestness and sense of absolute values, was fast fading. Gladstone knew it, often spoke of it, but he refused to abdicate.[18]

One politician who gave his views of Gladstone (together with, among other prime ministers, his views on Peel, Palmerston and Disraeli) was the former Labour prime minister of the 1960s and 1970s, Harold Wilson. For Wilson, Gladstone 'was a massive character, yet one of the most psychologically complicated personalities in the whole history of Britain's ... Prime Ministers.' Wilson rather followed Taylor's line of argument; he believed Gladstone became 'totally involved' in the question of Home Rule for Ireland and 'his obsession dominated his party, as he clung to the leadership throughout the seventies and into the eighties. An increasingly rebellious party simply did not dare to get rid of him'. It was Gladstone's 'obsession' with Ireland which, Wilson declared, prevented the 'principal desire of its younger members, social reform', being forced through.[19]

Gladstone's life, according to American scholar, Peter Stansky, in a short work published in 1979, represented 'a progress in politics'. Using material from Gladstone's speeches, which he feels 'were often grand and elevating' and which 'remain of crucial importance in determining the form and substance of his politics', he looks at Gladstone's views on issues arising throughout his career.[20] They include his speech in Parliament on 3 June 1833 on the question of slavery (about which he had mixed feelings) and other issues such as financial, religious, and foreign policy, down to his last speech in Parliament, on 1 March 1894, a denunciation of the House of Lords for its amendments to the Local Government Bill. For Stansky, whose philosophy has been outlined in an article in *History Today* for July 2002, Gladstone was one of those 'insiders' much admired by contemporaries, but who, deep down, nevertheless retained a sense of being 'outsiders'. He was 'born into a mercantile family but pushed into a patrician education' and into playing a major role in Victorian politics. Stansky sees Gladstone as one of those 'formidably endowed characters struggling to articulate and communicate what they believed to be the feelings of those less privileged than themselves'.[21]

Ten years later, Agatha Ramm produced a 'political portrait' of the Liberal leader. Ramm considers that Gladstone's life was 'unusual, not because he was a noble or even pleasant character, but because he was extraordinarily able, active and courageous', and because of the way his life was of a different 'shape' from most others. Gladstone, after all, did not experience a 'peak point of achievement or enjoyment' followed by a 'decline … towards its end': 'his was different in having two breaks, no easily discernible peak and hardly a decline'. By looking at Gladstone's intellectual development, it was possible to show how his political life evolved in ways viewed by some of his contemporaries as an inconsistent fashion. Gladstone's reforms 'disturbed the social equilibrium', but his financial policies had encouraged 'the harmony of classes'. He was 'a demagogue [but] also a great political educator'.[22]

Morley had made limited use of one enormous body of material Gladstone himself had left – his diary, in which he had made some 25,000 entries between 1825 and 1896. This had been handed to the Archbishop of Canterbury for safe storage in Lambeth Palace Library in 1928. Nearly forty years later it was agreed that all of the family papers would be made available to scholars and that the diaries themselves should be published. This mammoth undertaking, beginning in 1968 with the publication of the first volume edited by M.R.D. Foot, was only completed in 1994 with the publication of the last, edited by H.C.G. Matthew. It provided the opportunity for a closer than ever look at Gladstone's life and thoughts and resulted in the publication of two major biographies. Both appeared in two volumes, each one separated by a number of years. The first to appear was that by Richard Shannon, with the first volume, covering the years from 1809 to 1865, being published in 1982,[23] and the second volume, dealing with the years from 1865 to 1895, being published seventeen years later, in 1999.[24] Shannon's view is that Gladstone's political life was shaped by three main factors: 'his devotion to the principles and policies of Sir Robert Peel'; his 'discovery of "the people" as a great resource of beneficent public energy to be mobilised and manipulated to good political ends', and, 'more profoundly formative than either', his Anglican Christianity:

> His unswerving conviction ... of the manifest providential government of the world, and his growing sense of his own assigned role as an instrument, however unworthy, of God Almighty.
>
> It was this Christian providentialism which was, primarily and ultimately, most significant in explaining the contours and courses of Gladstone's life.

It is therefore necessary, in Shannon's view, to 'reintegrate his religion with his politics' and include his adaptations of 'populist Liberalism' to his 'deeper abiding loyalties to his Peelite inheritance' in order to show Gladstone 'wielding the mandate of heaven in an age of burgeoning democracy'.[25] This is done by following Gladstone's political and private life as revealed in his own writings, especially his diary, as well as of those of his contemporaries, and the result is a huge work.

Colin Matthew's biography is less massive. The first volume, covering the years from 1809 to 1874, was published in 1986, and the second, covering 1875 to 1898, appeared in 1995. In 1999 a combined volume appeared. For Matthew, Gladstone was an able politician who managed to adapt 'politically, religiously and socially to new circumstances', who prepared, like Shakespeare's King Lear, to 'shape his old course in a country new'. According to Matthew, Gladstone's chosen method was

> A radical conservatism, which fused at times with an advanced liberalism ... It was a method which deeply perplexed Conservatives, and often disappointed Liberals. For the former it was almost always too much, too soon; for the latter, it was sometimes too little, too late.

Matthew sees Gladstone as 'a chief representative of the Victorian age' which displayed 'the strengths and weaknesses of a liberal democracy at the height of its self-confidence'. This is summed up by the

> powerful individualism, the executive competence, the capacity for a sense of history, a feel for 'ripeness' and for national development; against these may be balanced for all the introspection, a curious lack of self-awareness.[26]

On the whole, Matthew's Gladstone comes across as a secular figure, cast rather in the Morley mould, struggling to lead 'liberalism' into the modern world.

There are, of course, no shortage of ways of viewing Gladstone. For the Social Democrat Lord Jenkins in 1995 he represented a proto-Social Democrat, the political heir of Sir Robert Peel and inspiration for Asquith and the Liberal Party of the twentieth century.[27] For Travis Crosby, an American historian, he appears much more interesting as a psychological case-study. Crosby points out, in his 1997 biography, that there were 'two Mr. Gladstones': the one who retained self-control in the most pressing situations, and the other who sometimes broke through and displayed violent outbursts of anger and aggression. Crosby suggests that what Gladstone did was to develop 'coping' strategies to deal with the stresses he faced. There are several ways this can be done. One way 'commonly followed' by Gladstone was 'a strategy of withdrawal': hence, he often suffered 'diplomatic illnesses', avoided Cabinet meetings or threatened resignation. Another way of 'coping', however, is to attack the source of stress – in Gladstone's case, often, his political opponents. As far as Crosby is concerned

> For Gladstone, anger was probably used on occasion to intimidate but more frequently to fend off threatening events or behaviour ... Anger can thus be viewed, in Gladstone's case, as a reasonably effective way of managing the various stresses of political life, especially within the House of Commons.[28]

For Eugenio Biagini, whose biography was published in 2000, Gladstone's leadership should properly be placed 'in perspective', since he was a 'unique historical character':

> Shaped both by the strongly Evangelical culture of early nineteenth century Britain, and by the formative experience of Peel's 1841–6 government. In some fundamental respects he remained a Peelite throughout his career, though from 1864 to 1868 he adopted an ambiguously democratic rhetoric in an attempt to modernize the Peel/Aberdeen government tradition and adapt it to the new realities of the extended franchise.

But from 1876 onwards Gladstone's 'extra-parliamentary performances and charismatic public speaking' became the 'key features of his strategy' as national leader. 'However', notes Biagini, 'his aim remained that of converting "the masses" to his version of the Peelite gospel'.[29] He is also careful to show how Gladstone was influenced by international influences, especially those from Italy and North America, and to stress the Grand Old Man's own influence on the present day.

There are, therefore, a large number of biographies of Gladstone, but even these do not by any means mark the limits of the attention he has received from writers. His career has been approached in several different ways. Sometimes it has been a particular theme in his public life that has attracted notice. As early as 1931, for example, F.W. Hirst, a 'radical individualist', published a study of Gladstone's economic and fiscal policy. In two volumes, published in 1927 and 1935, an American scholar, Paul Knaplund, investigated his foreign and imperial policy, while in 1934 J.R.L. Hammond, an economic historian with socialist leanings, surveyed the story of *Gladstone and the Irish Nation*.[30] For both Hirst and Hammond, Gladstone's policies stood as a model for those that ought to be followed. All of these subjects have been studied again in more recent years, while others, too, have emerged. For example, it has been possible to take a broader view on issues relating to Gladstone and the evolution of the Liberal Party, while specific events in Gladstone's career have also been closely studied. Books and articles have appeared on the reform crises of 1867–8 and 1884–5, the Bulgarian atrocities in 1875–8, and the British occupation of Egypt in 1882, among a myriad of other matters.

To all of this must be added Gladstone's own writings, publications of other document collections, official archives, and his starring role in all books dealing with nineteenth-century British politics and many other matters. It therefore becomes clear that the task of the historian is a challenging one. There is such a wealth of material available, that, as Colin Matthew states in the preface of his own major contribution to it, any attempt to write an 'exhaustive or definitive' biography of Gladstone 'would be silly'.[31] It therefore becomes necessary to decide what the most pressing questions are relating to this leading political figure of Victorian Britain.

QUESTIONS SURROUNDING GLADSTONE'S LIFE

From his earliest days in politics some anomalies surrounded Gladstone. First, was his decision to enter the political arena at all: it has never yet been definitively settled as to why Gladstone chose a political career ahead of one in the Church. Once the decision was made, helped by his father, there arises the question of his political allegiance. His earliest public pronouncements – in somewhat cautious defence of slavery and in outright opposition to parliamentary reform – placed him firmly on the Ultra-Tory side of the House of Commons. Yet his personal allegiance was increasingly devoted to Sir Robert Peel, whose cautious acceptance of Parliamentary Reform and some other reforming measures, made him among the Ultra's least favourite figures. Gladstone's devotion to Peel, and particularly his financial policies, came to outweigh his loyalty to the Ultras who initially backed him, and cost him their support, and he was deeply upset by Peel's death in 1850. His fiscal policy throughout the 1850s and 1860s remained firmly 'Peelite', and Gladstone stayed a member of the ever-decreasing band of 'Peelite' MPs for the next nine years.

For this reason, the evolution of the Liberal party in the middle years of the century was something in which Gladstone played only a limited role. Given Gladstone's less than enthusiastic views of Lord Palmerston, the Liberal leader, it seems curious that he decided to join his Cabinet in 1859. The reasons for this decision have to be investigated, as do the relationship between the two men and its effects on the future of Liberalism. The resignation of the Liberals in 1866 and the passing by the Conservatives of the Second Reform Act led, however, to a triumph for Gladstone. The first ministry, from 1868 to 1874, its successes and the reasons for its downfall, must be studied.

Gladstone's years of semi-retirement in the 1870s and the causes of his triumphant return in 1880, based on his groundbreaking tour of Midlothian, also require investigation. When the Liberals once again won the election, in 1880, the appointed leaders, Granville and Hartington, had, they believed, no alternative but to step down for Gladstone. But his next two terms of office seem to have been less successful than his first, climaxing in a disastrous split in the Party in 1885. Gladstone's role in this needs to be assessed, as does the importance to it of the Irish policy he eventually adopted. It was Ireland which dominated the last years of Gladstone's public life, and especially his last ministry from 1892 to 1894. One question which remains unanswered is whether it was his preoccupation with Home Rule which prevented the evolution of the Liberal Party into a force capable of winning elections in the reformed system after 1885. Another is the precise reason for his final resignation in 1894.

To summarise Gladstone's private life in the midst of all this political turmoil is another necessary task. Gladstone was an archetypal Victorian husband and father, and his relationships with wife and children were sources of both support and tension to him. But there was another, even more private, side to Gladstone's life. He was very keen to 'rescue' prostitutes from their lives of vice and depravity: so keen, he formed close friendships with a few of the women themselves. He was also, however, aware of the wickedness of some of his thoughts and felt the need to punish himself for them. On several occasions, Gladstone recorded the symbol of a whip in his diary. While he did not ask the women to use it on him, it is clear they were on his mind when, in the utmost secrecy, he used it on himself. The extent to which all of this affected his public life needs examination..

Gladstone was a most important figure in his day, although his public life had its successes and failures. To be a successful politician involves remaining in public life and, perhaps, more importantly, making an impact on it by securing the implementation of favoured policies. Gladstone certainly made an impact on Victorian society. Crowds flocked to his house at Hawarden castle to see him in action, chopping down trees, or to hear him speak in Midlothian or on Blackheath, or in any one of innumerable sites across the country. His success rate in his securing his favoured policies was less than perfect, however, and despite his greatest efforts some of the things he had set his heart on he could not get enacted.

This, then, is the task to be undertaken: to tell the story of a larger-than-life character, from his earliest days, through his terms of service – as a backbench MP, a cabinet minister and a prime minister – until he finally left the House of Commons and retired. I will try to reveal Gladstone's character and the motives for his conduct, and assess his success and his place in the evolution of the Liberal Party, Victorian Liberalism and Victorian Britain.

1

EARLY LIFE AND CAREER, 1809–1834

On 29 December 1809, Mrs Anne Gladstone, of 62 Rodney Street, Liverpool, gave birth to her fourth son. He was christened William Ewart after a business associate of his father, John Gladstone. This was a wealthy household in a town in England that had taken its full share in the commercial expansion of the eighteenth century, in which John Gladstone had also taken an active part.

The port of Liverpool had grown rich on the slave trade. For many years in the eighteenth century Liverpool had been the leading port in this trade in Great Britain, but it was far from being the only one in which Liverpool merchants were engaged. Shoes and other clothing, sealing wax, paper and a wide variety of foodstuffs were sent to or received from colonies. Industry in and around Liverpool also prospered supplying goods to trade, sometimes in exchange for slaves, while contacts with the American colonies (and later with the United States of America) involved numerous goods and artefacts. By the time of the first census in 1801 the population of Liverpool had grown to 77,000, and the city was the fifth largest in the country, one well known for its enlightened policy on urban improvements.

FAMILY BACKGROUND AND EARLY LIFE

William Ewart Gladstone's father had emigrated from the lowlands of Scotland to Liverpool in 1787 and had spent the next ten years busily engaged in a variety of business ventures. John Gladstone had begun following in his father's footsteps as a corn merchant, in partnership with another Scottish émigré, Edgar Corne, and from that base his interests widened. Other trading interests, in sugar and cotton, were coupled with ventures into shipping and insurance and, not least, into property. In 1803 he took a mortgage on an estate on the West Indian island of Demerara, which was run by slave labour. By 1799 his fortune stood at something approaching £40,000 (about £1.75 million in today's money) and it continued to grow steadily, standing at around £200,000 (about £8.8 million) in 1815 and reaching a peak of nearly £600,000 (roughly £26.5 million) by the time of his death in December 1851. John Gladstone was therefore an extremely rich man, who could afford to send his sons to university and keep them as unpaid backbench MPs as long as necessary to establish their political careers.

John Gladstone was, by all accounts, a strong character. Young William certainly believed so. His father, he thought, was a very affectionate man, who was very devoted to his family as well as to his work, though even he had to admit that John Gladstone was somewhat short-tempered. John Gladstone's ambition was not confined to the sphere of business. He entered into the social and the religious life of Liverpool and was responsible, with other emigrants, for establishing a Scottish Kirk in the city in 1799 and in 1815–16 paying for the construction of an Anglican church at Seaforth. This reflected the significant change in his religious opinion. Having been born into a family of Dissenters, it was at least partly due to the influence of both his wives, but especially of his second wife, Anne, whom he married in 1800, that by 1805 Gladstone senior had become a member of the Church of England.

This would have been both a religious and a social decision. As a member of the Church of England, John Gladstone could now enter fully into the social and – perhaps more importantly for him – the political life of the city. For he had one ambition in life even beyond making money: he wanted to be a Member of Parliament. It is not surprising that his political opinions tended to the right. As an almost self-made man from outside the established elite, he found the doctrines of the Whigs, with their stress on status and birth, deeply unattractive. Equally unattractive, though, were the precepts of die-hard Toryism, the creed of unthinking opposition to change represented by those such as Henry Addington, Viscount Sidmouth, prime minister from 1801 to

1804 and home secretary from 1812 to 1821. He sought, and eventually, found a political figure he could admire in George Canning, who, thanks in part to his backing and encouragement, came to Liverpool and began to sit as one the city's two MPs from 1812. Canning, later renowned as one of the guiding lights of 'Liberal Toryism', foreign secretary and briefly prime minister, was a Tory who was prepared to contemplate necessary changes to keep the ship of state upright. His equally liberal companion as MP from 1822 was William Huskission, another forward-thinking Tory. Ideally, John Gladstone would have liked to be Canning's partner, sitting with him for Liverpool in the House of Commons, but it was not to be. In 1818 he secured election to the unreformed House of Commons by bribing the electors of the rotten borough of Lancaster. This was one of those seats where the number of electors was so small, or where they were tenants of a particular landowner, that one individual effectively controlled who they voted for. As there was no secret ballot it would not be possible to hide who one voted for. The consequences of voting for the wrong candidate could be serious, including eviction, or they could be profitable since, as John Gladstone discovered, it was also possible to sell one's vote. This, however, was too expensive for him, so he transferred two years later to the equally rotten seat at Woodstock, a 'pocket borough' in the pocket of the Duke of Marlborough: whoever the duke wanted would be returned to Parliament. He sat for this seat from 1820 to 1826, and then, briefly, for Berwick on Tweed from 1826 to 1827, when he was unseated on petition. But he made little impression in the House, consulting Canning on those commercial matters that came up for discussion. It is difficult to avoid the conclusion that John Gladstone's parliamentary career was a great disappointment to him. It is also quite likely that this influenced his views when young William wrote to seek parental guidance for a career. Perhaps Gladstone *père* could live politically through Gladstone *fils*.

John Gladstone was the undisputed head of his family. His influence on his children was profound, and not least his influence on young William. But there was another source of authority in the Gladstone household. He had married twice: his first wife, Jane Hall, had died childless in 1798; his second wife, Anne Robertson, lived until 1839. Anne Gladstone was the daughter of Provost Robertson of Dingwall, and she was not always a physically strong individual (this did not prevent her giving birth to six children). But what she lacked in physical strength was made up for in her extraordinary moral presence. Anne Gladstone took refuge from her declining health and the sometimes domineering presence of John Gladstone in religion. She was an evangelical, or low church, member of the Church of England. It was she who lay in large part behind John Gladstone's decision in 1800 to marry in a Church of England service. But religion was much more important to Anne than a Sunday service at church. From her couch she inspired her offspring with her own strong religious views, and in this respect at least her husband let her have her way. His own religious opinions were shaped in accordance with his wife's, and the result was that the Gladstone household in Rodney Street was a very religious one indeed.

His mother certainly had an influence on William Ewart, her fifth child. When she lay dying, William noted her last days in detail (as indeed he later did those of his daughter, Jessy, and his father) and summed up his feelings on her life:

> She was not during her illness in a state of mental vigour to warrant its being proposed to her to receive the Sacrament. Though she was deprived of this joy, and we of this palpable manifestation of her faith, we cannot feel it a cause for permanent regret while we know that in her daily life she had realised that communion with her Lord, which the ordinance is intended to convey and assure.
>
> Sin was the object of her hatred – and she can now sin no more. Sin is the cause of all the sorrow in the world; she can now no more add to the sin nor the sorrow ... She was eminent in the discharge of every duty; she sorrowed for sin; she trusted in the atonement of Christ. But this was not all: these elementary sentiments of religion were matured in her by the power of God, and she was made partaker of the nature and very life of her Redeemer, and her will conformed to his.[1]

By the time William was born his older sister Anne was seven years old, and his three brothers – Tom (born 1804), Robertson (born 1805) and John Neilson (born 1807) – were also senior to him. Only his sister Helen (born 1814) was younger than he was.

While his brothers were to have only relatively limited influence on William, his two sisters, in their different ways, were to be far more influential. To the young William it was his older sister, Anne, who had the most important role. Young Anne Gladstone was William's godmother, a loyal member of the Church of England and well acquainted with some of that church's teachers. She had a considerable influence on the young Gladstone, counteracting some of the more low church doctrines of his parents, and by dying at only twenty-seven in 1829, continued to exert a powerful influence on him in later years. His younger sister Helen, by becoming an opium addict and, perhaps even worse for Gladstone, a Roman Catholic in later years, was also influential on him, though more as a source of worry than of inspiration. As will be seen, his brothers, too, played their part in his later life, but all three have been somewhat overshadowed by their younger sibling.

Gladstone's boyhood has been covered by all of his biographers, using his own recollections. From these we discover that he had a lively time as a boy, and that much of what he had to do was no different from that faced by other children over the years. His first public performance occurred in October 1812, election year in Liverpool. A group of dinner guests in the Gladstone house met the future prime minister who, at the age of two years, 'was taken down to the dining room, dressed if I remember in a red frock. I was set on one of the chairs, standing, and directed to say to the company: "ladies and gentlemen"'.[2] He went to Edinburgh and Glasgow for an excursion to Sanquhar in Dumfries to visit the family's roots at some time in the spring of 1814 and, a year later, he went to Cambridge and London for the first time.

In London, young Gladstone stayed with his uncle, Colin Robertson, and was upset because he was not allowed to roam the streets freely as he did when at home in Liverpool. He attended a thanksgiving service at St Paul's Cathedral, presumably for the victory over Napoleon at Waterloo, but neither the service nor the cathedral, which he did not visit again for over fifty years, seems to have made much of an impression on him. It was in this year that the Gladstones moved to a large country house overlooking the River Mersey, between Bootle and Crosby.

Gladstone's own judgement of his childhood, when he looked back in his old age, was harsh:

> I wish that in reviewing my childhood I could regard it as presenting those features of innocence and beauty which I have often seen

> elsewhere, and indeed, thanks be to God, within the limits of my own home. The best I can say for it is that I do not think it was a vicious childhood. I do not think, trying to look at the past impartially, that I had a strong natural propensity then developed to what are termed the mortal sins. But truth obliges me to record this against myself. I have no recollection of being a loving or a winning child; or an earnest or diligent or knowledge-loving child. God forgive me ... The plank between me and all the sins was so very thin.[3]

And there were other problems: 'I was not a devotional child. I have no recollection of love for the House of God and for divine service'. When he heard preaching at St. George's, Liverpool, he confessed to being bored and remembered asking his mother when the speaker would finish. He admitted to liking *Pilgrim's Progress*, but so he did *Arabian Nights* and particularly a book on Scottish chiefs. He prayed 'earnestly', at the age of seven or eight, but only 'to be spared from the loss of a tooth'; to avoid 'Dr. Perry of … Liverpool … a kind of savage at this work (possibly a very good-natured man too), with no ideas except to smash and crash'. He could not, he claimed, remember anything about his religious upbringing.[4]

To account for this unfortunate lack of religious scruples in his early age, Gladstone offered two possible factors: the first was simply that he had not taken things up very quickly, and the second was that he had drawn little benefit from teaching. None of his three older brothers had any direct influence upon him, nor did his teacher, a Mr Rawson from Cambridge. Rawson's School 'afterwards rose into considerable repute' – but Gladstone attributed this 'not so much due to its intellectual stamina as to the extreme salubrity of the situation on the pure dry sands of the Mersey's mouth'. Gladstone remembered that

> everything was unobjectionable. I suppose I learnt something there. But I have no recollection of being under any moral or personal influence whatever, and I doubt whether the preaching had any adaptation whatever to children. As to intellectual training, I believe that, like the other boys, I shirked my work as much as I could.[5]

Gladstone, then, looked back at his childhood, which he believed ended when he was sent to Eton in 1821, somewhat censoriously, but this can possibly be taken too much at face value. The older Gladstone, it would appear, was being too harsh and expecting too much of his younger self. He seems to have been a fairly ordinary child, displaying no evidence of particular intelligence, strength of character, or religious faith. He thought he should have displayed exceptional piety and ability while a child, and this view seems to have been reflected in the upbringing of his own children. His eldest son, Willy, in particular, seems to have suffered for not displaying the characteristics his father believed should be evident in all children, but especially his own. Gladstone's own parents, however, were proud of him, even at an early age, and were preparing for the next stage in his career.

ETON AND OXFORD

To confirm their arrival in the very highest circles of British society, something John Gladstone laboured to do through his attempts at parliamentary distinction, the Gladstone parents sent their boys to Eton. The school at this time had not received the attentions of the great public school reformers of the middle nineteenth century, like Thomas Arnold of Rugby. Its organisation and its curriculum both differed widely from those seen later. Here were found self-employed housemasters and private tutors, who taught pretty much what they liked when they wished, and Dames, the formidable women who oversaw the separate houses in which the pupils lived. A boy could hope to learn Latin, some Greek, and some modern language – French, almost certainly – from his teachers. But he would learn as much from his friends and common members of the Eton Society if he could secure election to it.

William Gladstone was not necessarily expecting a good time at Eton. There was no room at the school for ardent evangelicals, and his older brothers – Robertson, and especially Tom – had had a dreadful time there. Robertson had made his escape to Edinburgh to learn business: Tom had to stick it out. This helped William, who on entering the school became his fag. But William had some things that Tom rather lacked – a strong intelligence and a sturdy temperament. This mixture enabled him to survive almost unscathed the rough and tumble of school life and work his way, as intended, into the higher echelons of the school.

Some of the masters appreciated William Gladstone, just as he did them. His French master, Berthomier, for example, encouraged his lifelong interest in Molière. But it was Edward Hawtrey who, noticing William's abilities, brought him to the attention of the school's headmaster, Keate, and first gave him a positive desire and enthusiasm to learn. Keate himself, whose formidable reputation as a disciplinarian and a flogger seems fully deserved, appears usually to have appreciated and been appreciated by William, but not invariably. Once, in a church, he and his father had secured a pew in the gallery, and

> There was I, looking down with infinite complacency and satisfaction from this honourable vantage ground upon the floor of the church, filled and packed as one of our public meetings is, with people standing and pushing. What was my emotion, my joy, my exultation, when I espied among this humiliated mass, struggling and buffeted – whom but Keate! Keate the master of our existence, the tyrant of our days! Pure, unalloyed unadulterated rapture![6]

William reached the sixth form – a distinction his brother Tom had never achieved – at the start of 1827, and found here a very different Keate from the one he was used to, but only enjoyed it for some ten months.

William's character had also developed while at Eton. He had made some firm friends, most notably Arthur Hallam, James Milner Gaskell and Francis Doyle. With these boys William became a member of Pop, the Eton Society, which had been founded in 1811 as a debating society, and he began to read widely on issues, past and present, that were coming up for discussion. It is possible to say exactly what these were since on 16 July 1825 – if not before – William began the diary that he was to keep daily for over sixty years; in it he tells us exactly what books he had been reading and when, and a great deal else. The list is impressive, ranging from the works of Sir Walter Scott to Clarendon's seventeenth-century *History of the Great Rebellion* and William Paley's *Evidences of Christianity*, Milton's *Paradise Lost*, *Tom Jones*, and even, in 1826, a Roman Catholic prayer book.

William's public-speaking career began with a discourse on the education of the poor on 29 October 1825, when he made his first speech at the Society, which he found a much less nerve-wracking experience than he thought it would be. There is no doubt where his sympathies lay:

> Is it morally just or politically expedient to keep down the industry and genius of the artisan, to blast his rising hopes, to quell his spirit? A thirst for knowledge has arisen in the midst of the poor, let them satisfy it with wholesome nutrient and beware lest driven to despair.[7]

Among his more historically-directed speeches, he has to admit he had changed his mind about Sir Robert Walpole: while there were faults with some of his policies, the fact that he secured the Protestant succession and followed a generally peaceful foreign policy more than made up for them. The sympathies of both of these speeches underlay Gladstone's later career in some measure.

But William also did other things while at Eton. He was joint editor of a newspaper, *The Eton Miscellany*, which included articles on various issues, often connected with 'Pop'. Less intellectually, he both played and watched cricket, went sculling, and joined the Salt Hill Club, a social and dining club, in which Gladstone, known by his fellow members as 'Mr Tipple', visited a local inn to 'bully the waiter, eat toasted cheese and drink egg-wine'. He clearly did not spend all of his time at school labouring over his books.

Gladstone's education at Eton finished in December 1827. His school work was of a sufficiently high standard for him to have secured a place at Oxford University to study humanities, mathematics and physics. It was not necessary to have done exceptionally well at school to go to Oxford; many students simply had their fees paid for a few years' study there. Gladstone, however, aimed to do well and spent the months from January to October 1828 with a crammer, the Revd J.M. Turner, at Wilmslow. Turner seems to have concentrated on Gladstone's mathematics, which was soon to stand him in good stead.

While at Eton, he had been introduced to some of those who inhabited the upper echelons of society. He had acquired habits of public-speaking, based on a wide reading of an enormous variety of books. He had even – somewhat surprisingly, given the school's rather vapid Church of England leanings – been confirmed in 1826, and he had taken communion six times before he left.

But while he had not neglected his religious upbringing at Eton, he had also begun to develop an interest in another matter – politics. His friendship with Hallam had introduced him to a Whig outlook on society, and he had himself followed some of the key debates in the House of Commons. He was especially upset that the attempts to secure Catholic Emancipation, the repeal of Acts dating from the seventeenth century which disallowed Roman Catholics from holding political office or officers' commissions in the Army and Navy, had once again been beaten. His father's parliamentary career had come to an end when he was unseated in 1827: George Canning's had ended with his death in August of the same year. The stage was being set for a major political clash, as the hopes of those calling for reform were aroused by disunity within the Tory government.

The next stage in William's career had been decided by his parents: he was to attend not just any college at Oxford, but the one with the leading reputation in the university, politically, intellectually and socially – Christ Church. The university as a whole had not undergone one of its greater periods of scholarship in the eighteenth century. Until 1809 the dean of Christ Church was Cyril Jackson, whose aim had been to turn the college into a training ground for an elite governing and administrative class. In 1800, under the influence of Jackson and his associates, the university had introduced statutes governing examinations, with a competitive system, and the division of degree results into classes. He was not afraid to urge his young students to work hard and assert their abilities. He did not, however, press for great changes in the curriculum, and in many respects, the education at Christ Church was much the same as that at Eton, but of a somewhat higher standard.

Gladstone started his residence at Oxford on 10 October 1828, and although he was to meet many different people in his time there, he would not meet anyone who was not an Anglican. Indeed, to be admitted to the university it was necessary publicly to accept the Thirty-Nine Articles of the Church of England, and Gladstone had done this at the time of his matriculation on 23 January 1828. He divided his time while at the university in much the same way as he had done at school – in formal classes, in private study, in the students' union, at church, as well as on other, more recreational, activities.

Gladstone's formal education at Oxford was, generally, classical but it also included some theology and mathematics. In 1829, for example, he had lectures every day: on Sundays (appropriately enough) there was an evening 'Divinity' lecture, followed on Monday by some mathematics, which also appeared on Wednesday and Friday evenings. He studied the Greek historian Thucydides on Tuesdays and Thursdays and the Roman writer Juvenal on Fridays. On Tuesdays, Thursdays and Saturdays he followed a course on 'Romans in the second century'.

These formal classes introduced Gladstone to, or developed his interest in, a variety of individual writers and thinkers who were to have a lasting influence on him. These included the classical authorities Homer, Plato and Aristotle, and more modern writers, such as Bishop Joseph Butler, the eighteenth-century theologian, and the conservative thinker, Edmund Burke.

Much of their work was read and analysed in private study. While on a visit to Cuddesdon, near Oxford in 1830, for example, he noted in his diary:

> **July 6** Up soon after 6. Began my Harmony of G[ree]k Testament. D[ifferential] cal[culus] etc. in Mathematics, a good while but in a rambling way. Began *Odyssey* Papers .... Turned a little bit of Livy into Greek. Conversation on Ethics and Metaphysics at n[igh]t.
>
> **July 8** Greek Testament – Bible ... Mathematics, long but did little. Translated some *Phaedo*. Butler & construed some Thucydides at n[igh]t ... Shelley.
>
> **July 12** G[reek] Testament ... Butler – a very pleasant evening.[8]

It was this private study which shows how the youthful Gladstone took a lively interest in the events of his own day, and used his academic work to relate to what was happening in his own time. For example, while making notes on Aristotle's *Rhetorics*, he filled his notebook with material on Aristotle on one side and examples taken from speeches by leading parliamentarians such as George Canning and Robert Peel (and even Viscount Palmerston) on the other. He used this knowledge when he began to make public speeches to the Oxford Union in February 1830. It was a cause of some embarrassment to his Liberal biographer, Morley, that his hero's first speech there was a defence of the repressive Treason and Sedition Acts of 1795. His most notable performance occurred on 17 May 1831, and this time, too, he spoke in an illiberal sense. The country at this time was rocked by the crisis over the first Reform Bill, which had been introduced by Lord Grey's new Whig government on 1 March. Following the defeat of the measure, the government resigned and called a general election. At the time of the parliamentary candidates' nomination, Gladstone had

> mounted the mare to join the anti-reform procession and we looked as well as we could do, considering that we were all covered with mud from head to foot. There was mob enough on both sides, but I must do them the justice to say they were for the most part exceedingly good-humoured.[9]

He was soon to experience less good-humoured electoral mobs. Gladstone had prepared anxiously for his turn at the Union, which was due on 16 May. Unfortunately, much to his dismay, the debate was adjourned for twenty-four hours: he did not think he would make a better speech because of it. He found it difficult to decide what to put into the speech because there was plenty of material to choose from, but the speech was evidently a great success, at least to the extent that Gladstone and the anti-reformers, perhaps not surprisingly, won the debate.

Beginning in October 1829, Gladstone and his friends established an 'Essay Club', probably modelled on that of the so-called Apostles at Cambridge. The Essay Club – known also as WEG – was seen as an elitist group of students, drawn from various Colleges, and did not last long. Nor did it help Gladstone win a scholarship founded by Dean Ireland, for which he made two attempts – in March 1830 and again a year later. On the second occasion Gladstone tried to explain to his father what had gone wrong. The prize had gone to a candidate who had written brief answers, compared with Gladstone's, but he blamed Eton for not educating him for the kind of subject he was being asked to write on. (Some would argue that Gladstone in later years could have drawn a moral from the first of these points.) He also vainly attempted to win a prize for Latin poetry; even he had to admit later that his poetry was rather weak, and had only got better later, after he had read some of Dante's.

Gladstone's later view of the state of religion in the Oxford of his undergraduate days is quite revealing:

> You may smile when told that when I was at Oxford, Dr. Hampden was regarded as a model of orthodoxy, that Dr. Newman was eyed with suspicion as a low churchman and Dr. Pusey as leaning towards rationalism.[10]

Hampden was later excluded from a position at the university through the pressure of those who thought his views on the Anglican creed unorthodox, and both Newman and Pusey became noted for their High Church views. Gladstone had become much less of an evangelical during his time at Oxford. But it was not the university that had done this. For one thing, while he knew and thought highly of both Bishop Lloyd and Pusey, neither of them tried to persuade him to change his religious views, and, for another, most Oxford sermons were so poor as to be incapable of converting anybody. It was clergymen from outside the university who had more of an impact. In October 1830 the Scottish nonconformist Dr Thomas Chalmers visited Oxford:

> and I went to hear him preach on Sunday evening, though it was at the Baptist chapel ... I need hardly say that his sermon was admirable, and quite as remarkable for the judicious and sober manner in which he enforced his views, as for their lofty principles and piety. He preached, I think, for an hour and forty minutes.

By Gladstone's later standards, this was a brief enough oration.[11]

Gladstone's religious views, however, continued to underlay some – though not all – of his spare time activities as an undergraduate. On 14 June 1830, for example, he 'Gave a large wine party', followed a day later by 'Another wine party' and a day after that he was 'out of wine'. He also went for long walks sometimes. On the evening of 25 June 1830 he walked fifteen miles towards Leamington, continuing the walk the next day, when he made an early start, and covered eight miles to Banbury, before having breakfast, after which he walked the remaining twenty-three miles to Leamington.

The weight of Gladstone's conscience was strong, however. In September, he recorded his dislike of playing cards, partly because they excited him and kept him awake at night, and partly because they reflected the players' state of dissipation. And there was one thing even worse than playing cards, since that at least was doing something. But

10 May 1830, for example, was 'a wretched day. God forgive idleness'.[12] Gladstone was convinced that he would always have to find something to do.

At Oxford, at least in his last year, that 'something' was clear: he had to study to secure a good degree. The final examinations were by no means easy. Those for the Humanities School began on 9 November 1831, and started with three days of written examinations, a weekend break, two days of oral examinations and finally two more days of written papers. The first day's examination involved 'Strafford's speech into Latin – with Logical & Rhetorical questions – the latter somewhat abstract – & wearying'. Gladstone wanted support: 'God grant that He who gave himself even for me may support me through it, if it be his will: but if I am covered with humiliation, may I kiss the rod'.[13]

On 24 November, he heard he had received first-class honours in Classics. That left mathematics. Gladstone needed to keep calm: this was helped by an invitation to visit Cambridge to see his friend Hallam, and by a prescription for 'saline draughts'. He found it hard to sleep before the examinations, but again came through with first-class honours. His Oxford University career had ended triumphantly. Many years later he was to state publicly, 'I love her from the bottom of my heart'. [14]

But graduation marks not an end, but a beginning: what is the graduate to do? Like many students, Gladstone had always given serious thought to this question. On 4 August 1830, he confided to his diary that he was 'Uncomfortable again & much distracted with doubts as to my future line of conduct. God direct me. I am utterly blind.' To seek advice he wrote a long letter to his father. He concluded that he really had no choice in his future career: 'I can come to no other conclusion, at least unaided, than that the work of spreading religion has a claim infinitely transcending all others in dignity, in solemnity and in usefulness'.[15] What can we make of this? Did Gladstone really want to enter the Church? Clearly he was asking his father to give him some advice, and in response to this letter John Gladstone did what, in his heart of hearts, William had wanted him to do. While he did not explicitly advise Gladstone not to enter the Church, he advised his son to wait before making a decision, at least until he had completed his studies. He went on to remind William

> that the field of actual usefulness to our fellow-creatures, where a disposition to exercise it actively exists, is more circumscribed and limited in the occupations and duties of a clergyman ... than in those professions or pursuits which lead to a more general knowledge, as well as a more general intercourse with mankind, such as the law, taking it as a basis, and introduction to public life, to which I had looked forward for you.[16]

His father's wishes, therefore, seemed very clear and different from Gladstone's own: he should study the law and from there, move into politics. For it was the realm of politics that the young Gladstone himself had found 'fascinating. Perhaps too fascinating'.[17]

This fascination is clear from Gladstone's activities during the debates surrounding the Reform Bill. His orations at Oxford did not stand alone as evidence of his interest in politics. Just two months after the exchange of letters with his father and only one month before his final examinations, Gladstone spent several nights in London, attending for five nights debates in the House of Lords, which he found extremely interesting. While his own sympathies were with the opponents of reform, Gladstone was prepared to admit that the best speeches in the debate were those of the Whig leader Lord Grey and his lieutenants, lords Goderich and Lansdowne. But he was unnerved by the prospect of the bill passing, and afraid of the consequences. It is also notable that among the doodles on a letter dating from 1829, in Gladstone's writing, it is possible to see, in the company of eminent politicians 'Lord Viscount Palmerston, M.P.' and his friends A.H. Hallam, MP and M. Gaskell, 'the Rt. Hon. W.E. Gladstone'.

Gladstone reflected on his father's letter and his own experiences later in 1831, to write again to his father in January 1832 with further reflections on his destiny. He had come to the conclusion, he said, that he now intended to do what his father had suggested to him the year before. He would begin by studying the law, especially constitutional law, and then, when the opportunity offered, he would try and find an opening into political life. This was a highly conservative document in some ways, with Gladstone justifying his decision to abandon a career in the Church on the grounds that the changes being brought in by the

Reform Bill needed to be fought – and, of course, though this was less openly acknowledged, this is what his father (and his mother) wanted.

EARLY CAREER

Whatever the reasons for Gladstone's decision, then, by the beginning of 1832 it had been made: he was to be a politician – and a conservative one at that. But he was also to be a Christian politician, one who would never forget that he had, at one time, a real calling to be a clergyman. This, though, was to be in the future, for in February 1832 Gladstone, in company with his brother John, left England on a grand tour of the continent, just as so many young aristocrats and upper class young men had done.

His journey took him through Brussels and Paris to Italy: Florence, Naples, Rome, Venice and Milan. The effects of the tour seem to have been twofold. Gladstone discovered first of all, that the importance of the Church as a teacher – even, in this case, the Church of Rome – went beyond the Bible and the Prayer Book. Secondly, while he found the Catholic Church to have unexpected merits, he also found the Protestant inhabitants of the Vaudois in France disappointingly like other men and women, who did not all come up to his expectations. And whatever he did, Gladstone could not forget what was happening back home. It was not good.

While he was away, the Great Reform Act had became law after a stirring two-year debate. The fifteen years following the defeat of Napoleon had been dominated by Tory governments and the initial cry for reform had been stifled by a mixture of repression and concessions made by the government of Lord Liverpool. But the demand did not go away. In the later 1820s even the Tory Duke of Wellington found himself forced to make concessions – the repeal of anti-Catholic legislation was carried by the Duke and his lieutenant, Sir Robert Peel, in 1829. But neither was prepared to go any further and when the cry for parliamentary reform resurfaced in 1830, the Duke spoke out for all Tories: the constitution was perfect and could not be improved. This effectively marked the end of his government and his replacement as prime minister by Earl Grey.

The Whigs were the party of political reform and came into office determined that Parliament should, indeed, be reformed. In the end, the measure they proposed to the Commons on 1 March 1831 caused amazement and hilarity in the House, and it was defeated by one vote in Committee on 23 March. Following a general election, the Whigs were again victorious and made a second attempt, which passed the Commons in June, but this time was rejected by the Lords. At this the Whigs decided they would have to pressurise the king, William IV, to promise to create enough peers to secure passage of the legislation. The king was reluctant to do this, but popular feeling was most definitely on the side of the Whigs, and after another general election, he agreed. The third Bill passed the Commons and, led by Wellington, enough Tory Peers abstained to allow it through the Lords. The result was that fifty-six boroughs were disfranchised, and thirty lost one of their two members. Forty-two new boroughs were created; twenty returning two members and the remaining twenty-two one member each. Manchester, Bradford and Birmingham were now to return MPs. The electorate went up by some 80 per cent, or about 300,000 in all, but by over 1,000 per cent in Scotland (to 64,447), giving a total voting population in England, Scotland and Wales of some 650,000 men. England still dominated the Commons, with 71 per cent of members representing English constituencies, but of these almost half had electorates of under 900. The Reform Act was, therefore, in some ways, a radical measure, and as such it roused the ire of Tories within and, like Gladstone, out of Parliament. But in some respects it was also a conservative one: the changes it made were not really very radical, and Peel came to realise this and tried to educate his own party accordingly. The Act was conservative in that it did not offer anything like universal male suffrage; it did not change the terms of election or the means of conducting elections, and MPs were still not to be paid salaries. It was passed because many of the Whigs, especially their leaders, believed that some constitutional changes were necessary. These changes would reconcile many of the new rich middle classes to the system, and they would defuse some of the more radical demands. But it was also designed to ensure that the aristocratic Whig element in the Commons should remain in charge.

The House of Lords was busily debating the new Reform Bill, in Gladstone's absence, and when he was in Rome he read their discussions with horror. Still in Rome, he remarked on 4 June that he was becoming accustomed to receiving dreadful news, but even the beauties of

Venice paled before the news he described as 'disastrous but expected', received on 16 June: it was that the Reform Bill had been passed.

It seemed, however, there was not much he could do about it – that was until he received a letter from his Christ Church friend, Lord Lincoln. Lincoln had persuaded his father, the ultra-Tory Duke of Newcastle, that he knew just the man to represent his interest in the duke's pocket borough of Newark: young William Gladstone. Should Gladstone accept this 'stunning and overpowering proposal'?[18] He voiced some doubts to his father (the duke, for example, had not been an ally of Canning), but he eventually accepted, coming back to England on 28 July.

The Reform Act had made some changes to the Newark constituency, increasing the electorate from about 500 to about 1,600. This made Gladstone's (as well as the Duke of Newcastle's and John Gladstone's) task that much more difficult. His first job was to prepare an election address, which would be circulated to voters. This he completed on 4 August. In it he put forward clearly what he stood for: the union of Church and State, the defence of the Church of Ireland, improvements in the condition of the working classes and a 'dignified foreign policy'. One other thing he also included was his belief in 'measures for the moral advancement and further legal protection of our fellow-subjects in slavery'.[19] Gladstone was not, therefore, even at this stage in his political career, an ultra-Tory, opposed to any and all changes. If necessary, he was prepared to accept and even to propose some measures of social reform, even in the area of slavery. But the fundamentals of his political belief, the major role assigned for the Church and its intimate connection with the State, were clear to see.

Gladstone, however, did not get to Newark until quite late in September, over six weeks after his address was written. He was roused from his bed in Torquay, where he had been staying with his family, early on a Sunday morning and hastily travelled north. Gladstone was not very happy to be travelling on a Sunday, particularly for political reasons, but it seemed to be necessary. On this occasion, even though it was a Sunday, politics took priority.

Gladstone left long memoranda recounting his experiences in Newark. He arrived late in the town and he found someone waiting for him who fortunately turned out to be a friend. After a brief night's rest – which Gladstone noticed was not marked by the very uncomfortable feelings he had sometimes experienced at Eton and Oxford – he toured the town, having been told to kiss every lady's hand, even if they did not want him to, and all the daughters, too. To his surprise, he found that most of the women took an interest in at least local politics, even if they were not so concerned with national questions, and even though they did not have the vote. Clearly Gladstone's advisers believed the women would have a notable influence on their menfolk when the election arrived. He recorded his experiences as he toured the town in some detail. One woman shouted at him from an upstairs window:

> another tore my card and flung the pieces at my feet – a third on hearing 'Well, Ma'am, shall we have a vote here?' – 'I wouldn't give you one to save your life if I'd a hundred'. This was the worst by far. Of the men, only two or three were at all insolent ... Once I got *pity* – 'Well, Sir, I do assure you I'm sorry for you from the bottom of my heart, for you're among bad ones'.[20]

Gladstone reported that over seventy specific questions had been put to him: of these, eight concerned the ballot, three were about the abolition of stamp duty on newspapers, and two on universal suffrage, but by far the majority, about sixty, were about 'slavery', all of which he felt he had fielded successfully.

But, as well as recounting his experience, he used the opportunity to reflect on some more general issues. He believed most voters 'had properly speaking no knowledge or notions of *politics*' – rather, they drew their ideas from a newspaper and repeated questions that had been suggested to the others. This, however, did not necessarily matter: 'nor is it ... desirable that the people should learn to take an interest in general politics, except in as far as such is necessary to secure their good government.[21] Even so, Gladstone was concerned about several things. First, 'the tendency of the newspaper system will be I fear to pervert the minds of the people by introducing excitement into them'. Secondly, he thought that the thoughts of the masses mixed good and bad together in such a way that the struggle between them resulted in 'embittering feelings and debasing conduct in its relation to man's highest interest'. The result of this was that Gladstone's canvas 'brought home to my mind a deeper and more sincere hatred of the Reform Bill … than I had before entertained'.[22] Gladstone would therefore enter the House of Commons as an arch-Tory, at least as far as his attitude to parliamentary reform was concerned.

But why did people vote for him? At least one man suggested that he might vote for Gladstone if he was bought a drink. Others thought that if they received an improvement to their property they might vote for the Duke of Newcastle's man – and to Gladstone, this was perfectly acceptable: 'I am in no degree ashamed of votes given through attachment to a landlord'.

Many men, though, voted for Gladstone because they felt that, as tenants of the Duke of Newcastle, they simply had to. Earlier the duke had evicted some of his tenants because they had dared to vote against his candidate, arguing 'May not I do what I will with my own'. Gladstone knew this, and had to admit to himself that he found the argument hard to accept: 'A man may not always do, morally, that which he may do legally … The duke's argument *seemed* to be, that the legal right in itself conferred the moral right', but he convinced himself that the duke would not think like this, 'this is a proposition from which I believe his own kindly nature would recoil much more strongly, than of many who revile him'.[23] It was only later that he found out how much his father and Newcastle had paid out to cover his election expenses, and the revelation alarmed him greatly.

Gladstone, in fact only met the duke for the first time on 9 October 1832, and made a long record of their conversation. He discovered then that he shared a good many of the duke's convictions, especially in religious matters and in the outlook for society. The duke thought that the Church of England's doctrines were 'entirely and perfectly in accordance with the spirit of Christianity', and young Gladstone agreed, but he hoped divisions in the Church were at least being reduced. Newcastle also believed that 'if we desert God, as a nation, He will desert us' – and Gladstone agreed with this too, adding 'we seem to be approaching a period, in which one expects events so awful, that the tongue fears to utter them'. The duke accepted as much, and said he had made his view public in a pamphlet and had been called a fool for doing it. But, as Gladstone said, 'It is no disgrace to be called a fool by persons who look on such views as folly'.[24] Gladstone had expressed some reservations about Sir Robert Peel, the Tory leader in the Commons. He told the duke that he did not think Peel's latest speech, though it was on the right lines, adopted a sufficiently high ground. The trouble with Peel, Gladstone thought was that he would accept some changes, and worried too much what other people thought about him, which was also Newcastle's opinion.

Gladstone afterwards reflected on his time spent at Clumber, the duke's country house. He came to the conclusions that 'Birth, wealth, station, are as well as talent and virtue among the natural elements of power, and we must not war with nature's laws. Moreover, there are many among them still strong not only by bulk of property and influence, but by lofty understanding or unblemished character'.[25] Newcastle, he felt, belonged to the latter class: what his former tenants might have felt about him is another question.

Gladstone won the election, which took place on 13 December 1832, comfortably, topping the poll, and took his seat in the House of Commons on 5 February 1833. This was no mean achievement. It was unusual for MPs to be elected at such a young age (the minimum age for election was twenty-one and Gladstone was only twenty-two at this time). He had not been employed since graduation, and although he had taken at least one dinner at Lincoln's Inn in case he needed a professional qualification, he did not qualify as a lawyer. Moreover, like all MPs, he did not receive a salary, and hence depended entirely on his father for financial support. John Gladstone responded to this call, purchasing the lease on an apartment in the prestigious Albany, an apartment block for bachelors in the West End of London, and giving him £10,000 (nearly £45,000) of capital stock in one of his companies.

Clearly William Gladstone was seen in Tory circles as a young man who would strongly support them in a new parliament. With their help and the backing of his father, Gladstone had started on a parliamentary career that would last sixty-one years. He joined a Tory party that was still reeling from the battles over the Great Reform Act and reduced to a mere 172 MPs, compared with Lord Grey's ministry with its 486 supporters.

The Whigs remained in office until dramatically dismissed by the king in November 1834. By that time, Gladstone had made something of an impact on the House of Commons. His first major speech occurred on 3 June 1833 in reply to a government proposal to abolish slavery.

This was partly a personal matter. Lord Howick, the government spokesman, used John Gladstone's Demerara estate as an example of harsh administration. Gladstone, we are told by Morley, was unable to attract the attention of the chairman of the debate, though it seems almost as likely that the chairman saw a rather wild and angry young man trying to speak and thought it better not to invite him to. He had calmed down, at least outwardly, by 3 June, but as he had noted in his diary on 31 May: 'the emotions thro' which one passes, at least through which I pass, in anticipating such an effort as this, are painful and humiliating.'[26] He attended a meeting of MPs with West India interests at Lord Sandon's on the morning of the third, and then went to the House of Commons, where he spoke for some fifty minutes, in a style reminiscent of his addresses to the Oxford Union. He concluded with an emotional expression of sympathy for the West India planters, which was to become typical of his speeches in the House. This does not sound very attractive; even so, the speech was well received by the 'Rupert of Debate', Lord Stanley, and by Thomas Babington Macaulay, neither friends of Gladstone, and, perhaps most importantly, by none other than Sir Robert Peel.

The votes Gladstone cast at this time were in a general illiberal direction. He voted, for example, against the admission of Jews to Parliament, the abolition of flogging in the army, shortening the life of a Parliament, the secret ballot, the income tax and the admission of dissenters to universities. He continued his struggle with his conscience about his vocation; on 21 July 1833, he took a lone walk to Kensington Gardens and spent several hours there reflecting on what his future should be. He wrote on 6 October, on receiving the news of the death of his friend Arthur Hallam:

> This intelligence was deeply oppressive, even to my selfish disposition. I mourn in him, for myself, my earliest near friend: for my fellow creatures, one who would have adorned his age and country, a mind full of beauty and of power, attaining almost to that ideal standard, of which it is presumption to expect an example in natural life. When shall I see his like?[27]

Perhaps this sad event lay at the back of his mind when he reviewed the year on his birthday, as he always did:

> Twenty-four years have I lived ... where is the *continual* work, which ought to fill up a life of a Christian without intermission? ... I have been growing, that is certain: in good or evil? Much fluctuation: often a supposed progress ... Business and political excitement a tremendous trial, not so much alluring as forcefully dragging down the soul from that temper, which is fit to inhale the air of heaven.[28]

He continued, nevertheless, to discuss religious matters with a wide circle of friends and acquaintances and to read a large number of books, British and foreign, including works by Dante, one of his greatest literary loves.

He spoke again in the Commons on 28 July 1834 dealing with the Universities Bill, arguing against allowing the admission of non-Anglicans, and was happy to say the House received him in a friendly way, though he put this down to the fact that the members had been engaged in a debate on Indian affairs and were pleased with the change of subject. Next day, he went to a dinner at Carlton House, hosted by Lord Lincoln. Peel was there, and Gladstone noted that he was in a good mood and had expressed his appreciation of his speech of the previous evening. He apparently thought it better than Gladstone himself had done. Gladstone was greatly heartened by this exchange, which he reported to his mother. It pleased him for two reasons: one was the positive manner in which Peel had referred to his speech; the other, and an even more noteworthy one, was Peel's friendliness towards him.

By the autumn of 1834, therefore, Gladstone had made a useful start to his political career. While he continued to worry whether he was doing the right thing by entering the House of Commons, it is fairly clear that politics were the most important element in his life – certainly in his public life. He was a confirmed Tory with an impressive record of opposition to reform measures of any kind. He was noted in December 1834 in *The Globe* as displaying 'the most zealous adherence to the most antiquated and obnoxious principles of his party'.[29] There was nothing in his parliamentary career that would cause concern to his patron, the Duke of Newcastle. But Gladstone was also aware of the need to secure the support of Sir Robert Peel, and he had got some way towards this. Peel, of course, needed all the supporters he could get, and no doubt appreciated Gladstone's talents.

It is not surprising, therefore, that on his arrival back in England in December 1834 to form a government, he should have sent a message to Gladstone, who was staying at the new family home at Fasque in Scotland that John Gladstone had bought in 1829. A new and most important phase in Gladstone's career was about to open.

2

THE PEELITE, 1834–1852

By the end of 1834 Gladstone had reached a degree of prominence in the House of Commons, and was noted as a staunch opponent of reform. It came as a surprise to him, however, when he received a letter from Sir Robert, inviting him to London for an interview.

PEEL'S FIRST MINISTRY, 1834–1835

Of all the politicians who were to have an impact on Gladstone, there is no doubt that it was Sir Robert Peel who had the greatest political influence. As leader of the rump of the Tory party in the House of Commons, Peel was an obvious target for Gladstone's admiration. While he was pleased with any encouraging comments from his chief, he was not expecting it when Peel asked him to come to London. Following the dismissal of the Whig Lord Melbourne's ministry by King William IV in November 1834, Peel, who was on holiday abroad, had returned to England and had managed to form a minority government in December, resting on a purely Tory body of support in the Commons. Gladstone, as one of Peel's brighter young supporters, was obviously a candidate for junior office. Their interview, held after Gladstone had made a rapid journey south, took place as early as 20 December:

> He offered me my choice of the Admiralty and Treasury Boards: recommending, however, the latter: and he gave as the reason that I

> should be there in confidential communication with him, and that my relation to him would there afford me much general insight into the concerns of government.

Peel evidently believed this would introduce Gladstone to some of the higher duties of government which he would be able to put to use later in his career. But Gladstone was lacking in self-confidence and hesitated a little before accepting the post at the Treasury. He closed his memorandum on the interview with a typically self-deprecatory, or perhaps self-centred and proud, remark: 'O God! that I were better worth the having'.[1] It was reassuring that Peel was very kind towards him throughout the brief interview.

One of the difficulties facing Gladstone when he accepted office, like all those appointed to a ministerial post at this time, was the need to stand for re-election. Gladstone had, indeed, expressed concern about this at his meeting with Peel, but he realised Peel was going to call a general election in any case. When this took place in January 1835 the government's position was improved somewhat by about one hundred seats, though it did not give the Tories a majority. More important in the long run than the election result was that Peel, while unopposed at his Tamworth seat, had nevertheless issued a manifesto outlining his views on the nature and policy of government. Recent views of the 'Tamworth Manifesto' stress the role of the Conservative Party as the party of government. Gladstone himself was to inherit this idea, and it was to form one of the main bases of his political philosophy. The manifesto itself accepted the Reform Act as 'a final and irrevocable settlement of a great constitutional question'. It went on to stress that Peel would not 'undertake to adopt' policies that involved simple and immediate acceptance of all public demands for change. On the other hand, he would, if necessary, after 'a careful review of institutions civil and ecclesiastical, undertaken in a friendly temper' carry through 'the correction of proved abuses and the redress of real grievances'.[2] These ideas seem to have become more attractive to voters later in the nineteenth century, but they did not help the Conservatives to win the election.

Gladstone's own career advanced a stage further in January, however. On the 26th of that month he was once more interviewed by Sir

Robert Peel. This time, once again, to his intense surprise, the Prime Minister offered him a new post, that of Under-Secretary of State for the Colonies. Since the Colonial Secretary, Lord Aberdeen, sat in the Lords, this meant Gladstone would be spokesman for one of the great departments of state in the Commons. Gladstone, faced with this offer, was very uncertain what to do: he was pleased to be offered the post, but worried he was not clever enough for it. He was aware Peel held him in high regard, but he was afraid he had given him a false impression, exaggerating his abilities. He was, in fact, Peel's second choice for the job, but the first, Lord Sandon, had declined it. The Prime Minister would feel the loss of Gladstone's services at the Treasury to him personally, but Lord Aberdeen had asked for him particularly. When Gladstone had worried that his West Indian interests would cause difficulties with the colonial lobby, Peel thought these could be overcome. Most important for Gladstone, however, was that both Peel, whose manner was apparently 'affectionate', and Aberdeen, who was also extremely relaxed and kind, were obviously anxious to be his friends.[3] In time, he was to form very close relationships with both men.

The story of the Peel government was brief. Faced with the opposition in office, the disparate elements of the Whig party drew together and first defeated the Conservatives' proposal for House of Commons' speaker – which Gladstone told his father he thought a very shameful act – and then joined together in the 'Lichfield House Compact' to secure the ejection of the government.

Gladstone did his best to support Peel, but he found speaking in the House of Commons very difficult. On 31 March 1835 he contributed to the debate on the issue that finally brought down the government, which concerned what should be done with the surplus revenues of the established Anglican Church of Ireland. 'It was received by the House', he wrote to his father, 'in a manner extremely gratifying to me'. But he was, as so often, less satisfied in other ways:

> Backed by a numerous and warm-hearted party, and strong in the consciousness of a good cause, I did not find it difficult to grapple with the more popular parts of the question; but I feel miserably short of my desires in touching upon the principles which the discussion involved.[4]

What was worse, it did the ministry no good. Peel's government was defeated in the debate and he resigned the next day.

Even so, Peel had some cause for satisfaction. As he explained to his followers at a dinner shortly after his resignation, he had not taken office with any great hopes of success, though he had hoped to do some good, and some good had been achieved. The most important thing was that, while the Conservative government had not proven strong enough to run the country, it had shown itself sufficiently strong to be able to stop any other government – namely, Lord Melbourne's Whigs – from passing measures the Conservatives believed would harm the country. Moreover, the Conservatives had shown ability during their brief spell in office, and the extent of the disunity among the Whigs had been revealed.

YEARS OF OPPOSITION, 1835–1841

The next six years was the story of increasing Conservative power as they continued to win seats, both in by-elections and in the General Election of 1837 caused by the accession of Queen Victoria, which, together with defections from the government, reduced its majority to some thirty seats. Indeed, the Conservatives nearly took office in 1839, but the rather odd 'Bedchamber crisis', when the young queen refused to replace her Whig ladies-in-waiting with Conservative ones, prevented this. It was only after the elections of 1841 that Peel, at last, managed to return to office at the head of a majority Conservative government.

The Whigs spent these years pursuing an essentially cautious domestic policy, and an increasingly assertive foreign policy, the latter masterminded by the former Canningite Tory, Lord Palmerston. They did not abandon all reform, most notably with the Municipal Corporations Act of 1835, which meant town councillors and aldermen would have to be elected to office, and the Dissenters Marriage Act of 1836, which allowed members of the Nonconformist churches to marry in their own churches, without the involvement of the established Church of England. But the Whig government was trapped on the horns of a dilemma, which the Home Secretary, Lord John Russell, explained to his prime minister in 1837. Many of the government's more radical supporters expected them to pass a lot more measures than they were able to, given the balance of power in the Commons. If they did not do much, they would lose the support of their allies: but if they attempted to do more, the Conservatives would receive stronger support. As time went on, the Whigs certainly appeared to do less and the radicals and Irish on the left of the party tended to feel increasingly alienated from the government. The result of this was that the Whig government began to lean more heavily on Peel for support, but Peel would only support them if their policies were suitably conservative.

Gladstone's own career, in these years, followed fairly closely that of his party. He realised very soon after the fall from office what Peel's position was, and by all accounts sympathised with it, though he thought Peel's decision to dissolve Parliament following his defeat had been a serious mistake.

The General Election of 1837 went well for Gladstone, who was safely returned for Newark, but was politically disappointing for others in the Gladstone family. His father was defeated when he stood for Dundee, despite the promised support of some two hundred voters. Gladstone was also to experience what it was like to be something less than a popular hero with the masses, as when he left Dundee he was hissed by the crowd. His brother Tom, meanwhile, came bottom of the poll at Leicester.

These years were also turbulent for Gladstone personally. On 23 September 1835, his mother died after a long illness. This event clearly touched Gladstone deeply: his mother, along with his sister Anne, had been the strongest influences on his religious outlook in the early years of his life. Like all Victorian gentlemen, Gladstone had not given much thought to marriage while he was a student or immediately afterwards, but by the end of the 1830s he had begun to think the time had arrived to settle down and start a family. Alas, it was not to be that easy. He had approached two young ladies: the attractive Caroline Farquhar, the sister of someone he had known at Eton, in 1835, and Lady Frances Douglas, daughter of the Earl of Morton, in 1838. Both had, after long and difficult courtships, made their opposition to his approaches plain. Young Gladstone, indeed, was so intense, that he positively scared Miss Farquhar.

Once again, therefore, in part as a consequence of these failures, Gladstone began to devote more time to questions of politics. He attended a number of meetings of Conservative Party leaders during late

1837 and into 1838. The most important of these revolved around the question of whether or not to adopt Lord Durham's report on Canadian administration, which had proposed that the colonies should be granted 'responsible government' – the government in the colonies should be made answerable to the local people. Behind this, for Peel and his followers, lay the question of whether or not the government itself should be defeated. At the meeting on 16 January 1838 Peel urged caution: he thought the government should be defeated by the Conservative Party on solely conservative principles. In fact, the Conservatives managed to carry five amendments against the government on this question. Gladstone was delighted, and thought it reflected great credit on Peel and the Conservatives, showing them in a far better light than it did the Whigs. But by March, in the aftermath of the disappointments in his private life, Gladstone was in a 'morbid state', and his mind was increasingly occupied by what he conceived to be his most important contribution to politics.

The dominance of religion in Gladstone's political philosophy did not diminish during his years in parliament. As he admitted in a memorandum written as late as 1897, 'The primary idea of my early politics was the Church'.[5] In April and May 1838 he attended a series of lectures given by the eminent theologian, Dr Thomas Chalmers, and when he heard that figure declaim that the state had no business to meddle with the doctrines of the Church, he reacted strongly. By August he had completed the manuscript of a book entitled *The State in its Relations with the Church*. The theme of this work was that the state was duty bound to protect and support the cause of religious truth, and the Church of England had a monopoly of religious truth. By implying that the state should enforce religious orthodoxy, Gladstone was proposing a very reactionary policy indeed.

The book was published in December 1838. It certainly received some attention, and Gladstone thought he would help this by sending copies of it to Peel and other leading Conservative figures. But he was to be grievously disappointed with their response. When he dined with Peel on 9 February 1839 he commented that neither Peel, Stanley nor Graham even mentioned his book, though there was no appreciable change in their manner towards him. The truth was, Peel and his associates were horrified by the publication. Peel is said to have called it 'trash' and Graham said he could not understand it. But one person seemed to be able understand it well enough: the Whig, Thomas Babington Macaulay. Macaulay's review of the book in the *Edinburgh Review* in April 1839 famously described Gladstone as 'the rising hope of those stern unbending Tories' – and this was the last thing Peel wanted in his party. Even at this time, however, Gladstone had no real understanding of how much difficulty the book might cause him. In June 1839, after Macaulay's review was published, Peel was forced to admit to Gladstone that he regretted the book's publication. But although much attention has been paid to this work and Gladstone himself reflected on it at some length later, it did not really have that much of an effect on his career. When he tried to follow it up with another work in November 1840, entitled *Church Principles Considered in their Results*, the lack of reaction to it was such that Morley felt the work was 'stillborn'.

One of the main effects of writing *The State in its Relations with the Church* – coupled with an eye infection – was to persuade Gladstone to take a holiday, and in August 1838 he once more left the country. This trip was to have a momentous effect on his life. In Italy he met the Glynne family of Flintshire, one of whom was an unmarried 26-year-old woman, Catherine. Gladstone did not waste any time. On 17 January 1839, 'he proposed in what must be one of the most incomprehensible love notes ever penned'. The second paragraph of it consists of one sentence 141 words in length.[6] Catherine, perhaps unsurprisingly, hesitated, and Gladstone kicked himself: once again, he thought he had jumped the gun. But this time, in the end, he was to be successful. At a party on 8 June 1839 Catherine agreed to become his wife, and they were duly married at Hawarden, the Glynne family home in Flintshire, on 25 July, in a double ceremony with Mary, Catherine's younger sister, who married George, Lord Lyttelton. Like Gladstone's parliamentary career, this was to be a long-lasting relationship.

This marriage has been the object of much study, and in particular the question has to be asked whether or not it was a happy one. Given the revelations in Gladstone's diaries about his relationships with London prostitutes and the occasional self-scourging arising out of his feelings of guilt, it has lately been suggested that it was not such an idyllic one as it was at one time presented. Travis Crosby has stressed how, in the early days of the marriage, Gladstone was frequently away from his wife, and 'At times Catherine Gladstone was no more than an infrequent guest in her husband's rule-ridden house'.[7] In 1840 and 1841 Catherine had to try very hard to get her husband's attention: if he could not go to Brighton to be with her and their first son William – who was born on 3 June 1840 – could they not be in London with him? Gladstone eventually agreed to this arrangement. But this was in the earlier days of the marriage, and, as will appear later, Catherine decided she could make her own way in the world, backing her husband up when he needed it, but also undertaking things on her own behalf. This greater self-assertion on her part made the marriage in later years more of a partnership of equals and, given Gladstone's own enormous capacity for work and volcanic personality, this was no small achievement on Catherine's part.

Gladstone's marriage removed at least one of his sources of anxiety. The parliamentary sessions of 1839 and 1840 also passed with him taking a more involved part in the development of Conservative Party politics. In March 1840, for example, he attended a meeting to discuss the approach to be taken to the warlike policy of the government in China. Hostilities had broken out there over the import of opium by British vessels to China, the British government's support for merchants engaged in this illicit opium trade and their refusal to allow the Chinese customs' authorities to search British vessels. Gladstone noted that everyone at the meeting was in agreement. The material in the papers available to them showed only one answer could be given to the question of the justice or otherwise of Lord Palmerston's belligerent policy. That answer, undoubtedly, was that it was not just, and Gladstone was not slow to tell the Foreign Secretary as much. It was 'an unjust and iniquitous war … to protect an infamous contraband traffic' in opium. Justice was with the Chinese 'and whilst they, the Pagans, and semi-civilised barbarians have it, we the enlightened and semi-civilised Christians, are pursuing objects at variance with justice, and with religion'. He had one good reason for worrying: 'I am in dread of the judgement of God upon England for our national iniquity towards China'.[8] He also had no particular desire to hide his growing hostility to Palmerston. A lot of time was also spent in 1840 discussing the vexed question of the Canada Clergy Reserves, lands in Canada held on behalf of the Church: the government proposed selling these off, a proposal Gladstone strongly objected to. This was a more important question than it appears, as it involved the whole question of how to assess colonial religious policy in general.

Lord Melbourne's government had decided on a notable change of policy. They decided that their budget should include reductions in the import duties on timber, sugar and coffee. This was a direct attack on the interests of the West India planters and other colonial producers whose supplies were only cheaper in Britain because they escaped paying the same high level of import duties as those from foreign nations. Faced with this proposal on 1 May 1841 a meeting at Peel's discussed what steps to take. Gladstone was, by now, clearly accepted as a leading figure in Conservative ranks, as he was one of only ten people present. Others included Lord Stanley, Sir James Graham, Henry Goulburn and General Sir Henry Hardinge, all of whom were to take high office in Peel's administration. At this meeting and after wider consultation within the party on the next day, it was agreed that the government's proposed Sugar Duties Bill should be attacked. This, Peel thought, was both less risky than proposing a general vote of confidence and it would also, he believed, be more likely to succeed convincingly by attracting some support from dissident Whigs.

The government persisted in its efforts to secure the passage of this Bill together with its other financial proposals, and the result of this was that Peel during the course of May decided on a change of policy. While there were risks attached to the idea of a general vote of confidence – some Whigs who would support a vote against a reduction of import duties might not be happy to support a general vote that could lead to the downfall of the ministry – Peel decided to press ahead with it. Gladstone himself agreed with this idea. The vote, when it came early on 5 June, was close: 312 Conservative to 311 Whigs – one of whom was, by all accounts, completely insane – and, as a result, Peel pressed for an early dissolution of Parliament and an immediate general election.

SIR ROBERT PEEL'S SECOND MINISTRY, 1841–1846

The Conservatives won the election comfortably, by some eighty seats, and Peel duly became prime minister. Gladstone was equally comfortably returned for Newark. But there were some serious difficulties with Peel's parliamentary position, even before the Conservative Party split itself apart over the question of Corn Law repeal in 1846. Perhaps the most serious of these was the underlying differences of opinion between

Peel and many of his followers. One problem was that most of Peel's supporters seem to have been drawn from the rural classes, since most of their MPs were elected for English counties and small boroughs with under 1,000 votes. These MPs were staunch opponents of change, supporters of what was known as the agricultural interest, and many were the offspring of the aristocratic elite. Few of them were at all sympathetic to the economic and social changes that Britain was undergoing with the increasing impact of industrialisation, and they saw no need to respond to them. They were known as 'Protectionists' and supported the Corn Laws, which levied import duties on foreign wheat and allowed farmers to keep up the price of their own cereal. In years of good harvests and low prices, import duties were raised to keep out foreign wheat, though in years of bad harvests and high prices duties were reduced to allow more in.

The manufacturing interest, on the other hand, favoured free trade in all imports and exports. This meant all import duties should be abolished, hence, manufacturers could import raw materials for their factories more cheaply and therefore cut the prices of their products, helping boost exports. If the Corn Laws were repealed, this would reduce the price of wheat imports, and many free traders realised it would make it possible for them to lower wages and cut still further the price of their exports. Their political sympathies tended to be with the Whigs, though Peel was hoping to attract them to his own side by his policies. Peel had his own firm and clear ideas about what Britain needed and what he had to do; he was becoming more convinced of the virtues of free trade, and was not prepared to make too many concessions to his followers. Those who agreed with him and got on well with him were those who shared his outlook; those who did not found him aloof and unsympathetic.

The first thing Peel had to do was form a government. He placed Gladstone's former employer, Lord Aberdeen, at the Foreign Office, and a marked change to the tone of British foreign policy soon became apparent. The former Whigs Sir James Graham and Lord Stanley received important appointments as Home Secretary and Secretary for War and the Colonies. Henry Goulburn became Chancellor of the Exchequer, although everybody knew that this meant, in effect, Peel would do much of the work himself. Gladstone, however, was to be sorely disappointed.

On 21, 22 and 23 August he had attended meetings at Peel's house, and became fully involved with Peel, Graham, Stanley, and a few others, in discussions about the Conservatives' response to the Speech from the Throne. It was agreed that an amendment should be proposed, and this was duly carried on 27 August. The second of these meetings was on a Sunday and Gladstone had to go to some lengths to justify his attendance. But when on 31 August he had a private interview with Peel, he was only offered the post of Vice-President of the Board of Trade, with Lord Ripon as President, and no seat in the cabinet. At the interview, Gladstone, perhaps hypocritically, stressed to Peel his unfitness for the office, but added that he would take it on, if that was what Peel wanted, and he would try and prepare himself for the post as well as he could. But it was Peel's definite wish: Gladstone, like other young Conservatives such as Lord Lincoln and Sidney Herbert, received relatively junior posts, but they were clearly being groomed for the future. Gladstone, alas, did not see this at the time, and recorded his private views of the matter a few days later.

> Upon quietly reviewing past times, and the degree of confidence which Sir Robert Peel had for years, habitually I may say, reposed in me, and especially considering its climax, in my being summoned to the meetings immediately preceding the debate on the Address in August, I am inclined to think, after allowing for the delusions of self love, that there is not a perfect correspondence between the tenor of the past on the one hand, and my present appointment and the relations in which it places me to the Administration on the other ... I am sorry now to think I may have been guilty of an altogether absurd presumption, in dreaming of the Cabinet.[9]

Still, he thought God had placed him here, though he noted how Peel was uncomfortable with what he had to tell him. At this point he did not think Peel had given him his just deserts. Despite this disappointment, however, Gladstone remained a staunch supporter of Peel, defending him, for example, against charges of irreligion that had appeared in the *Morning Advertiser*.[10]

The fact was that, although Gladstone held a junior post, Peel made good use of his services. As early as October 1841 he suggested to his chancellor, Goulburn, that Gladstone should be added to two or three of the Treasury Lords to form an unpaid commission to investigate the expenses incurred in collecting the national revenue. This would help them become familiar with the minutiae of running the government. He was not afraid to tell Gladstone some of his innermost thoughts on policy, telling him of the need for accurate and detailed information to enable a change in policy to be made. Gladstone responded that his own views were changing. The effect of his enquiries was slowly to convince him that British agriculture was strong and did not need the level of protection from foreign imports it received at present from the Corn Laws. He was reassured a little later after talking with Lord Ripon that the cabinet were all aware that import duties on wheat were greater than they needed to be. Unfortunately, Gladstone's own proposal, which would have cut all duties once the price of wheat reached 61s. a quarter, seemed somewhat more radical than those of his colleagues, and following a meeting at Peel's house on 5 February 1842, he asked to see his chief. To Peel's surprise and dismay he asked to resign. Peel, said Gladstone, was 'thunderstruck', saying he thought Gladstone had already agreed to the proposal that duties should stay at 20s. when the price was 51s. a quarter and be reduced to 1s. at 23s., that was now to go forwards, and 'that if he had understood me to regard the structure of the upper part of the scale as fundamentally objectionable he would have made a different proposition to the Cabinet'. Now it was Gladstone's turn to be taken by surprise – 'I said I never could have presumed to think that any opinion of mine could have affected his proposition to the Cabinet' – and he withdrew his proposal. But the damage was done: 'I fear Peel was much annoyed and displeased'. He assured Peel he would tell no one, and only one person did he tell: 'I came home sick at heart in the evening and told all to Catherine'.[11]

Peel had his own plan for the finances of the country. On 11 March 1842 he introduced his first 'free trade' budget, by which the duties on more than three-quarters of imported goods were to be cut, and duties on coffee and sugar, as well as on all exports, were to be abolished. He intended to cover the apparent deficit that would result from this by introducing an income tax, although only as a temporary measure. This tax had first been used during the Napoleonic wars and had been one of the first targets of the economical reformers in the post-war period, being abandoned as early as 1816. On 8 April 1842, however, it was on this very question that Peel was able to display what Gladstone called 'conspicuous intellectual greatness'. When no one, not even Lord Stanley, the so-called 'Rupert of the Debate', could answer the charges of the opposition against the government's financial proposals, Peel rose and delivered a most successful speech.[12] Gladstone's appreciation of Peel, both as a statesman and as a leader, grew accordingly. But even at this early date, some of Peel's cabinet and party, notably Stanley himself, were becoming uneasy at his apparent promotion of the manufacturing over the agricultural interest.

Then Gladstone, unfortunately, experienced another private trauma. In the summer of 1842 his sister Helen became a convert to Roman Catholicism. From this event and the correspondence arising out of it, it is possible to see once again the immense importance of religion to Gladstone's life. Dr Thomas Wiseman had written to both Gladstone and his father on 6 June to announce Helen's conversion. On the 12th Gladstone had a long and painful interview with his sister. He was particularly upset and annoyed that it was Wiseman who had informed her father of Helen's decision, rather than she herself, about what was a very serious and solemn matter, but he could do nothing to prevent her loss from the Church of England. Gladstone also had to cope with the loss of part of a finger in a shooting accident on 18 September. Rather more happily, however, on 18 October Catherine gave birth to her first daughter, Agnes.

While this was going on Gladstone continued to work steadily at the Board of Trade. The result of his efforts was that he became steadily more convinced of the merits of Peel's free trade policies – so much so that in January 1843 he published in a periodical, the *Foreign and Colonial Quarterly Review*, 'a masterly exposition' of the government's commercial policy. Even though he knew some of the Conservative Party were getting restless at Peel's policy (he was informed that many of the county members had gone as far as they could with Sir Robert Peel on the question of the reduction of import duties on wheat), he strongly defended the policy of the government. Although he was far from abandoning his views on the religious duties of the state, Gladstone was also beginning to see the importance of political economy. Even so, when Peel wrote to him on 13 May with the offer of a seat in the cabinet, the younger man hesitated, as so often, before accepting. It was not that Peel did not try hard, telling him

> For myself personally, and I can answer also for every other member of the government, the prospect of your accession to the Cabinet is very gratifying to our feelings.[13]

(He later told Gladstone this unanimity and strength of feeling was unique in his experience.) But even after a long talk with Peel on 13 May, Gladstone was still unsure. He debated within himself whether it was God's will that he should join the Cabinet – or whether he should take what was probably the only other realistic alternative and resign from the government altogether.[14]

The big problem causing Gladstone to hesitate was the fate of two bishoprics in North Wales, Bangor and St Asaph. It was proposed by the Parliamentary Ecclesiastical Commission that they should be amalgamated, releasing one bishop for a new see in Manchester, needed to take account of the shift of population into more urban areas. Gladstone argued that Parliament had no business to interfere with the Church's internal arrangements, and the two bishoprics should be left alone. Peel, on the other hand, wanted to carry out the will of Parliament, but he wanted Gladstone in the cabinet at least as much. He struggled to convince Gladstone that the subject of the North Wales bishoprics should not present him with a difficulty while he assured him that his views were generally in sympathy with those of the cabinet, and his joining it should not present either him or them with any problems. This represents a remarkable, but, for Gladstone, a not untypical state of affairs. Peel was clearly very anxious to entice him in, but it is quite striking how far Gladstone went to make life difficult for himself. In the end, though – and one suspects not surprisingly – he accepted the offer. He attended his first cabinets on 15 and 20 May, and he was not overawed on either occasion.

For the rest of the year Gladstone remained in attendance at cabinet meetings and followed the government's deliberations closely. Two things dominated discussions. The first was India, where in 1839 a British army had been sent to occupy Kabul, capital of Afghanistan, as a counter to Russian moves in the area. The withdrawal of this force at the beginning of 1842 had ended in a catastrophic defeat at the hands of Afghan tribesmen in the Khyber Pass. Peel's government had sent out a new governor general, Lord Ellenborough. Ellenborough felt he should restore British prestige and did so with an expedition to Kabul.

Unfortunately, the disaster in Afghanistan meant British prestige elsewhere had suffered and the rulers of Scinde felt tempted – so the British believed – to stop paying the dues they owed. The man sent to sort things out – a wild general, Sir Charles Napier – had failed in his efforts to negotiate a settlement, but was more successful in the invasion of Scinde that followed. In March 1843 Scinde was annexed to the British Crown. That was all very well, but in London Peel's government was taken by surprise and the cabinet had some doubts about whether the Ameers of Scinde had done enough to deserve annexation. In June, Gladstone noted 'great perplexity' about Indian affairs: 'Peel again declared to-day the proceedings to be unjust and indefensible',[15] and later in the month made his personal feelings plain. While he accepted the idea of a vote of thanks to the army for its work in Scinde, he thought the business there would be very damaging to the ministry should the opposition decide to take up the matter. In the end, the government had little choice but to agree to the annexation.

The second main problem, or rather series of problems, facing the government in the 1843 session – namely, Ireland – was both nearer to home and destined to have greater effects on Gladstone's career. There was discussion over the legislation that needed to be introduced to counter the increasing Irish demonstrations calling for the Repeal of the 1801 Act of Union. The government's legal officers were asked to prepare measures forbidding mass meetings or any discussion of the whole repeal question. In the event it was decided that mass meetings should be banned, and one called at Clontarf by Daniel O'Connell, 'the liberator', was duly broken up. But in February 1844, in an effort to conciliate Irish opinion, Peel proposed something that deeply shocked Gladstone: an increase in the grant made by the British government to the Irish Roman Catholic seminary at Maynooth. This would have raised the annual sum voted by the British Parliament since 1801 from £9,000 to £26,000. Gladstone strongly objected to giving money to the Roman Catholic Church, and prepared a memorandum listing over fourteen points on which objections to it might be based. Although he was aware how Peel was strongly in favour of the increase, Gladstone himself would not be convinced it would do any good. Those in favour of the measure, he wrote,

> deluded themselves I thought with visionary hopes of improvement, of controul [*sic*], of conciliation, all of which by the means proposed

> are entirely beyond reasonable expectation. This is purchasing peace by the hour. There may be times when that is imperative: but it never can be imperative upon those persons who believe it involves a sacrifice of the future to the present and barters gold for brass, even though that gold be tarnished.

He went on

> I said it grieved me beyond any thing to place anything relating to myself personally in the way of the measure of the government that only a great and decisive change of sentiments could justify my participating in such an act, and that no such change had taken place.[16]

Gladstone stuck to his guns on the issue. When Peel put forward a compromise solution, that other non-denominational educational institutions should be established elsewhere in Ireland and also receive grants, he still found it impossible to reach a settlement. It was fortunate that the proposal got no further in the immediate future.

This incident shows clearly that Gladstone's mind was still dominated by the related questions of religion and the Anglican church. He followed closely developments in the Church of England over the period, and paid attention to the 'loss' to the Roman Catholic Church of Newman, and the 'dangers' faced by other High Church Anglicans. His other concerns at this time centred on his work as President of the Board of Trade. He spent some time discussing with cabinet colleagues import duties and trade negotiations with foreign powers such as Portugal and the United States and, in particular, the difficulties arising from duties levied on the Stade River.

One of his most noted actions of the 1844 session concerned his securing the passage of a Railway Act, to strengthen one passed in 1840. By this 1844 Act, Gladstone laid down limits to the profits each railway company could make and also, most famously, insisted that all companies should run at least one 'Parliamentary train' for passengers a day, charging them a rate of 1d a mile. Each of these trains should travel at an average speed of at least twelve miles an hour, stop at all stations and have the luxury of covered carriages for all passengers. The Act even allowed for the possibility of the nationalisation of the railway companies and gives a clear indication that

Gladstone was not, at this time, a doctrinaire, laissez-faire liberal, in economic terms.

Gladstone remained a loyal member of the cabinet during most of 1844. He had by this time made a considerable impact on some people, one of whom was Lord Stanley, who became leader of the Protectionists in opposition to Peel in 1846. Stanley's relations with Peel were worsening somewhat, but he kept a close eye on Peel's young lieutenant. When Stanley and Gladstone were discussing the dearth of young men of 'decided political promise' in the Commons, Stanley made a point Gladstone did not forget: 'He said to me, "you are as certain to be Prime Minister as any man can be, if you live – the way is clear before you" '.[17] It is no surprise that in the years following the break-up of Peel's Conservative Party, Stanley should have made persistent, though ultimately unsuccessful, efforts to persuade Gladstone back on to his side, nor that Gladstone, despite his continued loyalty to Peel, should have seemed so reluctant to sever his connections with Stanley.

But if Peel's relations with Stanley were worsening, his relations with the mass of his party were worse still. On 14 June 1844 the government suffered its most serious defeat yet in the Commons, and one on a commercial question at that. In this case, it concerned import duties on sugar, which Peel wanted to reduce. Conservative back benchers who favoured higher duties and free traders united to defeat the proposal. Peel was livid: he did not want to ask the Commons to vote again on the issue to get it to reverse its earlier decision, and he came to the conclusion that the only course open to the government was resignation.

Gladstone certainly did not want this, and tried to persuade Peel to moderate his tone somewhat. He felt some sympathy – not unnaturally – for him. He thought it was all too apparent that Peel and his loyal allies did a great deal of hard work, not helped by the backbenchers, many of whom only appeared to be roused out of their apathy when they opposed something the government was going to do. In this particular case, however, Gladstone thought they had been too hard on the backbenchers and it would have been wise to have made a concession to them. Peel did not go this far and, while he withdrew the threat of resignation, he did so in a speech to the Commons that Gladstone thought was very cold and reserved. This was one occasion when Gladstone was very upset with what he heard Peel say, and he thought it was Stanley who did most to save the day and get the vote reversed.

With the Maynooth problem ever present in background of his public life, Gladstone found plenty to do and no shortage of developments in his private life either. On 4 April his second son, Stephen, was born. Less happily, his relations with his sister Helen – by this time an opium addict – were becoming even more strained, and his brother Tom, with no success in politics, was becoming increasingly jealous of his younger brother. Both matters gave Gladstone cause for concern when he visited the family home over the summer of 1844. Things then took a turn for the worse politically, when a cabinet was summoned on 19 November with Maynooth and other Irish colleges high on the agenda. This time Peel wanted the cabinet's agreement to his proposals: that the grant to Maynooth College should be increased from £9,000 to £26,000 a year, and the college should be given £30,000 in one lump sum for repairs and improvements. Gladstone went on record to say he could not be a member of a government that took such a step. He admitted that the views he had declared in *The State in its Relations with the Church* made it impossible for him to be a part of the new proposals, and therefore he had no option left but to resign. Peel and his colleagues tried to persuade Gladstone to stay.

When the last Autumn cabinet of the year was held on 6 December, Maynooth and the government's Irish policy were once again discussed. By this time, Gladstone was convinced that he had to go and on 2 January 1845 sent Peel his letter of resignation. Peel did not quite understand what the letter meant and it was left to Sir James Graham to explain it for him. When Peel and Gladstone had a meeting on 9 January, the Prime Minister pulled no punches, telling him that he thought his loss would be very damaging to the ministry. This gave Gladstone some further pause for thought, but by 21 January he told Peel his mind was fully made up. He told the prime minister that he had considered the matter carefully and come to the conclusion that, if he voted for the measure and remained in the cabinet, people would say, quite justly, he could not be trusted. That would, he said, finish his career as a politician once and for all.

Gladstone's resignation did much to persuade some of the ultra-Protestants on the Tory side of the House that they now had a new leader. His resignation speech disappointed them, however. He explained that he had not resigned because he disapproved of the measure proposed in principle: he had resigned because it did not agree with some of the doctrines he had put forward in his earlier writings. Those views he had now changed somewhat, but he could not remain in office on that basis. He voted for the Bill, which passed its second reading in April and became law later in the year. It seems he was genuinely consistent in his attitude and his belief that it would be less damaging for him to resign from the cabinet and support the measure, than to remain in his post and do so, even though it was a government measure. It is not a straightforward point of view at all and sounds somewhat strained, but it is typical of the complexity of Gladstone's ideas. His publicly-declared motive was probably genuine, and so he was right, and his exclusion from government would not be for long.

Gladstone, however, was never short of things to do: if he had time to spare, he either filled it for himself, or found others to fill it for him. During the early part of the summer of 1845 his intellectual faculties were kept active with his studies in the theology of Bishop Butler, and on 27 July Catherine gave birth to a daughter, Catherine Jessy. It was at this time, too, that Gladstone began his 'charitable' involvement with prostitutes – something that has recently been brought back into public attention – when he held a conversation, 'not free from shame to me', with a young prostitute near Hawarden.[18]

He then had vague thoughts of taking a holiday in Ireland, but instead decided on a tour of the Continent. This could hardly be described as a holiday, however. A week before Jessy's birth, his sister Helen had left the country to seek treatment for her opium addiction in Baden-Baden. More and more alarming reports of her state of mind reached Gladstone, and in September he left for Munich, her last known residence, to try and 'rescue' her. The resulting chase sums up some of Gladstone's attitudes well. When he reached Munich and found his sister gone, he did not immediately pursue her, but instead lingered long enough for two long talks with the eminent Catholic theologian, Dr Ignaz Döllinger. He carefully recorded their discussions, which, according to Richard Shannon, 'marked an epoch in Gladstone's intellectual and religious life'.[19] Gladstone was pleased to see a liberal side to the Roman Catholic Church and to hear a perceptive Catholic's view of the problems facing Europe's Christian churches. He was encouraged to think there was hope, still, for his faith. There was little hope for Helen though. Gladstone managed to locate her and take her to Cologne, but she would go no further with him, and he returned to England in the month of November alone.

As the year drew towards its close political developments quickened. News of impending famine in Ireland – the result of a disastrous blight in the potato crop – had reached London over the summer of 1845. The Conservative Party, representing as it did the agricultural interest, could not do what was necessary to help relieve the situation, namely, repeal import duties on wheat, thereby providing cheaper bread for the Irish peasantry. But perhaps the Whigs could. On 26 November, writing from Edinburgh to his constituents, the Whig leader, Lord John Russell, announced his conversion to the repeal of the Corn Laws in order to allow free trade in corn. Peel, who had cause to believe that repeal had to be carried, but felt he was not the one to carry it, resigned office on 6 December and Russell began the task of trying to form a government. Gladstone was in close contact with Lord Lincoln at this time and it is hardly coincidental that the two men should have begun to discuss the Corn Laws. He told Lincoln that if the effect of the Corn Laws was

> to keep out the corn instead of bringing it in, I held myself at liberty to vote for its abolition and could justify the vote to my constituents and contend it was the same which they in my place must as fair and honest men have given.[20]

When Peel thought Russell was going to succeed in his task, Lincoln told Gladstone, who knew very well that if Peel should try to get such a measure through it would split his party, that the Conservative leader 'was in high spirits'. But as the month went on Russell's task grew harder – for one thing, men in the Whig party saw Peel's own dilemma and were keen to exploit it. Russell accordingly returned 'the poisoned chalice' to Peel, who began himself to try and re-form his ministry. Gladstone was aware that Peel's reconstituted government was not going to be very strong.

On 21 December 1845, Peel saw Gladstone and offered him the post of Colonial Secretary in place of Lord Stanley, who had refused to rejoin the government. He did not immediately accept, telling Peel he would like to see Stanley first, but in the end, having read the cabinet papers on the parlous situation in Ireland, he agreed to join. Peel was 'most kind, nay fatherly – we *held* hands instinctively & I could not but reciprocate with emphasis his "God bless you"'.[21] Unfortunately for Gladstone and Peel, the offer of a secretaryship of state meant that Gladstone needed to be re-elected. He seems to have been confident he would be able to secure re-election for Newark once more without difficulty, but this time the sour old Duke of Newcastle, mortally offended by Gladstone's change of attitude to the Corn Laws, put up a Protectionist candidate against his former protégé and beat him. Hence Gladstone, who remained without a seat until August 1847, spent his time as Colonial Secretary outside the Commons, and could only sit and watch as Peel's ministry tumbled to its fall, with Peel himself savaged by the Protectionists, Benjamin Disraeli foremost among them.

Gladstone was not a great success as colonial secretary. He had not given much thought to colonial affairs prior to this date, and relatively little thereafter. He believed that colonies were subordinate to the mother country, and therefore should accept what the mother country chose to do for them – even to the extent of accepting more criminals from home. But he also felt that colonies should take some responsibilities for themselves, and if, for example, they got involved in wars with local inhabitants, they should pay for them themselves. This was a confused attitude and not likely to be popular with any colonies, though Gladstone was colonial secretary for such a short time he had very little effect on colonial development.

Gladstone was not admitted to Peel's confidence for much of 1846: it was only a few days before a Coercion Bill for Ireland was introduced that Peel informed him of his intentions. Only then had Peel sent round a memorandum to the cabinet, in which he argued that, if defeated on the Coercion Bill, the government should resign, but he would not call for a dissolution of Parliament. The Duke of Wellington, in soldierly fashion, argued that they should fight on, even if they were beaten, and this agreed largely with Gladstone's own inclinations. Peel was able to secure passage of the Corn Law Repeal Bill on 25 June, though most of his supporters were from the opposition benches, and on the very same evening the ministry's Coercion Bill was beaten by a combination of Whigs, Irish and dissident Tories voting together to defeat the government. This convinced Peel he had to go. Accordingly, he summoned what Gladstone described as 'the shortest Cabinet I ever knew'.

> Peel himself uttered two or three introductory sentences. He then said that he was convinced that the formation of a Conservative Party was impossible while he continued in office. That he had made up his own mind to resign. That he strongly advised the resignation of the entire government. Some declared their assent; none objected. And when he asked whether it was unanimous there was no voice in the negative.[22]

THE PEELITE OPPOSITION, 1845–1852

Gladstone spent the next few days discussing the situation with former colleagues, Sidney Herbert, Aberdeen and Graham. Herbert believed that Peel was going to stay in Parliament, but act solely for himself, and would not bind himself to any particular party. Aberdeen, perhaps not surprisingly, recommended a cautious approach to the new ministry. Graham commented on the 'virulence' of the hostility against Peel and himself, but let Gladstone know, because of recent events, he ought to consider himself free to take any course he pleased. Over the next few years Gladstone was to act on this advice, to such an extent that he nearly alienated Graham and his other former colleagues and friends completely.

The fall of Peel's ministry represented the end of the old Peelite Conservative Party. Most of the backbenchers stayed loyal to the landed representatives, headed by Lord George Bentinck and the wily Benjamin Disraeli in the Commons, and by Lord Stanley, afterwards the 14th Earl of Derby, in the Lords. The Whig–Radical coalition, headed by Lord John Russell, was still capable at this time of forming a strong ministry, confirmed by their general election victory in 1847. As a result of this, those Conservatives like Gladstone who stayed loyal to Peel, found themselves in a quandary. Numbering only some 120 MPs before the 1847 election and about half that number afterwards, they could not form an independent ministry in the Commons, even if their nominal leader had wanted them to. But Peel himself continued to act as an independent MP and refused to give an effective lead to his followers. Several possible courses therefore lay open to them. They could act with one or other of the two main parties by assuming that their only difference with the Derbyites was over free trade and join them, as some did, or recognise that the growing liberalism of their position had made it possible for them to co-operate more fully with Russell's liberals. Failing either of those options, they could continue to act independently, supporting or opposing the government on the merits of the case, and possibly attracting to themselves a body of support from other parties that would enable them eventually to form another ministry themselves. Exactly which of these lines to take exercised Gladstone's mind for the next seven years.

But so, too, did more personal matters. The very first thing he had to do was to get a seat in the Commons. He achieved this in August 1847, when he became one of the two MPs for Oxford University, a very prestigious seat and following in the footsteps of his mentor, Peel. Just after this, in November, his daughter Mary was born. He had to spend a considerable amount of time late in 1847 and into 1848 trying to sort out the financial mess that was Oak Farm, an industrial estate that was overdeveloped by its manager with funds from a mortgage taken out on the Hawarden property. Gladstone had a personal interest in this. Sir Stephen Glynne, his brother-in-law, was owner of Hawarden and was unmarried. His younger brother, Henry Glynne, who was rector of Hawarden, had only daughters and his wife died in 1850. Thus, there was no male Glynne heir to Hawarden – and Gladstone rather hoped there would not be as he and Catherine had become very fond of the place. Gladstone had to spend up to a third of his private income to rescue the Oak Farm Company, and, even worse, he had to leave 13 Carlton House Terrace and settle into a smaller property at number six. He sold part of the Hawarden Estate to pay off the debts. Sir Stephen Glynne was moved out of Hawarden until 1852, when both the Gladstone and the Glynne families moved in.

Ill-health also dogged Gladstone in these years. In September 1847 he suffered an attack of erysipelas, a painful and debilitating skin infection that his daughter Agnes had also suffered from. His father had a slight stroke in January, and Gladstone spent much time over the next five years visiting him: an increasingly delicate task, as the old man hectored him, trying to convert him from his free trade convictions. Worst of all, in 1850 Catherine Jessy became ill, and on 9 April she died of meningitis. Gladstone was devastated by her death and recorded all the events of her last illness in a long and detailed memorandum.

One other event marked this period in Gladstone's personal life. Between 13 July and 10 August 1849 he was occupied by a frantic search across Europe for the wife of his friend Lord Lincoln. Lady Lincoln had fled to the continent with her lover, and in Italy she gave birth to a child. Gladstone pursued her, eventually catching up with her and gaining proof of her infidelity. Again, he was deeply upset (as was Catherine also): first, on the personal grounds of his admiration for Lady Lincoln, and secondly, by the astonishing wickedness of her behaviour in her betrayal of the sacred institution of marriage. When the divorce proceedings were heard in April 1850 Gladstone gave evidence to the court. Just over two weeks after his return to the country, on 28 August Catherine gave birth again to another daughter, Helen, a 'very plump and attractive' child. The pressure Gladstone was under led to his beginning self-flagellation as a means of relief and as punishment for the sin he had developed of reading what he saw as erotic literature, such as Restoration poems, some classical authors and French *faiblaux* or bawdy fables. His increasing contacts with prostitutes, as he tried to 'rescue' them for the House of Refuge at Clewer in Buckinghamshire, where they were to be trained and made respectable, also unsettled him. Like many men of his era, Gladstone refrained from having sexual relations with his wife while she was pregnant, a difficult thing for a man of his strong sexual drives, and Catherine's eight pregnancies during the first fifteen years of their marriage accounted for some six years of that time.

Given this unsettled background to his private life, it is not surprising that Gladstone's parliamentary activity was somewhat limited between 1846 and 1851. Indeed, his speech on the Jewish Disabilities Bill in December 1847 was his first parliamentary oration for nearly two and a half years, and, significantly, it was in favour of this liberal government measure, allowing Jews the same rights as Nonconformists and Roman Catholics in Parliament. He made another major speech in March 1848 on budgetary policy, consciously placing himself as a likely chancellor of the Exchequer – but for which party? In fact, Gladstone spent a lot of time discussing with his 'Peelite' colleagues, the financial and commercial policies of the Whigs. The economic policy of the Russell government was by no means opposed to free trade, and he decided in March 1849 that he would offer the government conditional support for their repeal of the Navigation Act. But in May he confessed to Aberdeen that he was not opposed to the idea of the protectionist Lord Stanley being given the chance to head a government.

In October he gave vent to even more personal views in a talk with Lord Aberdeen. He clearly did not approve of Peel or Graham's 'policy', such as it was:

> Peel's political position ... I described as false and in the abstract almost immoral – as he, and still more Graham, side on the opposition side of the House professing thereby to be independent Members of Parliament but in every critical vote they are governed by the intention to keep ministers in office and sacrifice everything to that intention. In this Lord Aberdeen agreed.[23]

It was during 1850 that Stanley and his followers began seriously to hope that they might be able to attract Gladstone over to their side. Graham began to suspect Gladstone might have come to an arrangement with the Conservatives, but in response to their advances Gladstone expressed himself very cautiously; he did not wish to oppose Lord Stanley's taking office simply for the sake of it, but at the same time he did not think he could yet co-operate with him. He remembered all too clearly how Stanley's followers had savaged Peel in the Corn Law debates, and felt it would be some time before he could forgive or forget it.

The first crisis in politics in 1850 did not directly involve Gladstone, however. Rather it involved a Portuguese money-lender living in Athens – Don Pacifico – and the Foreign Secretary, Lord Palmerston. Palmerston had used the British Mediterranean fleet to blockade the Piraeus and capture Greek merchant ships to the value of £30,000 damages for Pacifico, who had lost property during a riot in Athens. Not everyone in Britain approved of this policy. The Queen and Prince Albert, Peel, Stanley and Disraeli, and Gladstone, too, ranged themselves against the fiery foreign secretary; only Russell and his party were on his side, and the Prime Minister at least was only lukewarm in his support.

It took Lord Palmerston over five hours to explain to a crowded House of Commons why he had done what he had done. It was nothing to do with Don Pacifico personally: it was all to do with Britain's place in the world, and the duty of the British government to protect British citizens wherever in the world they happened to be. It was just as in

Roman times. Then a Roman could appeal to the mighty Empire: now, declared Palmerston, in one of the most famous perorations of all, 'a British subject in whatever land he may be, may feel certain the watchful eye and the strong arm of England will protect him from injustice and wrong'.

Like his allies in the debate, Gladstone was not unduly impressed by this doctrine and made two speeches against Palmerston. In the first he reminded the House that a Roman was the representative of a domineering, military elite and Britons should not model themselves on such a one. He also denounced Palmerston's ideas of Britain's right to interfere and to teach other nations how to behave. The second speech eulogised Aberdeen and his less charismatic or aggressive policy. There was little evidence here that he would ever find it possible to ally himself with Palmerston. But all of his efforts were to no avail: Palmerston eventually won the debate and, what was worse, some of the 'Peelites' had even voted for him.

If this was disappointing to Gladstone, worse still was to follow. On 29 June 1850 Peel was thrown from his horse, and he died on 3 July before Gladstone was able to see him. The distraught Gladstone tried to find some spiritual meaning in the event. If Peel had acted as his 'father figure' in politics, their relationship had not been especially easy since Peel had resigned office and showed absolutely no intention of taking it again. To Gladstone, still a young man with much to do, this was an inconvenience to say the least. In a sense, therefore, it is no doubt correct to say that Peel's death was an 'emancipation' for Gladstone, but he does not seem to have seen it like that. His first task following Peel's death was to find someone who could take on Peel's role, and he lighted on Lord Aberdeen, senior surviving 'Peelite'. But Aberdeen never quite had the authority of his late master: to that extent, at least, Gladstone was 'emancipated' and his own reputation enhanced.

The months after Peel's death were not particularly happy for Gladstone either. In October, his sister-in-law, Lavinia Glynne, died. He was also spending some time engaged in his night-time 'rescue work' in the capital. But this was dangerous for both private as well as public reasons. The temptation afforded by the young ladies Gladstone interviewed was very real, as was the possibility of blackmail should his activities become known outside an elite circle of friends and acquaintances. Then, to make matters worse, his daughter Mary began to suffer from an eye infection. There was nothing for it: the Gladstones would have to leave the country and where else could they go, but Italy? Besides, he had a public mission there, too: he hoped to collect evidence of the corruption of the papacy. But this result of the journey was to mark one of those minor revolutions in Gladstone's political life.

The Gladstones left England on 18 October and, by the middle of November, had reached Naples. Here they found both beauty, natural and man-made, and horror, mostly man-made. The Kingdom of Naples, which included the island of Sicily, was ruled by a Bourbon monarch, known to his own subjects as King 'Bomba', because he had restored 'order' to his territories by artillery bombardments. Naples was not, of course, a democracy – but those who were calling for political changes that might lead to the smallest 'popular' role in government, or for the possible unification of all the Italian states, found themselves languishing in chains in Neapolitan prisons. Gladstone was able to visit them there:

> Each man has a strong leather girth round him above the hips. To this are secured the upper end of two chains. One of four long links descends to a kind of double ring going round the ankle. This ring is never undone ... The second chain ... united two prisoners together. This likewise is never loosened ... The words ... are to be understood strictly.[24]

Gladstone also heard tales of a massacre perpetrated by the authorities, for which the soldiers responsible were decorated. He was assured by one of the prisoners that official British intervention on their behalf would be counterproductive while Palmerston was foreign secretary, but perhaps Aberdeen could be persuaded to do something using his contacts with the Austrians, the Neapolitan government's patrons, to put pressure on King Bomba. Gladstone began to consider what he could do.

On his return to England in February 1851, Stanley once again displayed his desire to lure Gladstone to his side, offering him the chance to join the minority government the queen had invited him to form. Gladstone, was, for a moment, anxious: some of his 'Peelite' colleagues might not wish to follow him over to the Tory ranks (or would not be welcome there) even if he found it desirable to go. But Stanley told him any government he formed would have to place a small import duty on wheat, which, for Gladstone, made it clear what he should do. For the sake of form, he consulted Aberdeen, and then gave Stanley his refusal, which he thought came as no surprise to him. Gladstone privately thought the whole thing was a waste of time; he would never abandon free trade on corn, and surely Stanley should have known it.

In any case he had other important things to do. For one thing, on 25 March he made a major speech attacking the Ecclesiastical Titles Assumption Bill. Pope Pius IX had just restored a Roman Catholic Church hierarchy in Britain, and Russell's government had asserted the illegality of this. To Gladstone, Russell was being illiberal, and he made his opposition to the measure plain, finally clearing himself of the reputation for religious bigotry he had acquired in the later 1830s. But he suffered two devastating blows in the immediate aftermath of this: two friends, Manning and Hope, announced to him their intention of converting to Roman Catholicism. Manning was removed as an executor of Gladstone's will, and it was many years before the two men communicated again.

The memory of Naples also still rankled. On 9 March he had written a letter to Aberdeen, asking him to take action. Aberdeen duly contacted Count Schwarzenburg, the Austrian foreign minister, who agreed to send an envoy to Naples. But before any official response was forthcoming, Gladstone, on 12 July, sent Aberdeen another letter, and to Aberdeen's dismay, losing patience with the lack of response, he published it five days later. The Neapolitan government, Gladstone announced to the world, was 'the negation of God erected into a system of government'. The letter astonished all who read it; some, including Aberdeen and Schwarzenburg, were annoyed, and the latter now refused to take any action. Others, including Palmerston, were highly delighted. Palmerston, indeed, had the letter printed in the Foreign Office, and despatched to British ministers abroad. Here was one inkling that Gladstone and Palmerston did, after all, have something in common, and that Gladstone might be viewed, in one more way, as a liberal.

Gladstone spent a good deal of time in 1851 working on the committee setting up the Great Exhibition and this brought him closer to Prince Albert. He addressed a meeting of Thames coal whippers at

Shadwell in May, another brief portent of things to come. He began to see in Benjamin Disraeli an enemy to equal King Bomba, especially as Disraeli's financial proposals seemed ever closer to coming to fruition as the protectionist Conservatives appeared to increase in strength. There were also two major events in his private life. The first, and most private, was his first meeting in June with a young prostitute called Elizabeth Collins. Although Gladstone was never unfaithful to his wife, some of his feelings for Collins were overtly sexual, and there can be no doubt that she knew it and took advantage of the fact. Gladstone struggled with his feelings about her for a long time before she decided she wanted to be 'saved', and it was many years, before she was eventually 'rescued'. The second, tumultuous, event occurred on 7 December when, after an illness, Sir John Gladstone died. Quite what effect this had on Gladstone psychologically is difficult to say, since most commentators agree that their relationship had never been especially close and had grown ever more distant over time. Undoubtedly, Gladstone felt the death of his mother and his daughter (and Peel) much more than he did that of his father. But, like Peel's death, this one too marked an emancipation for him. First of all, visits to Fasque stopped; the new baronet, Thomas, and Gladstone were by now, on very bad terms, and he did not visit there again until 1858. Secondly, Gladstone became richer, inheriting just over £150,000 – the same as his brothers John and Robertson, and more than his sister Helen. This inheritance helped him secure possession of the Hawarden estate. The Glynne brothers, Sir Stephen and Henry, had neither male heirs nor money enough to keep the estate in being. In 1852 when Stephen moved back into Hawarden, Catherine and William Gladstone took care of Sir Stephen's debts and a quiet legal arrangement was drawn up in 1855: the whole estate would go to young Willy Gladstone on the death of the last male Glynne. Despite his pangs of conscience at the treatment of the Glynne daughters, Gladstone soon began to act as owner of the castle, and he and Hawarden were truly inseparable.

Gladstone believed 1851 to have been his 'saddest year': certainly his church seemed to be under great pressure, and politically he had achieved very little. He could only hope that more could be accomplished in 1852: and he was not to be disappointed. On 2 December 1851, the Prince President of France, Louis Napoleon Bonaparte, nephew of the Emperor Napoleon I, had, by a coup d'état, declared himself President of France for life (just a year later he would put an end to the charade and make himself Emperor Napoleon III). Palmerston had, rather surprisingly, taken the step of announcing the British government's approval of his action without first obtaining royal assent for it. The Queen and Prince Albert were outraged and called on Russell to dismiss his wayward foreign secretary. Russell, himself annoyed at Palmerston's arrogant behaviour, agreed, and by Christmas he was out of office – and very angry with Russell.

This, however, also marked the beginning of the end for Russell's ministry. While Palmerston may have approved of Louis Napoleon's coup, many in Britain (including Palmerston himself) believed that the country was defensively in a very weak position. The revolution brought about by the application of steam power to ships had had its effect on naval warfare, and since the days of Peel's cabinet an increasing number of people had felt that Britain was becoming more open to attack from abroad. (Gladstone was one of the few who did not share in this fear, as later events were to demonstrate clearly.) To help defend the country a reserve force of militia had been set up earlier in the century, and Russell's cabinet agreed it should now be revived. But to raise it would cost money, so Russell introduced a budget calling for an increase in income tax to fund it. Gladstone and his Peelite friends could not approve of this; the Derbyites saw it as a good opportunity to attack Russell, and so also did Palmerston, despite his views on national defence. The result was that on 20 February 1852 a coalition of forces voted down the proposal in the Commons, and Russell resigned; Derby was invited to form a government.

DERBY'S FIRST MINISTRY, 1852

Gladstone and his Peelite colleagues spent a considerable time trying to decide on the attitude they should take to the new ministry. There was some division of opinion. Sir Henry Hardinge, a soldier, joined the government, accepting office as Master General of the Ordnance, while Lord Jocelyn said he would also join Derby, if Derby would only abandon Protection. Graham and Cardwell, on the other hand, had effectively already joined Russell's Liberal Party. Gladstone himself was cautious – too much so for his friend, the former Lord Lincoln, now Duke of Newcastle, who said he could not agree with Gladstone's evident desire to support or even possibly join the government. Newcastle himself hoped to lead a 'new' Conservative Party. Gladstone seems to have inclined towards Jocelyn's views. The key issue remained, as far as he was concerned, that of Free Trade against Protectionism. By the end of March, Gladstone thought 'the great bulk of the Peelites' were for joining Derby, 'avowing that Free Trade is their only point of difference'; but he went on

> Lastly, I myself, and I think I am with Lord Aberdeen and S. Herbert, have nearly the same desire, but feel that the matter is too crude and too difficult and important for anticipating any conclusion and that our clear line of duty is independence, until the question of Protection shall be settled.[25]

Gladstone, therefore, reacted cautiously to the activities of the Derby government. The basic difficulty was that he did not believe, for one reason or another, that Derby was even yet won over to free trade. There is little doubt that the main reason for this was his chancellor of the Exchequer, Disraeli, who argued the government's friends would not allow him to abandon Protection. As time passed Gladstone's attitude to Disraeli hardened perceptibly: each of the Chancellor's financial speeches, he remarked, was 'more quackish in its flavour than its predecessor'. Before the session broke up the government did manage to secure (with Palmerston's support) the passage of a Militia Act, in which Gladstone took little part. In July 1852, a general election was held.

Gladstone, far from worrying about losing his seat at Oxford University, took his wife and family, including his new son, Henry Neville, born on 2 April, on holiday to Wales. He came a comfortable second in the poll held on 14 July. On his return to London he attended a Peelite conclave. The election had not done them any good, reducing their numbers to about forty. Gladstone had hoped a closer union with Derby might be possible, but when the Peelites received a copy of the Queen's Speech relating to free trade, they were very disappointed. Even though free trade brought some benefits, these, it appeared to the Conservatives, were mixed blessings. Derby, even at this late stage, tried to appeal to Gladstone personally, when the two men met at a party at Lady Derby's on 27 November. But he refused to be drawn: he would have to see exactly what the Chancellor was proposing before he could begin to commit himself.

The final drama began on the evening of 3 December, when Disraeli introduced his budget, and was to last for two weeks. Disraeli's aim was easily pronounced, but almost impossible to achieve. He hoped to do enough to satisfy everybody: the Protectionists, who would not feel 'betrayed' again; free traders, who would feel their interests had not been too strongly attacked; Irish members; and, last but not least, the Peelites. Gladstone, though, seems to have been unimpressed with Disraeli's ideas from the start. On both 6 and 10 December he had made speeches against the Chancellor's proposals, but the big moment came early on the morning of the 17th. The government had not done too badly in the general election, although it had still not secured an overall majority, but Disraeli's final budget speech might have done enough to win over a large number of waverers. If, when he had stopped talking to a crowded House of Commons at 1.00 a.m., the House had divided, he might well have carried his budget. But this did not happen. Gladstone, rising furiously from his seat, demanded the attention of the House and, late though it was, he proceeded to harangue it for some two hours.

Gladstone's speech on this occasion is very important for a number of reasons. First, and most obviously, it destroyed Disraeli's reputation as a financier and sealed a personal hostility between the two men that was to extend for the greater part of the next thirty years. Secondly, it helped to secure Gladstone's own financial reputation. He was careful to point out that he was the rightful heir of Sir Robert Peel and an experienced political figure, who deserved a place in any government set up to succeed Derby. Thirdly, it raised his reputation among all those who, for whatever reason, were hostile to Derby. Like it or not, he was becoming a hero to the Liberal and even the more radical Left. Last, but not least, it helped secure the defeat of the Derby government. Derby resigned later the same day and the queen sent for two men: Lord Lansdowne and Gladstone's mentor, Lord Aberdeen. A new phase in Gladstone's life and career was about to open.

Gladstone had joined the Peelite Conservative Party and become a close ally of Sir Robert Peel, who recognised his talents and brought him into office, first as an under-secretary and then as vice president and, in 1843, president of the Board of Trade, with a seat in the cabinet.

Perhaps Peel did not move quickly enough for Gladstone, but the latter stayed in the cabinet until the Maynooth crisis forced him to reconsider his position and resign. But Peel's resignation over the repeal of the Corn Laws in 1845 and Russell's failure to form a ministry marked Peel's return and Gladstone's revival. He became Secretary of State for the Colonies, but only briefly. The Corn Laws were repealed, Peel was voted out and the Peelites became an independent group in the Commons until Peel's sudden death in 1850.

Russell's ministry from 1846 to 1852 caused a significant split on the left wing too. The dismissal of Palmerston led him to unite with Derby's supporters and the Peelites and defeat Russell. Derby's minority ministry could not last long and was brought down by a defeat in the Commons, a defeat to which Gladstone contributed a great deal, with his strident attack on Disraeli's budget.

These years show Gladstone reaching the top rank in British politics. During this time he had stayed loyal – so he believed – to Peel and his legacy. Now, if he played his cards right, he was once more going to get the chance to act as a government minister. It remained to be seen whether the next few years would be as active as the last ones had been for him, whether his career would continue to prosper and where he would end up.

3

THE RISE TO POWER, 1853–1868

Sixteen years after the fall of Derby's first ministry in December 1852, a liberal government took office, and at its head stood William Gladstone. But these sixteen years were marked by upheavals in the politics of the country, as well as in Gladstone's own career. Politics in these years were in something like a state of flux: it is difficult to label the various parties convincingly. Perhaps the most united group was the rump of the Conservative Party, formed from those supporters of Peel who had rejected his anti-Corn Law proposals, led by Lord Derby and, following his retirement, Disraeli, but even that showed signs of fragmentation. The 'Peelites', those who had stayed loyal to Sir Robert Peel, declined into one of the many disparate groups that eventually formed the Liberal Party. That party also comprised right-wing moderate Whigs and more left-wing radical elements, and, of course, the unclassifiable Palmerston. Bringing them together and keeping them together was far from easy.

THE ABERDEEN COALITION, 1853–1855

The downfall of Derby's ministry left the way clear for the queen to summon Lord Lansdowne and Lord Aberdeen to discuss his successor. Lansdowne – not for the last time – declined the post, leaving the way clear for Aberdeen. Whatever his personal feelings for Russell and his Whig and radical followers, the Peelite Aberdeen realised that he would not be able to form a ministry without their support. He was aware this would not go down well with some of his supporters – Gladstone included – but a series of meetings persuaded them all of the necessity for this course of action. The result was the formation of the Aberdeen coalition government, a combination of Peelites, Whigs and Radicals, and Lord Palmerston. Both Russell and Palmerston had hesitated before joining. The former thought his numerous followers in the Commons would never accept their relatively weak strength in the cabinet; the latter was well aware of the fundamental disagreements he had with the more pacific Aberdeen on foreign policy. But both were won over: Russell was promised the post of prime minister when Aberdeen resigned, which was not expected to be long, while Palmerston accepted the 'safe' post of Home Secretary – it was better than nothing. Gladstone, after some hesitation caused by an apparent desire on Lord John Russell's part to offer Sir James Graham the job, became Chancellor of the Exchequer.

Most people, then and later, have accepted that the Aberdeen coalition was a fair reflection of what 'the people' – that is, the politically active upper and middle classes – wanted. But it would have to do something dramatic to give itself credibility in the country, and people began to look in the direction of the Chancellor of the Exchequer to provide this. He had, after all, destroyed the last budget, now he should 'make a new one'. This was not easy, for Gladstone had to consider not only the hostile elements in the House of Commons, but also some of those within the cabinet. He had plenty to think about, having withstood a serious challenge for his Oxford University seat and securing victory by only 124 votes in the January 1853 election. He then began to work very hard on his budget, which he talked over with an approving Prince Albert on 9 April. The Prince 'followed me in the most intelligent manner and seemed to express great satisfaction with the plan'.[1] His presentation to the Prince took only one hour: it took three times as long to tell the cabinet what he proposed to do, and even longer, when the time came, to tell the Commons.

Gladstone intended to further reduce or abolish import duties on two lists of articles, carrying on Peel's tradition, and to cut excise and stamp duties. Like Disraeli, he proposed to levy income tax on all incomes over £100 a year (a reduction of £50 p.a.), but, unlike his predecessor, he intended to levy it at 7d in the pound (slightly less than 3 per cent), for the first two years, then at 6d (2.5 per cent) for two years, at 3d (1.25 per cent) for three years after that, and finally in 1860, to reduce it to nil. He also aimed to cut legacy duty on houses, but to extend it to include the value of inherited land as well as personal property. Most controversially, he announced his intention to extend the income tax to Ireland. This budget clearly demonstrated Gladstone's adherence to the principle of free trade, but he still firmly believed that income tax was a purely temporary measure and hoped it would soon be abolished. His decision to levy legacy duty on inherited land was an attack on the agricultural interest. Including Ireland in the income tax schedule was a necessary move in Gladstone's opinion, but given the volatility of Irish opinion following the dreadful famine of the mid-1840s, it was not perhaps the most tactful of moves.

Gladstone had to struggle to get the budget to the floor of the Commons. Some in the cabinet went along with it. Gladstone himself thought at the end of the second day's discussions that his friend the Duke of Newcastle, Lord Clarendon, the radical Sir William Molesworth and – perhaps of greatest significance for the future – Lord John Russell, favoured the whole plan. He thought Lord Aberdeen and another of his friends, the Duke of Argyll, were also more or less favourably disposed to it. But those opposed were a formidable force which included a former Whig chancellor, Sir Charles Wood, as well as Sir James Graham, Lord Granville, Lord Lansdowne, and, most outspoken of all, Lord Palmerston. Their main objection centred on the extension of the tax proposals to Ireland, and Gladstone had to work very hard to overcome this. On the next day, however, Lord Aberdeen put his whole weight behind Gladstone; he said 'it was better to take the whole: the more you cut off from it the worse the remainder hung together'. Argyll, too, 'fell in with an assent to the whole plan'.[2] Gladstone stuck to his guns and on 15 April he laid his cards on the table. In reply to a question from Graham he said:

> That all my proposals had been adjusted with a view to overcoming the great difficulty of differentiation and that speaking with great deference while I could not feel any security either in one alternative or another I thought the entire budget safer than a reduced one for the House or the country and I felt that if we proposed it the name and fame of the government at any rate would stand well.

> Wood seemed still rather to hang back; but the rest of the cabinet now appeared well satisfied and we parted well resolved and certainly more likely to stand or fall by the Budget as a whole than we seemed to be on Wednesday.[3]

While Gladstone himself calculated that the Conservatives could possibly gather some 340 MPs against the government 's own 310, they were highly unlikely to get this number together at any one time. In these circumstances the government had to go ahead. The budget presentation, finally made on 18 April, lasted, by Gladstone's own reckoning, four hours and forty-five minutes 'and my strength stood out well, thank God'. It was really the Chancellor who 'stood out'.[4] This budget speech brought congratulations from Prince Albert, and indirectly from the Queen herself, from Aberdeen, and what was especially heart-warming, from Lady Peel. He might, perhaps, have been even more pleased had he known then what the diarist Charles Greville believed: the speech

> has raised Gladstone to a great political elevation, and what is of far greater elevation than the measure itself, has given the country assurance of a *man* equal to great political necessities and fit to lead parties and direct governments.[5]

It is unfortunate that even Gladstone himself had to admit that the budget was not, in the end, to be the success he had envisaged, while the income tax, far from disappearing in seven years, has continued and gone from strength to strength.

Meanwhile Gladstone's private life, for once, reached the national stage. While engaged on one of his late night 'rescue missions' on 10 May 1853, he was approached by a young man by the name of Wilson who demanded he find him a job or he would tell what he had seen to the newspapers. He chose the wrong man. Gladstone could not get rid of him, so set off in search of a policeman, reported to him what had happened, and accompanied both men to Vine Street police station. Gladstone decided that he would have to press charges of attempted blackmail against Wilson to avoid similar events in the future, and, when the remand and committal hearings were held, he appeared to give evidence. It is very doubtful if many knew of his 'nocturnal rambles' and this event certainly stirred up some gossip, but it is perhaps a reflection of his public character that no lasting damage was done to his career or reputation by this revelation. No one, indeed, seems to have made any real attempt to make anything of it, and it certainly did not stop Gladstone seeing Elizabeth Collins and other prostitutes. Wilson was eventually sentenced to one year's hard labour, though Gladstone interceded with Home Secretary Palmerston on his behalf to secure his early release.

On one private matter Gladstone could perhaps express at least some satisfaction. On 7 January 1854 Catherine, after a difficult time, gave birth to a son, Herbert. It was to be her last child and it seems as if she was aware of this and deeply unsettled as a result. Gladstone had to spend some time with her at what for public reasons was a difficult period.

Gladstone found plenty to do as chancellor in late 1853 and 1854. Among other matters to deal with there were the questions of money for the new Palace of Westminster, the design of new Australian coinage, and the possibility of moving the National Gallery to Kensington. He spent time in the Scottish Highlands in August and September 1853 with the Duke of Sutherland and the Duke of Buccleuch and their families. On 12 October he made a speech to an assembled crowd in Manchester on the unveiling of the monument to Sir Robert Peel, and found the experience rather exhilarating. He involved himself with proposals for the reform of the civil service emanating from Sir Charles Trevelyan and Stafford Northcote, only to discover that the Whig-Liberals in the cabinet disapproved of most their recommendations. Gladstone also hoped, rather optimistically, to extend the underlying philosophy of these proposals – the abolition of anomalies and application of scientific theories to management and organisation – to his old university of Oxford.

The story of the Aberdeen coalition is overshadowed by the event which brought it to its end: the Crimean war from 1854 to 1856. This arose from the perception in Britain (and, to a lesser extent, in France) that the Russian Empire was expanding dangerously towards Constantinople. The British government had made it clear to the Russians that any attempt by them to seize control of the Bosporus and Dardanelles, which would give the Russian fleet access from the Black

Sea into the Mediterranean and Britain's sea route to India, would be resisted, if necessary by force. The power that controlled these straits, the Ottoman Empire, was not, as a Muslim power, particularly well liked in Britain, but it did its job as a guardian of this vital waterway and hence Britain would support it. The Turks were aware of this and when Russia began to put pressure on them by occupying Moldavia and Wallachia in the Balkans, they decided to resist the aggression, declaring war on Russia on 4 October 1853. The British and French Mediterranean fleets now lay off Constantinople, a visible symbol of the British backing for the Turks, while in France Napoleon III also favoured a firm stand against the Russians. But Tsar Nicholas I decided the time had come to deal with them, and the Russian Black Sea fleet defeated a Turkish force in the 'massacre' at Sinope on 30 November. The British public began to call for war.

Largely as a result of the pressure of these events, the coalition in London began to break apart. On 16 December, Palmerston resigned, citing in public the question of parliamentary reform, a bill on which Russell was endeavouring to bring in, but in reality he felt the government 's response to the Russians was too 'weak'. Even Gladstone wanted him back this time, partly because of the harm Palmerston's defection would do the coalition and partly because he felt it would send out a warning to St Petersburg. Palmerston duly returned, and Russell's proposed bill was dropped, but the leadership provided by the British government at this time was indecisive. The truth was that Aberdeen simply did not wish to lead the country into war. On 22 February he got into a long conversation with Gladstone:

> He then asked me whether I did not think he might himself withdraw from office when we came to the declaration of war. All along he had been acting against his feelings, but still defensively. He said all wars were called or pretended to be defensive. I said that if the war was untruly so called our position was false, but that the war did not become less defensive from our declaring it or from our entering upon offensive operation. Any man would require a distinct principle ... in giving up at this moment the service of the Crown. He said how could he bring himself to fight for the Turks? I replied we were not fighting for the Turks, but we were warning Russia off the forbidden ground.[6]

Britain, in alliance with France, eventually declared war on Russia in March 1854. Gladstone always maintained this was a defensive, and therefore justified, action, though he became less happy with it as his support for the Turks waned. A British and French army was despatched to the Near East to force a Russian retreat, but the Russians withdrew from Moldavia and Wallachia on their own initiative leaving the allied commanders, Lord Raglan and Marshall St Arnaud, and their superiors in London and Paris, in a quandary. In the end it was decided that an assault on Russia's naval fortress at Sebastopol in the Crimea would be a good idea; it should not be too difficult to capture and would hinder Russian Black Sea operations for years to come. But many in Britain saw the war as more than just a 'Crimean' conflict. To Palmerston, and those who thought like him, it was intended to deal the mighty Russian Empire a more damaging blow. Hence, allied warships were also to be sent across the North Sea to deal with Russian forces in the north and, if all went well, perhaps some of Russia's subject peoples – Poles, for example – could be encouraged to rise up against their masters.

All this, of course, would cost money, and Gladstone's budget plans for 1854 – as well as his longer term plans from the previous year – had to be adjusted accordingly. Most obviously, he increased the rate of income tax to 10½d. in the pound (just under 4.5 per cent), and he tried to issue some new Exchequer bonds, to be paid off over the next six years. But this time his policy was not a great success. He hoped the operations of war would be guided by fiscal considerations, a somewhat unrealistic hope. The costs continued to mount and had he not resigned, it would have been Gladstone and not his successor as chancellor, Sir George Cornewall Lewis, who secured the odium of adding to the national debt.

The military campaign in the Crimea, far from bringing glory to the government, descended into a shambles. Defeating the Russians at the Alma on 20 September might have led to the swift capture of Sebastopol, but it did not. Instead, the allies decided to besiege Sebastopol, and Russian attempts to relieve the fortress were defeated at the battles of Balaclava (25 October) and Inkerman (5 November). It is at the former that one of the most infamous operations in British military history occurred – the charge of the Light Brigade. This event, with the appalling conditions in which the troops lived and died at

Sebastopol and in hospital at Scutari, and the breakdown in supplies reaching the Army as winter intensified, came to the notice of the British public. The prestige of the Army – and of the government – suffered accordingly.

It is not surprising that the Aberdeen coalition did not last long into 1855. Towards the end of the previous year, Russell had displayed increasing restlessness. He proposed, first of all, that the responsibilities of the Secretary of State for War should be extended, and that the holder of the office, the Duke of Newcastle, should resign in favour of Lord Palmerston. Although Newcastle was later to accept this proposal in principle, the remainder of Russell's cabinet colleagues did not encourage him. But Russell then determined to go. When a backbench radical MP, John Roebuck, moved a motion of the House of Commons for a committee to investigate the conduct of the war in the Crimea, Russell, on 24 January 1855, took the chance to leave: 'he did not see how it could be resisted – that as it implied a censure on the conduct of colleagues he had no course but to resign'. At this point the cabinet agreed with him, and sent their resignations to the Queen. But, as Gladstone noted, the Queen 'declined to receive our resignations and urged with the greatest earnestness that the decision should be reconsidered'.[7] The cabinet decided to stay on without Lord John, and to try and resist Roebuck's proposal. The Commons, however, like Russell himself, had lost patience with the Aberdeen ministry, despite Gladstone's own spirited defence of his chief, and Roebuck's motion was carried by 304 votes to 148. Faced with this clear evidence of their unpopularity, the government resigned.

Aberdeen, who had spent much of his career as a Tory, had clearly become more Peelite in his outlook over time, and Gladstone had become more sympathetic to him. Indeed, he had not wanted him to resign unless it was unavoidable, and when negotiations began to form a new ministry he argued strongly that Aberdeen deserved a place in any new cabinet. That, at least, was the reason he gave to Palmerston when he turned down the former Home Secretary's initial approach.

PALMERSTON'S FIRST MINISTRY, 1855–1858

If Gladstone had to abandon Aberdeen, whom could he serve under? It seemed everyone wanted him. First to call on him was Lord Derby, who, as leader of the largest opposition party, the Queen had asked to succeed Aberdeen. Derby hoped to secure Gladstone, Herbert and Palmerston. But the three men discussed the possibility and left him disappointed. Other prospective heads of government were Russell, Palmerston, Clarendon, Lansdowne, and, even at this late date, Aberdeen. Gladstone, still unhappy at Russell's conduct, would not accept the idea that he should have the chance to become Premier. Even when Lord John paid him a personal visit on 3 February 'and sat … his hat shaking in his hand', Gladstone would not agree to join him.

To Lansdowne's suggestion that Clarendon could form some kind of coalition, Gladstone replied that 'if … the country was to continue under a coalition government it was in my opinion better to continue the old coalition under Lord Aberdeen than to form a new one'. As for Lansdowne, Gladstone, in one of those moments that he later greatly regretted, advised him he did not think he would find it possible to form a ministry.[8] Discounting Aberdeen, who worked hard to persuade Gladstone he did not wish to be in a government, still less to lead one, that really left only one man – and as Gladstone commented, 'the world is drunk about a Palmerston government'.[9]

Gladstone was not at all impressed at the prospect: 'Lord Palmerston is in no way equal to the duties which fall upon a Prime Minister'.[10] In joining him Gladstone felt he would have to be 'ready to overlook not merely the inferior fitness but the real and manifest unfitness' of Palmerston for the post, and the weakness of the new cabinet, especially when it was faced with the hostility of Russell and Derby and their followers.[11] It is clear that Gladstone had no liking for Palmerston and his judgements about him and his colleagues were harsh. Yet, despite his depth of hostility, in a decision which exercises historians as much as it did many of his friends at the time, Gladstone did elect in the end to join Palmerston, along with Herbert. In a meeting at Sir James Graham's home on 3 February 1855, a group of Peelites, including Argyll, Herbert and Gladstone, debated for some three hours what they ought to do. It may be that Gladstone hoped he and his friends would make Palmerston's government more Peelite than Whig in outlook and that he (Gladstone) could carry on the same fiscal policy as he had pursued while Aberdeen's chancellor. There was also an element of political calculation, seldom absent from Gladstone's decisions: the 'country' *wanted* a Palmerston government, so if he wanted to stay on as chancellor, he would have to join him. Last, but probably not least, at their meeting, Aberdeen had made his own views plain: he said 'he must strongly advise our joining'. Gladstone recorded what followed:

> Herbert and I went to my house and despatched our answers. Then began the storm. Granville [Gladstone's closest ally and confidant in his first and second ministries] met us driving to Newcastle's. Sorry beyond measure: he almost looked displeased, which for him is much. Newcastle: I incline to think that you are wrong. Canning: my impression is you are wrong. G. Harcourt, Sir J. Young, Elcho, Lord Ellesmere, J. Wortley, and various letters streaming in, all portending condemnation and disaster ... I think I see the reason of what we have done clear and broad before me.[12]

The decision to join Palmerston might have been, as Gladstone very quickly realised, a major political mistake on his part. If, however, he was to stay in office, he had no choice but to serve under him, even at the cost of what seemed to be a fundamental split in the ranks of the Peelites. Those who had not joined were isolated from Palmerston: some might join Russell, others Derby, but it looked as if the days of the 'Peelites' as a united force were over. It was not to be quite so damaging as this, though, since Gladstone and his friends' adherence to the Palmerston government was not to last very long.

Gladstone was not impressed with Palmerston as a prime minister. He was an 'eminent member' of the cabinet 'but nowhere has he that peculiar guiding influence which my experience of Sir R. Peel taught me to associate with the idea of premiership and which was not wholly wanting in Lord Aberdeen'.[13] The issue which led to the Peelites' early resignation was the one that had already brought down Aberdeen – Roebuck's proposed committee into the state of the Army in the Crimea. Palmerston's view was simple: let the Commons have their committee, provided it was fairly composed, and let it report. The government could take notice of its recommendations in due course. This, to Gladstone – still the executive politician, who felt the House of Commons should not interfere with government in this way – was unthinkable, especially as Palmerston had already assured him the government would not agree to the committee. Gladstone spoke his mind in cabinet as early as 18 February:

> I went so far as to say that if the inquiry into the state of the army were allowed by this government it neither could nor ought to enjoy a week's credit or authority in the House of Commons and intimated that I could not see my way to this concession under any circumstance.

Later that same day, to Prince Albert and the Queen – both of whom thought the government should accept the idea of the committee rather than resign – he said as much: 'without any positive and final declaration I intimated to each that I did not think I could bring my mind to acquiesce in the proposition for an inquiry by a select committee.'[14]

The issue soon became a trial of strength between Palmerston and his Peelites, led by the outspoken Gladstone. The Prime Minister argued that the Commons was 'becoming unruly' because it had begun to doubt the government's intentions on the Roebuck committee; granting the measure, declared Palmerston, would put the government back in charge. This argument cut no ice with Gladstone; the Commons should not expect the government to do simply what it wanted, and any concessions over the Roebuck Committee was an unwarranted surrender to it. When the cabinet met on Ash Wednesday, 21 February 1855, Gladstone presented his objections, but unsuccessfully. Despite some Royal pressure to stay, when it became clear Palmerston was going to accept the principle of the Roebuck Committee, Graham, Herbert and Gladstone all announced their resignations.

Quite what damage Gladstone and his two colleagues had hoped to do to Palmerston by resigning is not clear. The prime minister was able to reconstruct his cabinet without too much difficulty, Sir George Cornewall Lewis succeeding Gladstone as chancellor. Palmerston's acceptance of the committee and his policy of winning the war – at least, that is, of securing the capture of Sebastopol and then opening negotiations with the Russians – was popular in the country, so Palmerston's premiership and the war went on. Gladstone had obviously expected more to happen. At first he did not seem personally ill-disposed to Palmerston – probably because, as he told Prince Albert, he did not think the ministry would last very long, but, as time passed and the government showed no signs of collapsing, he became more outspoken against the prime minister. During 1855 and 1856 he became steadily more convinced that Palmerston was a bad prime minister, surrounded by a weak cabinet, leading a government from which nothing could be expected but 'legislative inefficiency, foreign brawls, large establishments, and heavy blunders'.[15] He did not confine himself to private denunciations of the government either. He published two articles in the *Quarterly Review*, 'The declining efficiency of Parliament' in September 1856 and 'Prospects political and financial' in January 1857, both of which strongly attacked the government in general and Palmerston in particular. (He also published an article on Homer, on which he had been working since the spring of 1856.)

During the course of 1856 Gladstone publicly opposed the government's proposals on education and expressed reservations about the Peace Treaty of Paris, signed on 30 March 1856, which ended the Crimean conflict, and gave Britain and France some success. It neutralised the Black Sea by forbidding warships of all nations to enter it and forced the Russians to dismantle the fortifications around Sebastopol.

It is not surprising, looking at Gladstone's public record over the years from 1855 to 1857, that Lord Derby thought he might be able to persuade him to join the Conservative Party. At the end of 1855, Derby's elder son, Lord Stanley, paid a social visit to Hawarden. This was a great moment for Gladstone, notwithstanding his own time spent in the castles of dukes, since it showed how far he had risen in the social scale in Lancashire society – and his father had never achieved as much. During 1856 Derby tried on two occasions to lure Gladstone over to his side. These brought no result; the main problem seemed to revolve around the leadership of the House of Commons. If the Conservatives took office, it would be Disraeli who would take this role, whereas Gladstone's allies, particularly Sir James Graham (and Gladstone himself), felt that he should have the job. This factor, and Gladstone's dislike of Disraeli, was sufficient for him to express to Derby his inability to co-operate more closely with the Conservatives at this stage. At the beginning of 1857, though, the Conservative leader tried again. This time Gladstone expressed openly his aversion for Palmerston and how strongly he disapproved of his policies, in particular because of the enormous expenditure of public money they entailed. When on 13 February, Lewis introduced his budget, the former chancellor was enraged. Accordingly, a week later, having told Derby and, through him, Disraeli, what he intended to do, Gladstone launched a stinging attack on the budget. Lewis, he declared, had failed to balance revenue and expenditure and to reform the tariff: he had 'thrown overboard, condemned, repudiated', the financial policies of the last twenty years. The Conservatives joined in, and it looked to many as though, at last, Gladstone had joined the Conservatives.

But in politics appearances can be deceptive, and in this case they were. The problem was, while Gladstone thoroughly disliked the prime minister and his apparent lack of principles, and while he felt alienated from the party Palmerston was leading, he did not really feel very much greater attraction to the Conservatives. While he was quite well-disposed to Derby personally, he had no liking for Disraeli, nor for many of Derby's backbench supporters, and they were no more keen on him. Moreover, all the time he was negotiating with Derby about Palmerston's budget, he had also begun to seek support from another direction: any support at all for his campaign to remove Palmerston suited Gladstone, and the Conservatives were deluded if they thought he was seeking out only their help. He had begun to talk to Richard Cobden, sometime leader of the anti-Corn Law League, and the subject of Peel's eulogistic final speech in the Commons. Cobden represented a different constituency to Gladstone – a more middle-class and popular one – but some of his ideas coincided well with his. Both men could approve of cuts in public expenditure and a peaceful foreign policy; both, therefore, could easily oppose Palmerston.

Palmerston's foreign policy was hardly peaceful. In January 1857, only six months after the end of the Crimean war, British troops had embarked on a military campaign in Persia to counter threatening moves by the Shah in the direction of British India. In October 1856, Chinese authorities had boarded a British ship, the *Arrow*, and taken twelve of the crew prisoner, accusing them of piracy. After a protest by the British they were released, but the Chinese refused to apologise and, as a result, a British fleet bombarded the forts guarding the mouth of the Canton river. On 3 March 1857, Cobden introduced to the House of Commons a series of resolutions condemning this action, as well as the Persian campaign. He was supported by both Disraeli and Gladstone.

Palmerston responded in a typical blustering speech, condemning in his turn coalitions of self-interested politicians, but on this occasion it was to no avail. Gladstone remarked that the division, 263 to 247 against the government, did 'more honour to the House of Commons than any I remember', and he even admitted, to the privacy of his diary, to being 'excited'. The British House of Commons did know right from wrong, after all, and Gladstone was confident that the British electorate would, too, when Palmerston resigned.

Gladstone believed Palmerston's ministerial career had reached its conclusion, but unfortunately things did not turn out that way. While Gladstone held his seat at Oxford University unopposed, the election on the whole was a triumph for the older man. The electors liked his assertive foreign policy and his pride in Britain's power and influence; they also liked the enormous cut in income tax Lewis had just made. Cobden and his close associate John Bright both lost their seats in the election. Gladstone's brother-in-law, Sir Stephen Glynne, lost his too (despite Gladstone's best efforts on his behalf) and Palmerston emerged with a clear majority of between eighty and ninety seats.

This result was a severe blow to Gladstone, and in March he expressed to Herbert some of his anxieties. He explained that while he was still loyal to Herbert, and he remained totally opposed to Palmerston, he did not want to lead Herbert, or to be led by him, into Derby's hands. Things were so bad he thought he would stay away from Parliament altogether; if he did attend the Commons, it would be as a private member, and not as a possible leader of the Peelites. When Palmerston's government proposed its estimates in June 1857, Lord Stanley observed that Gladstone, 'either from ill-health, pique or prudence, stays away'.[16] Gladstone had learned an important lesson, though. Whether he liked it or not – and he most certainly did not – Palmerston and his policies were popular with the electorate. But while he was dismayed by the election results, he did not display any intention of leaving politics altogether. In the circumstances, however, it would take something exceptional to bring Gladstone to Westminster, and this, in 1857, was provided by the government's Divorce Bill. This had passed the Lords without too much difficulty (though at one stage an amendment was carried proposing that if one of the 'guilty parties' should attempt to marry the other they should be jailed or fined), but it touched a nerve with Gladstone. The Bill proposed the liberalisation of divorce procedures and allowed divorced persons to remarry in Church, if they chose. To Gladstone this was, once again, the state interfering with the rights of the Church. It is reported that on 14 August, he made no less than twenty-nine speeches in opposition to one clause, and seventy-three speeches against the Bill altogether – though to oppose the measure so strongly, given his help to Lord Lincoln in his divorce case, seems ironic. Some changes were made to the Bill before it was passed, though Gladstone in the end missed this. His sister-in-law, Lady Lyttelton, had been desperately ill and Catherine had gone to be with her and give her any help she could; she summoned Gladstone to Hagley just before Lady Lyttelton died there on 18 August. He and his wife then returned to Hawarden, where he spent time, in between reflections on the iniquity of Palmerston, on his Homeric studies.

Apart from the Divorce Bill question, Gladstone did not spend a great deal of time concerning himself with political questions in 1857. He seems, for example, to have taken no particular interest in the great 'Mutiny' that broke out against British rule in India in May of that year. But early in 1858 events nearer home took a sudden and dramatic turn. On 14 January a group of Italian nationalists, led by Felice Orsini, threw bombs at Napoleon III and his Empress, Eugenie, as they made their way to the Paris opera. While the Emperor and his wife escaped unhurt, several onlookers were killed. It was discovered that the bombs and the plot itself had been manufactured in England, and a group of French army officers called on Napoleon to deal with the plotters' backers on the other side of the Channel.

Napoleon himself was not anti-British, but Palmerston was aware he should do something to appease the French on this occasion. Accordingly, the Conspiracy to Murder Bill was drafted, which proposed to make it illegal to plot the assassination of any foreigner on British soil. But the Premier had blundered badly on this occasion. He became unpopular with those 'patriots' who had just recently cheered him, and when the Bill was introduced the Conservatives, led by Disraeli, strongly attacked it as truckling to a foreign power; Gladstone, whatever his feelings about the Bill, which he seems to have opposed on principle, saw his chance and joined in the assault. Palmerston lost the vote by 234 to 215. As many as eighty of his own supporters had turned against him, accusing him, of all people, of weakness in the face of a foreign threat. He resigned at once.

THE DERBY MINISTRY AND MISSION TO THE IONIAN ISLANDS, 1858–1859

Derby was once again called on to form a ministry. He immediately tried to attract Gladstone into it, offering him any post he liked in the new cabinet, and adding he would also include Herbert in it, should he wish. Gladstone met Herbert, Aberdeen and Graham to decide on his response. He replied quickly to the invitation in the negative:

> I could not render you service worth your having ... The difficulty is even enhanced in my case by the fact that in your party ... there is a small but active and not unimportant section who avowedly regard me as the representative of the most dangerous ideas.[17]

It is no coincidence that at the same time as this letter was written, Gladstone also received one from John Bright, warning him of the danger of allying himself too closely with the Conservatives.

Despite his out-and-out refusal to join Derby in February, Gladstone pursued a fairly noncommittal course towards the new ministry for the next few months. He made one rather remarkable speech in May, bringing in a motion which called on the government to support the calls of the Romanian people for unity and independence from the Ottoman Empire. But Gladstone's case was not helped by some stinging attacks he made on the Ottoman Empire (which the Crimean war had just been fought to defend) and Islam, and his equally strident support for Russia. The result of the speech was to unite both the government and Palmerston and his supporters in defence of the Crimean policy, and the proposal was soundly beaten.

But the Derby ministry soon faced a crisis of its own. Their attempts to settle the government of India had led to a dispute between the President of the Board of Control in London, Lord Ellenborough, and the Governor General in India, Lord 'Clemency' Canning, notorious in some quarters for his apparently 'soft' treatment of the Indian mutineers. Ellenborough resigned in May, and Derby, aware that Gladstone had made some speeches in defence of the government's Indian policy, made one more effort to draw him in. This was perhaps the most serious of all the attempts he made to recruit Gladstone. For one thing, the emissary was an eminent Conservative politician, the Home Secretary,

Spencer Walpole. For another, Derby made it clear that he was quite prepared to accept other Peelites besides Gladstone into office. Furthermore, on this occasion, Disraeli made it clear he would, if necessary, give up the leadership of the House of Commons. Last but not least, Disraeli himself took the trouble to write to Gladstone, urging him to accept the offer.

Gladstone, with Derby's backing, approached Aberdeen and Graham for their advice, but then on 26 May he sent Derby yet another refusal: 'I have not seen, and I do not see, a prospect of public advantage or of material accession to your strength, from my entering your government single-handed'.[18] Underlying all this lies Gladstone's continuing dislike of many Conservatives, and their dislike for him. Disraeli still did not attract him, and it may well be that Disraeli's letter actually discouraged rather than encouraged him. His antipathy to Palmerston remained strong. (They had taken opposite sides on the Indian question and Gladstone had later argued in opposition to Palmerston that Britain should not oppose the project to build a Suez Canal, which had just been put forward by a French backed consortium.) But his Peelite friends were more liberal, and his own feelings too had become more sympathetic to the liberal cause – if only Palmerston was out of the way. But Derby even now did not give up all hope, and one rather strange incident was now about to occur as a result of his continued – though increasingly illusory – hope of attracting Gladstone.

Beginning in September 1858, Gladstone took a summer break, first at Hawarden and then in Scotland, visiting first the Duke and Duchess of Sutherland at Dunrobin, where he tried his hand at deer stalking, and then Lord Aberdeen at Haddo. While there, at the beginning of October, he received a rather curious letter from Edward Bulwer-Lytton, the colonial secretary. It suggested that Gladstone might like to undertake a special mission to the Ionian Islands, a British Protectorate since 1815. Gladstone did not immediately respond or return to London. First, he paid a visit to his brother Tom at Fasque, where a reconciliation happily took place. He and Catherine then saw Willy off to Oxford University and followed this with a visit to Robertson in Liverpool. Only then did he go to London to discuss the Ionian Islands project with Bulwer-Lytton. The government proposed to Gladstone that he visit the islands to prepare a report on their future.

The problem there was that the population, mainly Greek in origin, had begun to express a strong desire for union with that country. In 1849 an uprising of a sort on Cephalonia, one of the most important islands, had been brutally suppressed, but the underlying restlessness had continued. The British High Commissioner from 1855, Sir John Young, had been driven to suggest that at least some of the islands should be handed over to Greece, which suggestion had rather unfortunately been made public before Gladstone had even arrived to prepare his report.

The decision whether to go or not was not an easy one for Gladstone to take. Among the factors against it were those expressed by Sidney Herbert – it showed Gladstone acting as an ally of the Derby ministry (which, of course, is why they wanted him to go), and it would also take him out of Parliament at a crucial time. It would be difficult to achieve anything, and failure in the Ionian Islands would only expose Gladstone to ridicule, bearing in mind his work on Homer – *Studies on Homer and the Homeric Age*, published in March 1858, had been received with amusement and astonishment. Aberdeen suggested Bulwer-Lytton had known that Gladstone's interests would tempt him to accept the offer. It was clear, though, that Catherine could do with a holiday, and both she and daughter Agnes announced they would be pleased to go. He also felt some desire to help out Young, a Peelite and Eton and Oxford friend. Accordingly, on 5 November he was appointed High Commissioner Extraordinary to the Ionian Islands.

Gladstone and his party travelled via Brussels, Berlin and Vienna, and then to Trieste; from there they sailed for Corfu, where they landed on 24 November. The results of Gladstone's visit, however, might well have been disastrous. First, he fell out with Young, and in the New Year succeeded him as High Commissioner, not realising this meant he would have to stand down as an MP. He accordingly changed his mind and quickly made arrangements for his successor to be named, and the choice fell on a soldier, Sir Henry Storks. In the meantime, before Storks's arrival, Gladstone addressed a special assembly on Corfu, in Italian, trying to explain and justify his proposed reforms. They ignored him and simply proposed an address be sent to the Queen calling for union with Greece. Storks finally arrived on 16 February, and the harassed Gladstone and his family left Corfu three days later.

Fortunately for Gladstone, the effects of this visit were however very limited. He prepared three volumes of reports for the government, but these sank without trace. The Ionian Assembly rejected his proposals after several days of debate. More seriously, his reputation in Britain suffered another blow. *The Times* said that his 'acts of eccentricity' were not unusual, so that 'after all the experience we have had, we have no right to be astonished at anything Mr. Gladstone may do'.[19] Herbert was furious with Gladstone because of the mess he had got himself into, and only Disraeli got anything out of the episode when he suggested Gladstone should be crowned King of the Ionian Islands. In fact, just four years later, the British relinquished their hold on them and they were united with Greece.

The family returned home via Venice, Piedmont and France, and Gladstone noted with dismay the ominous militarisation of Piedmontese society. Count Camillo di Cavour, the Piedmontese prime minister, had used Orsini's attempt on Napoleon III's life to remind the emperor of his early days in Italy and his friendship for the cause of a united Italy. Much of northern Italy, particularly on the eastern side of the peninsula, including Lombardy and Venetia, remained under the control of the Austrian Empire. To the south, pro-Austrian rulers governed the duchies of Parma and Modena, while the Pope acted as secular ruler of the city of Rome and its surrounding territories. In the extreme south the kingdom of the Two Sicilies, which comprised the Island of Sicily and Naples, was ruled by an Italian dynasty, but Gladstone had seen for himself in 1851 how repressive this regime was and how it treated friends of the cause of Italian unity.

Cavour seems to have had his eyes fixed on driving the Austrians out of their north Italian territories. The kingdom of Piedmont had failed to do this on its own in 1848, and Cavour hoped he could now get French help for his cause. He paid Napoleon a visit and this, coupled with Orsini's dramatic pleas and heroic bearing before his execution, convinced the French emperor he should act. The summer of 1859 was marked by a bloody campaign by French and Piedmontese forces in northern Italy, ended by a peace treaty at Villafranca.

Napoleon had struck a blow against the Austrians, who ceded Lombardy to Piedmont, and in return he secured Nice and Savoy for France. But he had also set in motion a campaign for a united Italy. An army under the celebrated republican revolutionary Guiseppe Garibaldi drove out the Neapolitan dynasty, and, rather than let Republican forces conquer the whole peninsula, Cavour had despatched his own kingdom's troops to meet up with those of the red-shirted leader. By the end of 1861, therefore, shortly after Cavour's death, Italy was a more or less united kingdom. The Austrians had lost Lombardy; the Pope had lost his possessions outside Rome and the pro-Austrian dynasties in the centre of Italy had lost theirs too. But it took Prussian help to finally free Venetia from the Austrians (in 1866) and Rome from the French garrison (in 1871).

While these dramatic developments were taking place in Italy, in Britain politics were about to undergo another transformation. Derby's government had to do something to justify its existence. They struggled, with Palmerston's assistance, to secure the passage of a bill reforming the country's militia forces and then turned their attention to a parliamentary reform bill. It was not promising much of a reform, however, and all it did was to convince all prospective Liberals in Parliament – or nearly all – that any hope of real reform was not possible with them in office and the time had come for them to be removed. Gladstone, however, thought that as only two years had passed since the last General Election, the Conservatives should be given another chance. Clearly he did not want to see Palmerston back in office, but, on 31 March, the Reform Bill was defeated, despite Gladstone's silent support, and, to his annoyance, Derby decided to resign and call another General Election rather than fight on.

The General Election had come at a bad time for the Conservatives. The unsettled international situation did much to convince the public that Palmerston would be a more suitable national leader than Derby, and the future of Italy was a matter of concern to all liberals, further helping to cement their unity. While Palmerston stood for Italian freedom from Austrian rule and its unity, so did the majority of his parliamentary followers, and so, too, did Gladstone. It was this consideration, at least as much as any domestic issue, which did most to bring about a genuine liberal reunion, and it is generally agreed that the birth of the Victorian Liberal party can be dated, precisely, to 6 June 1859, at Willis's Rooms in London. At this meeting almost everyone present agreed what steps should be taken to bring about the dismissal of Derby and his replacement by Palmerston. Perhaps most significantly, Lord John Russell agreed that he would serve as a minister in a cabinet led by Palmerston, a reversal of their roles in the Whig ministry from 1846 to 1852, and an admission by Russell of his diminished political status, but putting his own supporters behind Palmerston. More radical liberals, like Cobden and Bright, also accepted this idea, as did Herbert, on behalf of the few remaining Peelites. Only one man of significance on the Liberal side was not there, Gladstone, but his absence made no appreciable difference to the course of events. When Parliament reassembled a motion of no confidence in the government was proposed and passed by 323 to 310 votes, and Derby resigned. The Queen and Prince Albert would have liked to have made Lord Granville prime minister, but now the Liberal Party had the power to impose their chosen candidate, the seventy-one year old Lord Palmerston.

PALMERSTON'S SECOND MINISTRY, 1859–1865

Palmerston began to construct his ministry after Granville gave up his half-hearted attempts. Russell, the old Whig, insisted he took the post of Foreign Secretary. Herbert, the Peelite, became Secretary for War, a post of importance given the crisis in defence that had arisen from the Orsini affair and French warship construction. The Whig Duke of Somerset became First Lord of the Admiralty and the Duke of Newcastle Colonial Secretary. None of these appointments caused particular surprise, but there was one that did: this was that Gladstone had decided to join the cabinet as Chancellor of the Exchequer.

This decision on Gladstone's part, which historians agree was one of the most momentous in his career, took many of his contemporaries aback and has been intensively studied since. Quite why he joined the cabinet of a prime minister whom he had spent the last four years heartily attacking, both in private and in public, baffled many people, even among his own family. His niece, Lucy Lyttelton, recorded in her diary: 'Uncle William has taken office under Ld Palmerston as Ch. of the Exchequer, thereby raising an uproar [in] view of his well-known antipathy. [But] he agrees at present with Lord P.'s foreign policy.' This, unsurprisingly, reflects Gladstone's own opinions:

> The overwhelming interest and weight of the Italian question, and our foreign policy in connection with it, joined to my entire distrust of the former government in relation to it, led me to decide without one moment's hesitation, to accept Palmerston's offer.[20]

But he went on: 'In finance there was still much useful work to be done.'

Historians' views have differed somewhat. Some consider that Palmerston's public commitment on the side of Italian unification, confirmed in a speech in his Tiverton constituency in the election campaign, had won Gladstone over. The Italian question certainly seems to have done a lot to unify the rather disparate 'liberal' group that met at Willis's Rooms and clearly had a significant role to play in Gladstone's own decision. But it is difficult to avoid the conclusion that other factors were at work in Gladstone's mind as well. Whatever his reluctance to admit it, Gladstone had plans, and he had ambitions. He had thought seriously about the possibility of joining Derby and the Conservatives, and he had retained a liking for the flamboyant earl. But he could not get on with Disraeli. The previous four years had convinced him that if he did not join the Liberals – even if Palmerston remained in charge of them – he would not join anyone. In isolation, out of office, none of his plans would be achieved. Like it or not, then, to carry on in politics, he had to join this government, and he had to tolerate Palmerston. Many years later, Gladstone remarked that his time as Palmerston's chancellor was 'the most trying of my whole political life'[21] – but it was also the foundation of his reputation as the 'People's William', the man who was to be the personification of popular liberal politics into the 1880s and a towering figure in British political life.

The first three years of the new ministry were the most difficult from Gladstone's point of view. He found himself locked in conflict with the prime minister on two closely related matters, economic policy and defence policy. While Gladstone's ideal combined an improvement in Anglo-French relations with cuts in public expenditure, Palmerston's was to secure the former by means of 'putting England in a state of defence', but that would increase costs. The budgets of 1860 and 1861 witnessed terrific battles between the two men and their supporters before they were finally agreed.

Gladstone took the first steps. In November 1859 Richard Cobden was despatched to France to attempt to negotiate a treaty reducing import duties on French goods and export duties on British coal, iron and machine tools. The deal was sealed in January 1860, thanks not least to the Emperor's personal wish to do something to improve Anglo-French relations. Palmerston was not opposed to the treaty either, but he did not think that by itself it was enough. Under Derby's government the British public had begun to form a Rifle Volunteer Corps to defend the country from a French invasion, and by June 1860 there were some 150,000 volunteers enrolled. In July 1859 a Royal Commission had been appointed to 'consider the Defences of the United Kingdom', which, when it reported a year later, recommended the expenditure of no less than eleven million pounds on fortifications to defend the country's naval dockyards. Meanwhile, expenditure on the Royal Navy itself was also growing. To counter French ironclad warship construction, Palmerston demanded that the Navy build twenty of these vessels, and naval estimates, too, began to rise.

As early as February 1860 Gladstone had begun to warn Palmerston that he could not stand by and let estimates rise so far and so fast. The Premier responded that nothing need be done at present, but made it clear he favoured both a large navy and strong fortifications. Gladstone reacted furiously against the recommendations by the Defence Commission that the fortifications should be financed by a loan: that, he said, would be 'a betrayal of my public duty'. Gladstone, it seems, found it hard to believe that Palmerston was genuinely convinced of the need for these works and thought that he was accepting the proposals just to secure popularity. When Gladstone began to hint at resignation, Palmerston responded decisively, warning him

> If he resigned nobody would believe a man of his ability and experience and statesmanlike position left the gov't because he would not have the country defended, they would say and believe however unjustly he was afraid of the financial consequences of his budget and running away from them.

He also warned Gladstone of the long-term consequences: 'Out of office he would be thrown into companionship with Bright, which would be ruin to him as a public man.'[22]

When the matter was discussed in June and July 1860, the dispute between the two men deepened. Argyll, Gladstone's friend, tried to persuade Palmerston that some compromise could be reached, but neither man seemed to heed his suggestions. Gladstone warned Herbert on 20 July he was not prepared to accept a loan to fund the fortifications, and when the cabinet agreed to this the next day it was only after the

Chancellor had left the meeting. When Parliament debated the question on 23 July most of the House of Commons supported the government, except for a number of radicals. This could not have been lost on Gladstone, nor could the fact that both Argyll and Herbert had taken the Prime Minister's side. Palmerston's warnings had struck home: he would either have to support the fortification loan, or retreat once more into parliamentary isolation and see his cherished plans fall through. Advised by Graham that his resignation might endanger the Cobden Treaty, on 25 July Gladstone wrote to Herbert asking for details of the sea defences at the naval dockyards – a clear implication that he had decided to stay in the cabinet. On this occasion, Palmerston had called Gladstone's bluff.

In addition to his failure to prevent the vast expenditure on fortifications, Gladstone also failed to carry one other important element in his financial arrangements for 1860: the abolition of the duties levied on paper. In 1859 he raised the income tax (which under his 1853 plan was to have been abolished in 1860) from 5d (just over 2 per cent) in the pound to 9d (3.75 per cent) in the pound, its highest ever peacetime figure. He spent a lot more time planning what to do in 1860. The Cobden Treaty cut some import duties and Gladstone proposed a total of 371 of them should be abolished: he also proposed to abolish the paper duties. In all, he gave up some £3 million of revenue. To make up for this he added £1 million to minor taxes and collected the other £2 million from lapsed government funds and by raising the income tax by 1d from 9d to 10d. Palmerston was particularly opposed to the repeal of the paper duties and spoke against it in cabinet on one occasion for some forty-five minutes. But Gladstone would have none of it, and this time he had the support of the rest of the cabinet. He introduced his budget on 10 February and, a month later, the Paper Duties Repeal Bill.

Despite being Foreign Secretary, Russell decided the time had come for him to introduce a further measure of parliamentary reform. This confused the issue of voting: not all of the government's supporters were at all keen on this proposal, which would have lowered the franchise qualification and redistributed twenty-five seats from smaller boroughs, and it was withdrawn after a somewhat languid debate on 11 June. Meanwhile, Gladstone's budget and Paper Bill struggled through the

Commons, the latter being accepted by a majority of only nine votes. As then applied, the rules of the House of Lords allowed them to reject any Commons measures they did not deem to be a 'finance bill'; when they decided the Paper Duties Repeal Bill did not fall into this category, they refused to pass it.

Palmerston was not displeased; he told Gladstone to accept the Lords' verdict and no one should resign as a consequence. Russell agreed with the Premier, though he took the matter more seriously. But Gladstone was furious. He insisted that the Commons should pass a measure condemning the Lords' action, though to placate Palmerston he promised that 'the mildest means of correction should be adopted'.[23] Palmerston agreed and was prepared to take some notice of this Lords' attack on the Commons' privileges, but Gladstone thought that he did not go far enough, and in the cabinet discussion he had the support of both Russell and Argyll. Accordingly, when Palmerston announced in the House of Commons a Resolution condemning the Lords, 'and yet speaking in defence of their conduct', Gladstone was more outspoken, 'Most earnestly and eloquently condemning them, and declaring that action and not resolutions became the House of Commons'. He was 'loudly and tempestuously cheered by the radicals, and no-one else'.[24] But perhaps 'ruin' would not face him after all if he could attract a significantly large body of support from this quarter, even if he lost Whig support he might survive.

Gladstone won the Paper Duty struggle in 1861. His idea was quite simple: the repeal measure that year should be included as part of the budget statement, and so the Lords would not be able to reject it. But the result was possibly his greatest dispute of all with Palmerston, still opposed to the proposed repeal. Gladstone this time won the cabinet onto his side following three days of strenuous debate on 10, 12 and 13 April. He knew, however, that early in 1861 fifty-one Liberal MPs had signed a letter to Palmerston calling for reductions in government spending, and so he would also have support in the House of Commons for his proposal to try and keep limits on public expenditure. It was agreed that the income tax should be cut by 1d, back to 9d, but even with the Paper Duties repealed this would leave a surplus. On 15 April Gladstone introduced the budget; Russell publicly gave it his support, and in the crisis debate on 30 May it was decided by 296 to 281 votes that the repeal of the paper duties should be included in the measure.

Gladstone was delighted; this, he wrote, was 'One of the greatest nights in the whole of my recollection'.[25] Palmerston, on the other hand, was not pleased, displaying his irritation by entering into a heated exchange with Gladstone about a minor Treasury matter, and becoming all too aware of his increasing stature in the country.

With this crisis out of the way, relations within the cabinet settled down. The 'invasion panic' abated, demands for defence expenditure declined (though Gladstone argued consistently throughout the ministry that they remained too high), and an uneasy calm ensued. The budget of 1862 got through relatively easily, although Gladstone had to threaten to put another penny on the income tax to secure a suitable reduction in the naval estimates. In April 1863 he was able to take 2d off the income tax and a year later another penny.

Gladstone's relationship with Palmerston and his cabinet colleagues was one of the main elements in his political development over the years of Palmerston's second ministry, but it was not the only one. It is generally accepted that over these years Gladstone developed many of the characteristics that made him the leader of popular liberalism in later times. One of the most important elements in this was his increasing awareness of popular feeling. Palmerston had led the way here, but his audience had been somewhat different to Gladstone's. When in April 1862 Gladstone visited Manchester and addressed a largely working-class audience, condemning extravagance in public spending, he was bidding for popular support in his battles with the prime minister and the heads of the spending departments. At the same time the populace was becoming anxious to see Gladstone. Arrangements were made in the later summer of this year for him to visit Newcastle, on what was something like a triumphal exhibition. It is a pity, then, that the visit is notorious for the speech he made at Newcastle, in which he addressed the question of the American Civil War, which had broken out in April 1861.

This conflict, between the northern, or Union, states and those ten of the southern, or Confederate, states that had declared themselves independent of the American Union and set themselves up as an independent confederation, was being fought for a number of reasons. The two groups had drifted apart in their economic and social development, with the North becoming steadily more industrialised and economically more powerful. The South was fighting against the steady encroachment of northern businesses and for what it believed was the right of states to leave the American Union if they chose. Another major issue dividing the two groups was that of slavery, with the South defending it and North becoming steadily more hostile to it, until their leader, President Abraham Lincoln, on 1 January 1863 declared it abolished.

Given the economic strength of the northern states it was expected they would win any conflict, but in fact it was the Confederates who took the initiative. Most of the British upper classes, Gladstone among them, had no love for the Union and believed the Confederates were in the right. In the battle at Bull Run in July 1861 and the Seven Days battles from 26 June to 2 July 1862, the Confederate army defeated Union forces. In the light of this, Gladstone, on 7 October, declared openly his view that the Confederate states had 'made a nation' and, though he later attempted to deny it, he argued that their government should be granted international recognition. He went on to urge the cabinet to attempt to mediate in the war. But while this speech did some harm to Gladstone's reputation with those British radicals, like Bright, who strongly supported the North, it does not seem to have affected his relationship with the working classes too much. Just as they were seeing in Gladstone a new hero, he was beginning to see in them a new source of support. The tide of war turned in favour of the Union after the battle of Gettysburg on 1–3 July 1863, a catastrophic defeat for the Confederate army. Although the Confederacy struggled on, it was forced to surrender in April 1865. The American Civil War was to trouble Gladstone again, however.

The war had caused serious harm to the Lancashire cotton industry in 1861 and 1862, as northern warships blockaded ports exporting southern cotton to Europe, and to help relieve this the Gladstones had organised work on their Hawarden estate. (Catherine, for example, had taken in ten unemployed factory girls to be trained for service.) Despite their problems, Gladstone was impressed at the self-discipline shown by these workers. This was a contributory factor to a famous declaration he made in May 1864. In a speech in the Commons on 11 May 1864, he stated that 'every man who is not personally incapacitated by some consideration of personal unfitness or of political danger is morally entitled to come within the pale of the constitution'. Faced with a furious outcry, even from some on the Liberal benches, Gladstone hastily backtracked. He had not, he said, spoken in favour of universal manhood suffrage, or at least not immediately, but it is difficult to see what else he could have meant in the longer term. Whether or not anyone who heard or read this speech approved of it depended entirely on where they stood in relation to parliamentary reform. Those who favoured a radical measure of reform had their admiration for Gladstone heightened; those who did not, or who were cautious about it, had their suspicions of him confirmed. He had certainly travelled a long way from his days of outright opposition to any measures of parliamentary reform that he had displayed when he first made his appearance on the political scene in the 1830s.

In any event, Gladstone had done enough with his public pronouncements to alienate the electors of Oxford University. When, in July 1865, another general election was held, he was defeated. This did not matter: he had already seen what was coming and accepted nomination for one of the seats for South Lancashire, where he arrived 'unmuzzled' from the restrictions of the university. Interestingly enough, he had been approached by representatives of this constituency as early as 1861, but had decided against it then. The 1865 election, however, confirmed Gladstone's liberal – even radical – credentials. But in October the unthinkable happened: the elderly premier was taken ill at his country seat of Brocket and died, and British politics was about to come to life again. The election had given the Liberals a majority of about seventy, but the party remained a coalition of forces. Russell, who succeeded Palmerston as prime minister, was now relieved of his Foreign Office responsibilities and remained committed to parliamentary reform. Gladstone, who had clearly seen the way the wind was blowing, offered his services to Russell, on condition that he became Leader of the House of Commons (and, by implication, would succeed the elderly Russell as prime minister when the time came). Russell, who had seen a much more liberal Gladstone emerging in the 1860s, was pleased to accept his offer. The only other significant change from Palmerston's cabinet was that Lord Clarendon succeeded Russell as foreign secretary.

THE RUSSELL AND DERBY MINISTRIES AND PARLIAMENTARY REFORM, 1865–1868

It was generally agreed that a parliamentary reform bill should be introduced, but quite what form it should take – in particular, how widely the franchise should be extended – was a matter for debate. Gladstone, despite his 1864 declaration, seems to have been more cautious than Russell, at least initially. The bill eventually introduced proposed lowering the franchise qualification in towns to include those paying £7 per year in rates, or above, rather than at least £10 a year and £14 per year in the countryside, which would have had the effect of increasing the electorate in England and Wales by a mere 400,000 to around 1,500,000. In addition, small boroughs were to lose forty-nine seats; these would be redistributed elsewhere. The only effect of such a modest measure, or so it seemed, would be to increase the Liberals' already dominant position in the boroughs; it would not enfranchise the whole of the working classes, nor give them predominance among the electors.

When Gladstone introduced the bill on 12 March 1866 he must have expected opposition from the Conservatives: after all, the measure had the support of Bright and presumably, therefore, of other radicals. But it did not have the support of everyone on the Liberal side. A number of Palmerston's supporters believed he had done a good job, and the system was working well: it did not need to be 'improved'. This opposition was grouped around the backbencher Robert Lowe and others, who became known, because of their open and steadfast opposition to change, as 'Adullamites', named by Bright after the followers of King David who took refuge from Saul in the cave of Adullam. The Conservatives had been trying for some years to open up a split in the Liberal ranks, and with one so evident as this it is not surprising that they began to try very hard to bring about the defeat of the government. As leader of the Commons, Gladstone came under considerable pressure and was forced to work very hard. He also found himself taking a much more liberal position. On 6 April 1866 Gladstone went to Liverpool – the heartland of Lord Derby's land holdings and influence – where he attacked the earl's son as a 'selfish aristocrat' and made it plain the government was determined to press ahead with the Reform Bill. But on the second reading the government's majority, against a proposed amendment by the Adullamite Lord Grosvenor, was only five votes. The Liberal majority of the 1865 election had disappeared. The government's case was not helped by the collapse of the city banking house Overend & Gurney, and the resulting financial crisis, and it lost the votes on two further amendments in May. The last affront came on 18 June, when an amendment proposed by another Adullamite, Lord

Dunkellin (the son of a notorious property owner in Ireland), was carried by eleven votes. Nearly fifty Liberal MPs had joined the Conservatives this time and voted against the government.

The government now had a choice of courses of action open to it: it could once again simply ignore the vote and stay in office; it could call for a vote of confidence; it could announce the dissolution of Parliament and hold another election, hoping to return with a secure majority; or it could simply resign. Gladstone and Russell initially favoured the second of these, but most of their colleagues had had enough. Despite the reluctance of the Queen to travel from her retreat at Balmoral and to accept the resignation, Russell was insistent and the government resigned.

Matters developed in an unexpected fashion over the next year. For one thing, the resignation of Russell's ministry seems to have attracted the attention of the masses to the reform question. Ten days after the government resigned, a large crowd gathered outside Gladstone's house in Carlton House Terrace calling volubly for 'Gladstone and liberty' and making it plain that he was their hero. On 23 July a rioting mob pulled down the railings in Hyde Park, making their determination to secure a measure of reform plain to the upper-class inhabitants who lived nearby. While Gladstone was anxious to disassociate himself from this kind of behaviour, he had done enough – for example, by attending the first dinner of the Cobden Club, founded in memory of Richard Cobden who had died in 1863 – to make himself a focus of popular liberalism. But between September 1866 and January 1867 he took himself and his family to Italy, where he had an audience with the Pope. This was an astute move on his part. He was all too aware of the divisions over reform apparent in the Parliamentary Liberal Party, and he had taken himself out of the way, leaving the question in the hands of Lord Derby's minority government.

Derby and Disraeli, for their part, took a realistic approach to the reform question. Disraeli, in particular, was anxious it should be the Conservative Party that passed a reform act, and less anxious about what the terms of that act should actually be. Having failed to attract the Adullamites to their side, the government introduced its own proposals in February 1867, though its own unity was to be seriously tested. After some hesitation Disraeli persuaded his colleagues to accept household suffrage in the towns. But the ultra-Tories, led by Lord Cranborne and

General Jonathan Peel, Sir Robert's younger brother, resigned from the cabinet on 1 March rather than accept such a radical measure of reform, and it was very apparent that any proposal would be difficult to get through the Commons.

Disraeli's hope was that the split in the Liberal ranks would be sufficient to enable him to ensure the passage of his measure through the Commons. Gladstone's, on the other hand, was that he could restore the unity of his party and either bring about the rejection of the Bill or pass sufficient amendments against it so that a more liberal act would result. The important thing in the latter case was that it would still be the government's act, and for that reason the House of Lords would be prepared to let it pass. But neither course proved easy for him as a dangerously large number of Liberal MPs refused to follow him. First, the Liberals could not unite sufficiently to secure the outright rejection of the Bill. Then, at a party meeting on 5 April, he tried to bring in a measure allowing all householders with a sufficient level of income the right to vote, but this led to the so-called 'Tea Room Revolt' three days later, when a group Liberal MPs decided to inform Gladstone they could not support this proposal, and he had to abandon it. Worst of all, on 13 April there occurred 'a smash perhaps without example', when some forty-five Liberal MPs – by no means all 'Adullamites' – voted with the government and defeated another of Gladstone's proposed amendments by twenty-one votes.[26]

It is not surprising that Gladstone began to be disillusioned with some of his party. He was coming to the conclusion that a more radical proposal was the answer; some Liberals might not like it, but they could be dispensed with. With popular feeling still on his side – symbolised by a visit to Gladstone on 12 May by members of the Reform Union, an active middle-class organisation – he clearly decided the time for a more radical stance had come. He need not have bothered; in a remarkable about-turn, Disraeli himself announced his acceptance of an amendment which enfranchised some 400,000 householders who 'compounded' the payment of their rates by including the cost in the rental they paid for their property.

The second Reform Act, as finally passed by the Commons on 15 July 1867, after a debate in which Gladstone deliberately took no part 'for fear of doing mischief on our own side', was a more radical measure than that which had been proposed by the Liberals in 1866. In the boroughs, the principle of household suffrage was accepted; in the countryside, a £12 rateable value was demanded. As a result of this, the number of electors nearly doubled, reaching almost 2,000,000 in England and Wales, and a modest 253,000 in Scotland.

At Christmas 1867 Earl Russell, now aged seventy-five, decided the time had come for him to retire from active politics, and two months later, in February 1868, the Earl of Derby was driven by ill-health to the same conclusion. The result was to set up a classic political rivalry, already prefigured in the struggle for reform. Russell's successor was already, in effect, chosen. Gladstone's position as Leader of the Commons and then effective head of the party in opposition, made him the obvious choice to succeed Russell, even though he had made enemies in it. The only other possibilities – among them Gladstone's friends Sidney Herbert and the Duke of Newcastle, and his sometime rival Cornewall Lewis – had all died (Herbert in 1861, Lewis in 1863 and Newcastle in 1864). His backing in the country, however, more than compensated for the dislike of some of his parliamentary followers. Derby's successor, too, was obvious: Benjamin Disraeli had, at last, made his way to 'the top of the greasy pole', and became prime minister.

But Disraeli's first term as prime minister was not to last long. The Conservatives were still in a minority and it was only a matter of time before a general election would have to be called. Disraeli hoped to make it a long time, claiming it was needed to prepare the registers to include all the newly-enfranchised electors. He no doubt hoped that the splits that had opened in liberal ranks during the reform crisis would continue to widen, and he also hoped to profit from the popularity following a foreign policy success. In April 1868 a British army under General Robert Napier had destroyed Magdala, capital of the Abyssinian Empire and his mission, to free British captives, including the British consul, held by the Emperor, had been a resounding triumph.

Gladstone, on the other hand, needed to find something that would hold the Liberal party together and which he would be able to use to attack the government. He was well aware there were some things, such as local government reform that it might be better not to chose. The issue he did eventually settle on was one about which he had strong personal feelings, but it was also one around which other Liberals, as well as Irish MPs, could rally: the disestablishment of the Anglican Church of Ireland.

Ireland had not been much in the news since the terrible crisis occasioned by the famine in the 1840s had passed. But many Irish people still laboured under very difficult conditions, and many had left Ireland, often to settle in North America. It was among these that the nationalist Fenian movement had first been established. There was an attempted Fenian 'uprising' in 1867, marked in England with a raid on Chester Castle in February and the shooting of a policeman in Manchester in September. Worst of all, on 13 December there was an escape attempt from Clerkenwell Prison, which resulted in an explosion and the deaths of several people nearby. This led to the execution of three Fenians and an awareness on the part of Gladstone and others that all was not well in Ireland.

Gladstone, though, took a more thoughtful approach to the Irish problem than advocating simple repression. He was aware that the main grievance of many of the Irish people was the conditions on which they rented land. But rather than attack property rights – a very touchy subject indeed – Gladstone realised there was something else that symbolised the disaffection of many Irish people: the position of the Church of Ireland. Since most of the Irish population were Roman Catholic, while many of those who were not were Presbyterian dissenters, there was little support for this Anglican body; the fact that it was an 'established' church, supported by the state and held large amounts of property, only added to their sense of grievance. A good many Liberals were themselves Nonconformists, and shared the view that the Anglican Church in England should itself also be disestablished: if the Church of Ireland was disestablished then that, at least, was a start. Additionally, while those on the right of Gladstone's party were not necessarily convinced of the rightness of the proposal, or that it would do any good in Ireland, they felt it would at least do no harm and the question would be a useful attack on the government. The elderly Russell gave his support to the idea, too. Finally, the Conservatives themselves were divided over the issue, so any proposal about it would help to split them.

The result of all this was that Gladstone prepared and, in April 1868, tabled in the House of Commons a series of resolutions calling on the government to disestablish the Church of Ireland. The government's attempt to prevent the House discussing the resolutions was defeated by a large majority of sixty-one votes. Gladstone had evidently succeeded in uniting the various elements in the Liberal Party behind him, and he had caught Disraeli. Disraeli now decided, rather than resign outright, to dissolve Parliament, and a general election was scheduled for November. It remained to be seen whether the voting public had been as convinced as the Liberal party with Gladstone's proposals.

GLADSTONE'S RISE TO POWER, 1853–1868

The last sixteen years had been crucial to Gladstone's political evolution. He had begun them as a follower of the late Sir Robert Peel, courted by the Conservatives rather more than by the Liberals. His dislike of Palmerston had developed in intensity and the chances of his leaving most of his Peelite friends and going over to Derby had appeared, at one time, to be very real. But he could not take the final step: his detestation of Disraeli and the loathing many Conservatives felt for him had prevented this. Besides, there was one thing he and Palmerston could agree on: unity for Italy. Hence, after the rather curious Ionian Islands incident, he had decided to go with Palmerston.

Gladstone's time in Palmerston's cabinet had not been easy though. He was totally out of sympathy with both Palmerston's anxieties over defence and his desire to end the slave trade. Gladstone's battles for economy in the early 1860s were unequalled by anything in his career, either earlier or later. But he also realised he could outlast the elderly premier, so he held on. As time passed, though, he came to sympathise more and more with popular liberalism, and he began to see in at least some of the nation's working classes a new respectability which could be contrasted with the apparent corruption of many of the rich. And popular liberalism began to see in Gladstone a new representative. His support for parliamentary reform was clear, but his radicalism on the question was often exaggerated by the voting public. However, this did him no harm. His battles in 1866 and 1867 placed him firmly in line to take over the Liberal Party, which he duly did on Russell's retirement, and he then managed to assert himself as an effective leader of it.

Gladstone could at least look back on a contented private life. His relationship with Catherine had developed to the extent that she was now able to lead a more independent existence, both supporting and being supported by William. Their financial situation, too, was somewhat more secure in these years, while his children were growing up and there would soon be the question of their futures to consider. Even at the age of fifty-eight Gladstone's life still had a long way to go.

4

THE FIRST MINISTRY, 1868–1874

When Gladstone took office as prime minister in December 1868, he stood at the head of a relatively united Liberal Party. He was elected on a platform which promised a wide range of reforms, many of which had been on the cards for some years but which Palmerston's nominally Liberal and, of course, Derby and Disraeli's Conservative governments had not seen fit to pass. High hopes existed among many Nonconformist middle- and working-class electors that Gladstone would be able to deal with these measures and Britain would at last see some much-needed changes to her social and political fabric.

THE LIBERAL PARTY AND THE GENERAL ELECTION OF NOVEMBER 1868

The election of November 1868 did not turn out as Disraeli's Conservatives had hoped it would. They had always been in a minority in the House of Commons and Disraeli's belief when he went to the country was that his party would benefit from the divisions which the Reform Bill debates had opened up in the Liberal ranks. Unfortunately for him, it was not to be: from a majority of some seventy seats in 1865, the Liberal majority in the new House of Commons increased to around 110. Most English county seats had voted Conservative, while most English boroughs returned Liberals – by this date, a fairly usual state of affairs. Westminster and Middlesex saw Conservative gains, mainly, it would appear, as a result of the increasingly numerous middle classes in these areas voting for them. Lancashire, too, was essentially Conservative in feeling, though in this case it seems to have been very much a product of anti-Catholic and anti-Irish feeling – sentiments which Gladstone was acutely aware of. His South Lancashire constituency had been divided into two new divisions under the terms of the 1868 Reform Act, and he was nominated for South West Lancashire. He does not seem to have believed assurances he was given about his good chances by local party workers. Since it was possible at this time to stand for election in more than one constituency at the same election, Gladstone took advantage on this occasion and arranged to stand for the Greenwich seat in South East London. When the time came, Gladstone lost his South West Lancashire seat but managed to secure election in Greenwich. The most striking Liberal gains were made in the so-called 'Celtic fringe'. Of the thirty-three seats in Wales, Liberals won twenty-three, and, even more strikingly, they managed to capture no less than fifty-three of the sixty Scottish seats.

The 1867 Reform Act did not significantly change the social composition of the Liberal Party. Nearly half of the 384 Liberal MPs were drawn from the aristocracy and gentry, while almost a quarter could be classed as merchants and manufacturers. About sixty MPs were representatives of Nonconformist churches, such as Unitarians, Congregationalists or Baptists, or of Quakers, or Jews. A roughly equal number of MPs also seem to have generally sympathised with the Nonconformists, probably because many of their electorate were like-minded. From these figures, it would seem Gladstone would have to tread carefully, especially over religious questions, and this, of course, involved allied matters such as education and general social discrimination, particularly as these non-Anglicans had a radical reputation when approaching matters of this kind.

THE CONSTRUCTION OF THE CABINET

Gladstone was felling trees in the woods at Hawarden when he received a telegram on 2 December telling him that the Queen's Private Secretary, General George Grey, was coming to see him. An eyewitness, Evelyn Ashley, described what followed:

> 'Very significant' ... I said nothing, but waited while the well-directed blows resounded in regular cadence. After a few minutes the blows ceased, and Mr. Gladstone, resting on the handle of his axe, looked up, and with deep earnestness in his face, exclaimed, 'My mission is to pacify Ireland'. He then resumed his task, and never said another word until the tree was down.[1]

This heroic account of events rather ignores the fact that four days previously Gladstone had had a conversation with Lord Halifax about some of the difficulties of forming a ministry, and had presented Grey with a memorandum on this subject ready for the Queen. In other words, he was already prepared for the summons and also prepared to say something suitable for the occasion when it arrived.

Gladstone had had thoughts about forming a cabinet well before December 1868. As early as June that year he had discussed possibilities with his new confidant, Lord Granville, and at that time he felt that there was one other man, besides themselves, who should be guaranteed a post in the new cabinet. This was the Earl of Clarendon, who, Gladstone thought, would make a good foreign secretary, albeit rather a Palmerstonian one in outlook. But as it turned out Clarendon was one of the people the Queen was very anxious not to have in the cabinet. When Gladstone had the first of two meetings with her on 3 December, she accepted only some of Gladstone's proposed nominees: Granville as Colonial Secretary, the Peelites Edward Cardwell as Secretary for War and the Duke of Argyll as President of the Council (though he ended up as Secretary of State for India). Hugh Childers, a Palmerstonian Liberal, was put forward to become First Lord of the Admiralty. The Queen hoped Clarendon could be persuaded to accept another role rather than that of foreign secretary, but in the end he was appointed to that post. The key post of Chancellor of the Exchequer went to Robert Lowe, former leader of the Adullamites, in preference to George Goschen, felt by some to be the more able financier, who became President of the Poor Law Board. Lowe's appointment, which did not turn out well, was clearly an attempt by Gladstone to reconcile some of the disparate elements in his party. The other, appealing to a different group was his appointment of the Radical John Bright as President of the Board of Trade. Gladstone had expected some difficulties with the Queen about the Quaker Bright's appointment, but she had been quite taken with him at their first meetings. Bright, however, was much more reluctant to join than the Queen was to accept his services, and it took some persuading to overcome this. Henry Bruce, the Home Secretary, was a Welsh coal and iron master, a representative of the 'Celtic' wing of the party. The aristocratic 'Whig' representation in the cabinet was added to by Earl de Grey (the Lord President of the Council), the Earl of Kimberley (Lord Privy Seal), the Marquess of Hartington (Postmaster General) and Chichester Fortescue (the Chief Secretary for Ireland). Fortescue was married to the formidable society hostess Frances Waldegrave, a valuable ally in Gladstone's relations with the aristocracy.

The cabinet, as finally formed in December 1868, was therefore an attempt by Gladstone to reflect the make-up of the Parliamentary Liberal Party, and it included more of a 'middle-class' element than its predecessors. Six of its members – Bright, Cardwell, Goschen and Lowe, together with Bruce and Childers – can be classified as 'middle-class', while eight were aristocrats or had aristocratic connections. (It might have been even more aristocratic had Earl Russell, the Duke of Somerset and one or two others not turned down the offers made to them.) The Peelite influence remained strong and there was a small, but significant, radical presence too. It was, on the whole, a talented and fairly well-balanced team, which had several pressing tasks ahead of it.

LEGISLATIVE REFORM: THE EDUCATION SYSTEM

One of the best-known reforms enacted by Gladstone's first ministry is that named after its leading proponent, William Edward Forster, the vice-president of the Committee of the Privy Council for Education, which was passed in 1870. But Forster's Education Act only applied to England and Wales, and was not the first of its kind introduced by Gladstone's government. A year earlier the Duke of Argyll had introduced an education reform measure for Scotland into the House of Lords. Gladstone had little to do with this bill, but he had not failed to see the opposition it had run into. The Lords did not like the prospect of a 'national system' of education, provided and paid for by the state, and believed the Roman Catholic Church and the Church of Scotland should remain providers of education. They feared the measure was a precedent for a similar one to be enacted later in England and used the opportunity to amend it drastically before sending it down to the Commons. There it had foundered, only to pass (in a modified form) in 1872.

While this was still going on, in October 1869 Gladstone proposed that the cabinet should discuss the question of education in England and Wales. It was broadly agreed that something had to be done, since at this time there existed no national system of education whatever in Britain. Those schools that did exist were provided by the churches, and the state had for some time provided them with some modest grants of money to help supplement their limited voluntary sources of income. The result of this was that many children lived in areas where no schools existed and received no schooling at all.

Disputes over the issue had sharpened in 1869 with the foundation of the National Education Union, which favoured the existing church-run 'system' and the National Education League, which pressed for a universal, 'non-sectarian' or 'secular' system funded entirely by the state. The latter, composed of Nonconformist and liberal elements, pressed the government to take decisive action urgently.

In November, Forster and Lord de Grey introduced a detailed paper dealing with it to the cabinet. The agreed measure laid down that where current voluntary provision was insufficient, local boards should be set up to provide schools paid for by modest contributions from parents, parliamentary grants, and, what was crucial, a local rate. It also stated that denominational (meaning Church of England) religious instruction would be part of the curriculum in the new state schools, though parents would have the right to withdraw their children from these classes. The bill upset Anglicans, who saw it as a blow at the rights of the Church of England. It also generated an enormous and voluble opposition from Nonconformists, who aimed at the elimination of religious teaching from all state-funded schools, and an effective state system that would supersede the local voluntary, church-run schools. This Nonconformist opposition could be found at its strongest in the Liberal Party, and the ministry found itself under increasing attack from its own supporters as the session progressed.

Gladstone himself wanted to preserve as much as he could of the Anglican element of the bill and, not surprisingly, its passage was slow and laborious, delayed both by the opposition to it and by the Irish Land Bill which was being discussed at the same time. It was introduced on 17 February 1870 and had its second reading over three nights, 14, 15 and 18 March. Then there was a delay, while ministers grappled with the difficulties raised by the opposition. When the cabinet finally reached agreement on 14 June it was that the new state system should supplement the old voluntary one (but that, at Gladstone's own insistence, the grant to the voluntary schools was to be doubled and that they could apply for building grants). In the end, the government had to accept the Cowper-Temple compromise over religious education, named after the late Lord Palmerston's illegitimate son, which laid down that all religious teaching in the new state schools should be 'undenominational', though how truly undenominational it was in the event was soon open to question.

Gladstone was aware that to get this kind of measure past the Commons would require Conservative 'acquiescence' at least, since he realised, quite rightly, that he could not rely on the Nonconformists in his own party. The Conservatives, for their part, were happy to widen the split they had seen opening in the Liberal ranks. They accepted the call for a national education system, swallowed any reservations they might have had about its 'undenominational' character, and simply enjoyed seeing Gladstone and his ministers wilting under the attacks of their own backbenchers. Many Liberals were bitterly disappointed by the religious dimensions of the measure, which was denounced by Bright as 'the worst Act passed by any liberal parliament since 1832'.[2] Whether their opposition to it arose out of genuine religious feeling, or whether it was simply a struggle for social position, was not the issue that taxed Gladstone: his main worry was that the Conservatives had been given new heart by it.

During the course of the debates Gladstone had hoped he could regain some lost ground with his supporters. Having carried his proposal by fourteen votes in the Commons that school boards should be balloted for, Gladstone stood firm against proposed amendments by the Duke of Richmond in the Lords. But he made his party motive plain to Granville:

> Any further contest ... will lose public time, but will exactly suit our party purposes: the tenacity with which we have held to this point has almost atoned in the eyes of some of our supporters for the equal tenacity with which in some other matters we adhered to views which were agreeable to the Opposition.[3]

The Act, as finally passed, laid down that new rate-supported schools, run by school boards elected by local ratepayers, including women, would be established in areas where no other schools existed. It also stated that all children aged up to thirteen years should attend a school, although at this stage it was not made compulsory, and it represented the first hesitant step towards a truly national system of primary education. By 1883 over 3,500 School Boards existed (although so did 11,500 voluntary schools) and central government money spent on education had risen from £1.6 million in 1870 to £5.1 million, while local government expenditure on it also rose from £2.2 million to £3.2 million in ten years from 1875 to 1885. In 1880 attendance became compulsory, while in 1891 school fees were abolished. On balance, therefore, although Forster's Act is justifiably famous as an educational measure, and stands as a tribute to Gladstone's tenacity and determination to see through a bill which he was not especially keen on, and which does not appear as a particularly grand measure in the story of Liberal unity.

It may be partly as a result of the struggle over Forster's Bill that in 1871 Gladstone changed his mind over another matter connected with education. The Nonconformists had long been pressing that the old universities of Oxford and Cambridge should allow non-Anglicans to hold teaching posts at them, as they had, since the mid-1850s been forced to admit non-Anglican undergraduates – partly at Gladstone's own prompting. But in 1866 he had voted against a proposal allowing non-Anglicans to teach there, which had been rejected. Even in 1870, Gladstone had felt these venerable, and, as he saw it, Anglican, institutions had every right to maintain their opposition to the change.

> For me individually it would be beyond anything odious, I am almost tempted to say impossible, after my long connection with Oxford, to go into a new controversy on the basis of what will be taken and alleged to be an absolute secularisation of the colleges ... I incline to think this work is for others, not for me.[4]

But as pressure grew, he decided, partly perhaps as a means of reconciling his Nonconformist critics, that the government would adopt as its policy the abolition of the restrictions. The Lords tried to prevent this, but Gladstone, as ever, stood firm and in 1871 the change was made law. Despite the fears expressed by the old elites, the effects on the universities were not at all disastrous and they continued to function largely as before.

ARMY REFORM

If the story of Forster's Act shows Gladstone fighting to secure the passage of the measure against some of his own party, and to some extent his own inclination, his dealings over army reform were equally contentious, but for somewhat different reasons. Gladstone felt the Army had to serve two functions: it had to be cheap, and it had to be efficient. He had no doubt that both of these things could be achieved if the Army was well administered, and in Edward Cardwell, he believed – correctly – that he had the man for the job. But the difficulties of dealing with any measure of army reform were great. For one thing, it might offend some people in very high places. The Queen's cousin, the Duke of Cambridge, was Commander-in-Chief and did not greatly favour the ministry's ambitions for the Army, while the Queen herself had reservations about them. The Conservative Party was not in favour of them, either, and this feeling was reinforced by the presence in the Commons of a number of serving army officers, most of whom had purchased their commissions. This system meant that army officers paid money for their rank and any promotion similarly had to be purchased. This meant anyone with money, whatever their level of competence, could buy an army rank and it did nothing for its efficiency. It also meant that compensation would have to be paid to officers if they were forbidden from selling their rank to others. Not surprisingly, however, it was one of the main targets of Liberal army reforms. Any measure of army reform, therefore, was liable to run up against strong opposition.

As early as 1868 the Liberals' first significant measure of army reform, the abolition of the punishment of flogging, had been enacted. In 1870 Cardwell had amended the terms of enlistment. From a term of service of twenty-one years in 1815, reduced to twelve years in 1847, soldiers were now to enlist for six years in the regular Army and six years in the Reserves. Also in 1870 the Queen signed an Order in Council which publicly placed the Commander-in-Chief under the authority of the Secretary of State for War.

The 1870 session had been a hectic one for Gladstone and his colleagues, but in February 1871 he suggested to Granville an almost equally challenging schedule, including a further measure for army reform. Cardwell had worked hard on the proposal over the winter, and while Gladstone had personally taken no hand in its preparation he did his utmost to secure its passage. This was the abolition of army purchase, and, even though it was coupled with a measure of compensation for the officers affected it aroused fierce opposition. To those who opposed Gladstone, as well as to the Prime Minister himself, this was more than a simple matter of army reform. He was, as he told his Greenwich constituents in October, 'assailing class interest in its favourite and most formidable stronghold', and he hoped that he could use this as a means of wakening the wealthy classes from their 'torpor'. The bill was introduced on 16 February, but only passed its third reading in July. The government's majority was reduced to fifty-eight: all of the Conservatives and twelve Liberals voted against it. If the passage through the Commons had been difficult, it was clear that getting the measure through the Lords was going to be impossible, and they rejected it some two weeks later, on 17 July.

But it was not always wise to try and thwart Gladstone when he had taken a cause to heart, as he had taken this. Many of the opponents to the abolition of purchase did not realise that it existed only on the basis of a Royal Warrant, and Parliament did not have to be consulted about its continuance. If the Queen's prime minister should advise her to cancel the Warrant, she could do so, and the officers concerned would receive no compensation for the price they had paid for their commissions. On 20 July Gladstone told the Commons he had advised the Queen to take this step, and she had accepted his advice. The result was a resounding defeat and an embarrassing climb-down for the Lords. Rather than see the army officers lose their compensation when this measure was enacted, they reconsidered their views of the Army Regulation Bill and voted it through.

Cardwell continued his work until the downfall of the Gladstone government. His other most famous change besides the abolition of purchase was the 'territorialisation' and 'linked-battalions' organisation of the infantry regiments. This meant that all regiments would be localised in a county, recruiting (nominally at least) all men from their own county. In addition, all regiments would consist of two battalions, one serving abroad, the other at home, recruiting and training men to replace that on active foreign service. But Cardwell, as a good Peelite, also tried to cut costs, and to this end recalled many British battalions from overseas service.

Quite how much effect all of these reforms had has recently been debated. Certainly, the Army's record in the colonial campaigns that marked the end of Victoria's reign was mixed, to say the least, and the disastrous opening to the Boer War of 1899 shows that there was still some way to go before the British Army could claim to be the equal of the Prussians. But there is no denying the increasing importance of professionalism which these changes helped to bring in.

As far as Gladstone was concerned the army purchase question shows him at his most decisive. Other measures, such as a bill to introduce the secret ballot had failed to get through the Lords in 1871, but the abolition of purchase was something he became determined to secure that year: it seemed as if more than just the prestige of the government was at stake. It is possible to see here one of the many faces of Gladstone the politician: he was playing the Peelite executive statesman, who knew what was best for the country. He would see the measure through, even if some members of his own party had reservations about it. He was also acting as the middle-class politician taking on the aristocratic world, trying to get them 'up-to-date' and efficient, even against their wishes. For their part, many of the aristocracy had their underlying distrust of Gladstone confirmed. He simply forced this measure through, but his means of doing so created distrust among his own supporters too.

The question also helped to damage Gladstone's relations with the Queen. His relations with Victoria had been good in the 1850s and early 1860s, as Prince Albert had taken a liking to him. The death of the Prince had, if anything, brought the Queen closer to Gladstone. But they had drifted apart somewhat in the later 1860s. In particular Gladstone became alarmed at the Queen's persistent reluctance to appear in public, on occasions such as the state opening of Parliament. Another problem was connected with the Prince of Wales. He had begun to acquire a reputation for profligacy, and although this did not help his relations with his mother it did not improve his public reputation either: republicanism began to get a serious hold among some elements in society.

Gladstone hoped that he could deal with several of these problems in one go. In June 1871 he suggested to the Queen that a royal residence should be established in Ireland, and that a member of the Royal family

– he suggested the Prince of Wales – should take up the post as representative of the Sovereign in Ireland, in place of the Lord Lieutenant currently there. Gladstone tried hard to convince the Queen of the merits of this proposal, but she was not impressed. She agreed initially to think it over, but in the end came down firmly against it.

Shortly after this, in November, the Prince went down with typhoid (the cause of his father's death) and became very ill. By the middle of December, however, he was on the road to recovery, and Gladstone suggested to the Queen that there should be a service of thanksgiving at St Paul's Cathedral attended by her and other members of the royal family, who would make a public procession to the cathedral. He stressed, once again, that there were several reasons why this would be a good idea:

> I then dwelt upon the extreme solemnity of the occasion: not only for the Prince, as any one after such an illness must be decidedly a better or worse man for it, and not only for the Queen and Royal Family, but for the future of the monarchy and of the country as connected with it.[5]

This time the Queen gave way, and the procession and service, which took place on 27 February 1872, were a great success (especially for Disraeli, who was well cheered on the occasion). But relations between the prime minister and the monarch were not really improved by it. Gladstone was not a model courtier: he was not afraid to tell the Queen what he thought she should do, nor was he afraid to argue his case at length. The Queen, for her part, found Gladstone's speeches and his policies, especially towards Ireland, increasingly irritating.

OTHER ADMINISTRATIVE REFORMS

While education and army reform were two of the most challenging reforms brought in during Gladstone's first term as prime minister, they were far from the only ones. Another notable reform was the introduction of the secret ballot. Gladstone himself had earlier accepted Palmerston's view that British voters should do their duty and vote fully in public view: the secret ballot was in some way 'unmanly', some even declared it was 'unEnglish'. As he had told his Greenwich constituents in December 1868:

> I have at all times given my vote in favour of open voting, but I have done so before, and I do so now, with an important reservation, namely, that whether by open voting or by whatsoever means, free voting must be secured.[6]

But it may be that changing political realities again brought a change of view in their wake. It is possible that Bright only accepted office in the cabinet on the understanding the ministry would introduce a bill bringing in secret ballot. With the extension of the suffrage under the 1867 Reform Act, also, Gladstone and many of his colleagues came to believe that the newly-enfranchised poorer voters were less likely to be independent than the wealthier ones of old. A backbencher's bill to introduce the secret ballot was brought in in 1870, but made no progress and was withdrawn, but Gladstone took the opportunity to declare publicly his change of mind.

As with army reform, the more the measure was opposed, the more determined Gladstone came to be to see it through. In 1871, the Ballot Bill was reintroduced, this time by Forster, like Gladstone a recent convert to the secret ballot. After lengthy debate in the Commons – where the bill took eighteen days to pass the Committee stage – Gladstone helped to secure its passage on 8 August, only for it to be defeated in the Lords two days later, on the plea of lack of time. Gladstone was now determined not to give up. When the measure was again introduced and passed the Commons in 1872, it was sent to the Lords with vague threats attending it. He warned Bishop Moberly, bishop of Salisbury, of the 'very serious evil' that might arise should the Lords again reject the measure, and informed Glyn, the Liberal Chief Whip, that the Lords might 'know … what the country thinks' if they did:[7] there would have to be a general election unless they toed the line. Thanks in part to 'Puss' Granville's smooth negotiating skills, a suitable compromise was worked out – the Act would only be effective for a few years and would then have to be renewed – so the Peers agreed, by a mere nineteen votes, to accept the Parliamentary and Municipal Bill on 18 July 1872. It is difficult to say precisely how much effect the Act had in Great Britain, but in Ireland its effects were immediate. In much of the country the political influence of the Anglo-Irish Protestant landlord was broken, replaced, in some measure, at least, by that of the Roman Catholic priesthood. This was to have profound repercussions on Gladstone's later career and the future of the Liberal Party.

Gladstone was also supportive of some other reforming measures, even if he was not fully involved in their preparation (and this, considering the weight of other demands on his time, is not surprising). One of these was the reform of entry into the civil service, enabled by an Order in Council in June 1870. Gladstone had had an interest in improving the efficiency and effectively reducing the cost of the civil service since the days of the Crimean War and the report and recommendations of Sir Stafford Northcote and Sir Charles Trevelyan. This had introduced the ideas of graded entry and competition for places in the civil service, but it was Lowe, the Chancellor of the Exchequer and the main advocate for reform in the 1868 ministry, who wanted to extend these further. While Gladstone did not have to worry about the details of the legislation on this occasion, he did have to calm the hostility of Clarendon at the Foreign Office and of Bright. Gladstone gets the credit for the resulting compromise: it was agreed that entry to all departments would be by open competition, where the head of that department agreed. From now on, to ensure the 'right men' for the job were found, candidates for the higher section, providing the future senior civil servants and policymakers, were examined primarily in classics and mathematics, while those for the junior section would be assessed in bookkeeping, copying and English history. This ensured that the successful candidates for the senior section were much more likely to be drawn from the universities of Oxford and Cambridge, and would undoubtedly 'fit in' with the ethos of the service. This system provided the basis of civil service recruitment that has lasted until the present day, but it was slow to be adopted. Clarendon still did not agree to it, so while the Colonial and War Offices immediately opened their doors, the Foreign Office remained the only Department of State where entry was still entirely by nomination, and the Home Office delayed admitting 'open' entrants until 1880.

Gladstone's ministry also dealt with matters directly affecting the working classes. In particular, Bruce, the home secretary, began to consider the reform of the laws under which the Trade Union movement operated. Gladstone has been credited with laying down the new law's principle: 'punish violence … in all economical matters the law to take no part'.[8] The Trade Union Congress had first met in 1868, and its members had demanded that the government recognise the legal right of unions to exist, to find a way to protect their funds from confiscation by firms when their members went on strike, and to allow strikers to picket firms with which they were in dispute. It was no easy matter to draft a law which satisfied all these demands, and in the end two separate ones were passed in 1871. The Trade Unions Act apparently satisfied the first two requirements, while the Criminal Law Amendment Act dealt with the problem of picketing, but neither worked especially well. Picketing remained effectively disallowed, so the power of collective labour was curtailed, and a court case in 1872 revealed that unions' funds were liable to seizure because they were guilty of conspiracy.

Faced with the increasing hostility of a growing labour movement, Gladstone decided in September 1873 that the government should investigate the operation of the trade union laws, and he told Lowe, Bruce's successor as home secretary, to look into it. He appears to have played no role in the study Lowe undertook and brought before the cabinet in November, and in any case his government resigned before any of Lowe's proposed measures could be brought forward. Not surprisingly, perhaps, his own view of trade unions was ambivalent. He was prepared to grant them extra rights, but he was not prepared to go too far, and when workers in his own coal mines aimed to introduce a closed shop, for example, he stood firm against it. His standing in the eyes of the working classes was not helped by Bruce's Licensing Act of 1872. This Act granted magistrates power to enforce shorter opening hours on pubs and restrict the issuing of licences to publicans. Despite Gladstone's own apparent preference for 'free trade' in liquor, the decision to restrict the sale of beer was his government's and brewers and the Conservative Party made a good deal out of it.

IRELAND

The Gladstone ministry had, from its earliest days into 1872, passed a steady stream of reform measures. Gladstone, while he had taken the lead in seeing these through and become especially involved when the House of Lords had put up strong resistance, was not, however, the brains behind them. As he had told General Grey, his primary duty was 'to pacify Ireland', a task which was to take pre-eminence in this ministry, as it was indeed, to take pre-eminence in his next three terms as prime minister. But it was to be a difficult task: vested interests on both sides of St George's Channel were to ensure that. There were also problems with it in the Liberal Party itself, and these were to become greater over the years.

Gladstone was aware that the Irish tenant farmers felt several different grievances. Underlying all of these was the position of the Protestant elite over most of rural Roman Catholic Ireland. Gladstone was determined to put an end to the 'Protestant ascendancy', and he thought one way this could be started was by attacking the position of the established Protestant Church of Ireland. This was not only a clearly identifiable target, it was something with which many Nonconformist Liberal backbenchers could easily sympathise.

It was the first thing Gladstone turned his attention to after the formation of his ministry; it was, after all, the thing he had defeated the Tories on in 1868. As early as 13 December he saw the Queen and 'stated the case of the Irish Church. It was graciously received'. This was no small relief to Gladstone, who could easily imagine the Queen reacting fiercely against his proposals. On Christmas Eve he 'went to work on draft of Irish Church measure, feeling the impulse', a draft on which he continued to 'work much' at on Christmas Day, and in the evening he managed to complete it. He revised it and sent it out to be copied for the cabinet meeting on the 26th.[9]

In January 1869 he spent several days at Hawarden, passing some of the time working on Homer and felling trees, but spending more time drafting papers on the Irish Church question and discussing the matter with various visitors, such as the Viceroy, Lord Spencer, and his invaluable ally in the negotiations with the Queen, Lord Granville. He finally saw the Queen at Osborne House on the Isle of Wight on the 23rd. At this point the Queen's initial calmness began to desert her. The paper 'appeared to be well taken' on the 23rd, but the next day, she made no mention of it during a long audience, and a week later Gladstone was in receipt of a letter from the Queen, which 'showed much disturbance, which I tried to soothe'.[10]

Granville, too, tried to calm the Queen's fears, and at his suggestion she was visited by the Bishop of Peterborough. Rather than settling the matter, this led the Queen to suggest that the English bishops should intervene to negotiate a settlement, based on the idea that property belonging to the Church should be divided into two: that predating the

Reformation should be handed to the Roman Catholics, that from after the Reformation should be retained by the Anglicans. Gladstone, politely but very firmly, shut the door in the Queen's face:

> It would be more than idle and less than honest, were Mr. Gladstone to withhold from your Majesty his conviction that no negotiation founded on such a basis as this could be entertained, or, if entertained, could lead to any satisfactory result. Neither could Mr. Gladstone persuade the cabinet to adopt it, nor could the cabinet persuade the House of Commons, nor could cabinet and House of Commons united persuade the nation to acquiesce, and the very attempt would not only prolong and embitter controversy, but would weaken authority in this country. For the thing contemplated is the very thing that the parliament was elected not to do.[11]

The Queen retreated and began to work hard to persuade the Archbishop of Canterbury, Archbishop Tait, to come to a deal with the government. After the cabinet had completed their work on the Bill on 8 and 9 February, Gladstone paid a visit to the Archbishop's palace in Lambeth and explained the Bill to him, though without successfully converting him. His next task, following this rather inauspicious start, was to see the measure through the Commons.

On 1 March Gladstone introduced the Irish Church Disestablishment Bill in a major speech to the House. He declared that, from 1 January 1871, the Church of Ireland would cease to be the state church in Ireland, and would be disendowed of its lands. The Church would thereafter be governed by its bishops and a representative group of clergy and laity. All annual public grants to religion in Ireland – including that to Maynooth College – would cease. Much of the £16 million raised by disendowment would be devoted to public works in Ireland, except for those already covered by the Poor Law. The remainder would be granted to help the Church of Ireland to pay its own clergy, and be used as compensatory sums to the Presbyterian churches and to Maynooth College.

The crisis of the second reading was reached on 24 March. Gladstone secured a parliamentary triumph: a majority in his favour of 118 (368 to 250 votes). This was a larger majority by far than in 1866, when the Liberals had been turned out of office by a mere eleven votes, while in 1841 Peel had defeated the Whigs in 1841 by only one vote. The reaction to it was mixed. Gladstone himself believed it was a good start; it was such a large majority that it would help propel the Bill through the Committee stage in the Commons and, hopefully, have some effect on the behaviour of the Lords when they came to discuss it. Disraeli was apparently unimpressed; he assured Archbishop Tait that Gladstone's was only a 'mechanical majority' – though he went on to admit defeating the Bill was a 'lost game' in the Commons. Most importantly, however, it would seem that the Queen's hesitations were overcome by the scale of Gladstone's success. The Bill easily secured its passage through the Commons, with even the proposal to compensate Maynooth College out of the Church of Ireland's funds being voted through by a majority of 107. The final reading, on 31 May, saw a Liberal majority of 114.

Armed with this, Gladstone and the Queen began to pressure the Archbishop of Canterbury to make sure the measure passed the Lords by getting the Church of England bishops to abstain, at least, from opposition. Granville had a meeting with the Archbishops of York and Canterbury before the second reading of the Bill in the Lords, and they declared an intention to abstain in the vote. Granville began to see trouble ahead should the bishops oppose it, and began to hint to correspondents that the government might be prepared to accept some amendments to the Bill. In the end, the second reading was carried by thirty-three votes, but only one English bishop voted in favour of it and it would not have passed at all if thirty-six Conservative peers, including the influential Marquess of Salisbury had not also voted in favour of it. The House was very full, a reflection of the importance attached to it by the Peers.

While Salisbury, according to Granville, was not necessarily going to follow the Liberal lead, he was not going to oppose the measure, but this at least gave some grounds for hope that the Lords would see it through. Salisbury, though, could not prevent the Lords producing amendments to the Bill in the Committee stage – particularly ones relating to the control of the residue of the funds released by the disendowment proposal, and the use, or not, of a measure of 'concurrent endowment', or giving money to the disestablished Catholic and Presbyterian churches simultaneously.

With these amendments, the Bill returned to the Commons on 12 July. Gladstone, as was only to be expected, urged resistance, and by the 16th he was able to report that 'the amendments made by the Lords …

had been completely disposed of by the House of Commons. The last division, taken on the disposal of the residue, had, chiefly through mere lazy absences, reduced the majority of the government to a mere 72.' As he told the Dean of Windsor, in an effort to bring the Church of England into line, 'the clause for concurrent endowment was condemned in the House of Commons without a division' such was the strength of feeling against it.[12]

The Lords, however, fought back and once more returned the Bill. Gladstone was under considerable strain between 20 and 25 July, and in constant communication with Granville and others about its future. He spent 'an anxious day, a sad evening' on the 20th, and two days later 'was obliged to take to my sofa'. Although the Conservative peers eventually accepted the government's proposals – Gladstone sending the Queen a note at 7.00 p.m. on 22 July to say so – this caused some health problems for the prime minister:

> 22 – The favourable issue left me almost unmanned in the reaction from a sharp and stern tension of mind. 23 – My attack did not lessen. Dr. Clark came in the morning and made me up for the House, whither I went 2–5 P.M., to propose concurrence in the Lords' amendments. Up to the moment I felt very weak, but this all vanished when I spoke and while the debate lasted. Then I went back to bed. 25 – Weak still. I presumed over much in walking a little and fell back at night to my lowest point.[13]

He did not recover very quickly, and Archbishop Tait found him, even at the beginning of September, still looking very ill.

The result of the Disestablishment of the Church of Ireland Act was the end of the union of that church with the Church of England from 1 January 1871. It would receive some £10 million of revenue, but lose about £5 million to secular purposes. The measure was one of Gladstone's greatest triumphs, not so much because of its terms, but because of the way in which he had taken on the in-built Conservative majority in the House of Lords and had won. He was helped by the fact that Salisbury and thirty or so of his supporters had actually supported the Bill, but the clerical peers certainly had not. He had been strongly supported by his own party in both Commons and Lords, and this time it had been enough.

The fate of the Irish Church Bill was symptomatic of the difficulties faced by any non-Conservative prime minister in the House of Commons. Even with a united party behind him (Disraeli had failed on this occasion, despite his best efforts, to open any splits in it) and even with a measure that seems to have been genuinely popular in the country, Gladstone had found it difficult to get the Act passed. If he was going to try and secure the passage of bills about which some of his own party had reservations, he would find the job much more difficult, if not impossible.

This Act was the beginning, rather than the end, of Gladstone's plans for Ireland. After all, the disestablishment of the Church of Ireland was 'but one of a group of questions' including 'the land of Ireland' and 'the education of Ireland', which, according to Gladstone, formed

> the many branches from one trunk, and that trunk is the tree of what is called the Protestant ascendancy ... We therefore aim at the destruction of that system of ascendancy which, though it has been crippled and curtailed by former measures, must still be allowed to exist. It is still there like a tall tree of noxious growth ... Now at length the day has come when, as we hope, the axe has been laid at the root of that tree.[14]

To carry forward the attack on the tree now meant tampering with Irish property rights, a sensitive issue at any time. Even before the Irish Church Bill had run its course, Gladstone had been considering the Irish land question. As early as 24 May 1869 he was trying, as gently as possible, to deflect the thin-skinned Bright from his proposal to 'make the State a great Land-Jobber', providing a state fund from which tenants could buy up their tenancies from their landlords (one of several issues that caused Granville to voluntarily miss the Derby). By September, the land question was 'assuming an aspect of greater difficulty'.[15] Gladstone spent a good deal of time reading around the subject of Irish land, and it was brought home to him that the main difficulty facing the Irish tenant farmer was the ease with which his landlord could evict him. The rent paid could be increased for any reason, and, if the tenant was unable to pay the increase, he could – and understandably would – be evicted, and he would not be paid compensation for it. The landlord could find someone else to take his place without too much difficulty.

Gladstone, perceived, as he told the Chief Secretary for Ireland, Chichester Fortescue, that 'It is very desirable to prevent the use of augmentation of rent as a method of eviction'. He also thought it only right that, if a tenant was evicted, he should be paid 'compensation for disturbance', and he should also be paid compensation for any improvements he had made on the land. Just how this could be arranged was 'a question full of difficulty'. He also warned Fortescue that 'the proposition, that *more* than compensation to tenants for their improvements will be necessary in order to settle the Irish land laws, will be unpalatable, or new, to several, and naturally enough.'[16] Gladstone decided that a cabinet committee would have to be set up to look into the whole matter. He was informed by Granville that some in the cabinet (including Chancellor Lowe and Foreign Secretary Clarendon) were likely to 'take a purely moderate landlord view' of any measure though 'none will break up the cabinet' over it. Granville was right, and when the proposal was discussed in cabinet on 3 November, Gladstone thought it 'very stiff'.[17]

He had hoped, in the early stages of negotiations, that he would be able to secure a measure which would extend to the whole of Ireland the practice of Ulster. There, tenants received protection from unjustified eviction once they had been in residence for a number of years. If the tenant was evicted, he would be paid compensation, whether or not he had made improvements to the property. This increase in the rights of the tenant – the obligation to pay all tenants compensation on their eviction – would be a drastic blow to property owners, including some of Gladstone's own cabinet. Hence, it took him until 25 January 1870 to win the support of all of his colleagues. 'Cabinet', he noted in his diary, 'The great difficulties of the Irish Land Bill *there* are now over. Thank God!' [18] The Prime Minister explained the aims of his legislation in a letter to Cardinal Manning, taking rather less time than the three and three-quarter hours it took him to outline it to the Commons. The idea, he wrote, was 'to prevent the landlord from using the terrible weapon of undue and unjust eviction'. It would do so by forcing him to pay the tenant compensation, either under terms already existing (as in Ulster) or on a sliding scale to be established. 'Wanton eviction will', Gladstone hoped, 'be extinguished by provisions like these' and they should prevent demands for 'unjust' increases in rent.[19] The Bill secured its second reading on 11 March, by a clear majority, but it did not complete its passage through the Commons until 30 May. Even though the Conservatives had expected legislation along these lines, they did not let it through quickly or easily, and Gladstone had to take the lead in securing its passage, since none of his colleagues had the necessary knowledge, or, in some cases, the desire, to see it pass.

It is ironic that this Act, which had taken longer to pass than the Irish Church Disestablishment Act, was not especially effective. 'Wanton eviction' was, indeed, discouraged, but unscrupulous landlords could still easily find reasons for evictions, both justified and unjustified. No definition of an 'unjust' rent increase was laid down either. Tenants were not very impressed: the Act only gave legal rights to tenants, which in Ulster they already enjoyed. In a disputed case, the burden of proof was put on the tenant and going to the law was both time-consuming and expensive, commodities the average tenant farmer did not have. It did, however, mark a beginning. It gave some Irish tenant farmers some rights they had not before possessed. It gave Gladstone a better reputation in Irish eyes, which he was to build on in later years. It also showed that the Westminster Parliament could pass legislation that would try and improve the lot of the average Irish farmer and served as an indication that more concessions could be extracted from it if more pressure was put on it.

Gladstone tried another thing to reconcile the Irish at this time, but it was difficult for him to persuade his colleagues to accept it; the British public was not pleased by it and, by the time it was done, the Irish public had also lost patience waiting for it to happen. This was the release of Irish Fenian prisoners held in British gaols. Gladstone had actually suggested a 'Fenian amnesty' when he prepared an agenda for the cabinet meeting on 2 February 1869. The government in Ireland stood firm against this, and unrest there had made it necessary to pass a Peace Preservation Bill in March 1870. By September of that year Gladstone was determined some different action should be taken. He put a blunt question to Chichester Fortescue:

> Now that you have large powers in Ireland for the maintenance of order, and that the agitators have ceased to knock at your door, and our chief legal remedy has been sanctioned & applied, may we not

> proceed to release and put out of the country the handfuls of wretched Fenians whom we still keep in prison?[20]

But the Irish government continued to drag its feet, and oppose their release.

The result of this hesitation was serious. If Gladstone had managed to release them as a goodwill gesture it would have helped his Land Act be accepted in a more positive fashion in Ireland. It has recently been suggested that his failure to do so cast a blight over the whole of his Irish policy; it certainly did not help it. Of more immediate importance, though, for the future, both for Ireland and for liberalism in Britain, was the reception of his next major piece of Irish legislation – a bill for the reform of Irish university education.

The situation of the universities in Ireland was complicated by religious factors, and by 1871 there were three universities in Ireland. These were Dublin University, a Roman Catholic foundation, dating back to the fourteenth century; Trinity College, Dublin, a sixteenth-century Protestant foundation; and the Queen's University, dating only from 1845 and consisting of three affiliated 'Godless Colleges' – Belfast College, Cork College and Galway College. These three colleges were deliberately designed to exclude religion from their endowment or their teaching. Trinity College, had, in recent times, effectively taken over Dublin University.

Towards the end of November 1872 Gladstone brought up the Irish universities question in the cabinet. In January 1873 he spent time at Hawarden with Dr J.K. Ingram, a Protestant don from Trinity College; on the 17th this lasted 'almost from breakfast to dinner'. He prepared 'an abstract of historical facts about it' and on the 31st 'spent many hours in settling the Irish University Bill' with the cabinet (finally getting it through on 8 February).[21]

As finally drafted, the Bill endeavoured to establish a 'neutral' university centred on a new University of Dublin, which would not teach theology, philosophy or modern history. Belfast, Cork, and Galway Colleges, and the Catholic Dublin University would be affiliated institutions of this new university. It was, in short, a large-scale and sweeping proposal on which Gladstone laid the responsibility for a complete review of Irish education. He also told the House of Commons, when he introduced the Bill on 13 February, that the measure was 'vital to the honour and existence of the government'. In point of fact, it was the 'honour' of Gladstone himself, as prime framer of the Bill, that was most at stake.

The debate on the Irish Universities Bill was a dramatic one. Gladstone hoped that most Protestants, including the Nonconformists in his own party, would find the measure acceptable. He also hoped the more 'reasonable and moderate Roman Catholics' would support it, and the Bill got off to a good start. The debate opened in the Commons on 3 March. Thanks in part to Gladstone's opening speech, at least one MP, Home Secretary Bruce, thought there would not even need to be a division on the second reading. But, with the publication of a strident denunciation of the Bill by the Catholic Archbishop Cullen of Dublin, opposition began to pick up as Disraeli saw his chance of an alliance with Irish Catholic members against the government. Gladstone himself blamed the Roman Catholic bishops for his problems. By 8 March he was reporting to the Queen that twenty or twenty-five Irish members might stay away and 'when to these are added the small knot of discontented liberals and mere fanatics which so large a party commonly contains, the government majority, now taken at only 85, disappears'[22] A day later he told Victoria wearily that this measure might mark his chance to leave office, if it should not pass.

The end came in the early hours of 12 March. In one of their great confrontations, Disraeli closed for the Conservatives in a speech of some two hours; Gladstone responded with one of his finest efforts, but it was all to no avail. The government was defeated by three votes, 287 to 284. The Conservative majority included ten Liberals from English and Scottish seats and thirty-five Irish members; twenty-two Irish members abstained, even though they knew that if the government was defeated the consequences would be serious. Later that day, the cabinet discussed what to do, following their defeat: 'with a general tendency to resignation rather than dissolving'; and on the 13th they decided to go.[23] The result of this, however, as we shall see, was quite unexpected.

FOREIGN POLICY

Before taking the story of Gladstone's ministry to its conclusion, it is worth looking at its foreign policy and at Gladstone's private life during its course. The former is dominated by three events: the Franco-Prussian war from July 1870 to February 1871; the Russian repudiation of the 'Black Sea clauses' of the 1856 Treaty of Paris in November 1870, while the war was going on; and the negotiations and final settlement of the United States' *Alabama* claims against the British government, finally reached in September 1872. Most of this occurred following the death of the Earl of Clarendon in May 1870 and involved his successor, Earl Granville, who worked closely with Gladstone in foreign as well as domestic policy matters.

The Franco-Prussian war began, as far as most British people were concerned, suddenly and unexpectedly. Indeed, when Granville took over as Foreign Secretary he was informed by the Foreign Office staff that there was very little going on in Europe for him to worry about. But there had been some dramatic changes on the continent of Europe in the recent past, most engineered by the chancellor of the newly-established North German Confederation, Otto von Bismarck. Bismarck's views on foreign policy were quite different from those of Gladstone and Granville. He believed diplomatic questions would be settled by 'blood and iron'. Since the mainspring of his policy was the finest army in Europe of the day, that of the kingdom of Prussia, commanded by its finest general, Helmuth von Moltke, and since his country's economy was growing at a tremendous rate, he had reason to be so confident. Across the Rhine, a few people in France had begun to be nervous, but most remained confident that France had the best army.

The conflict arose over the future ruler of Spain. The Spanish requested a junior member of the Prussian ruling Hohenzollern family as king; the French demanded the Prussians turn down the request (which they decided to do anyway). But the French did so in a less than polite manner, requesting an assurance from the Prussian King Wilhelm that he would never consent to such an arrangement. Bismarck had been working to bring about a confrontation with France and he saw this as his opportunity. When Wilhelm refused, in a telegram despatched from Ems, to give the French the assurance they wanted, Bismarck edited it and published the revised 'Ems telegram' in the German press. This made Wilhelm's reply less polite than it had actually been and was a deliberate move by Bismarck to upset the French. The manoeuvre worked perfectly, and on 19 July 1870 a French declaration of war was received in Berlin.

Gladstone and his government could do very little about this. Gladstone himself had hoped on 14 July that the withdrawal of the Prussian candidate would bring an end to the crisis, but really he knew little about what was passing. At this point, the British were more on the side of Prussia, hoping that Wilhelm would publicly declare his support for the withdrawal of the candidature and France would abandon her request for a public acknowledgement that it would never be renewed. But this hope was overtaken by events, and all Britain could do when war came was declare her neutrality and watch events develop. As early as 29 July Gladstone was inquiring of Granville what Britain should do to ensure the preservation of Belgian neutrality, agreed by the Treaty of London of 1839, against either party – both France (on 9 August) and Prussia (on 11 August) agreed to treaties accepting it.

On 4 August the French were defeated at Wissembourg, and three days later, after a major battle at Spicheren, they began a general retreat. Gladstone was amazed at what had happened:

> The news stuns me. It is not merely a great action lost and won. It is the greatest blow apparently which France has received as a military Power for more than a hundred years, in the vital point of credit & reputation ... But further it raises the question whether it will be followed by a revolution ... What is perhaps most of all remarkable is the stupid way in which France has managed the whole controversy.[24]

French military operations did nothing to improve Gladstone's impression of them. On 18 August they suffered another major defeat at Gravelotte-St Privat. On 2 September, after yet another defeat at Sedan, Napoleon III and his army of over 80,000 men surrendered to the Prussians and their allies. Moltke then ordered his army to advance on Paris. But the war was not over: as Gladstone had earlier suggested might happen, the defeat was followed by a revolution. With Napoleon a prisoner, a Republican Government of National Defence was established in Paris; it began to organise new armies to defend the country, and the war went on.

Gladstone decided at this point to outline his government's position in an article in the *Edinburgh Review*. It was very clear that, whatever was happening, Britain had no real say in it, and Gladstone tried to justify the government's apparent lack of action. When the Prussians began to demand the cession of the French provinces of Alsace and Lorraine, however, Gladstone himself began to demand that Britain should do something. He felt the question of the 'transfer of territory and inhabitants by mere force calls for the reprobation of Europe' and European states should get together and denounce it. He thought it was not simply a matter of concern to the countries involved, but to all European powers. 'It appears to bear on the Belgian question in particular'. But the cabinet was unimpressed by his argument, and felt Britain should stand aside. Gladstone thought this a very unfortunate attitude to take, warning Granville 'that this violent laceration and transfer is to lead us from bad to worse, and to the *beginning* of a new series of European complications'.[25] But in the end, by the terms of the peace treaty – initialled at Versailles on 26 February 1871, and signed at Frankfurt on 10 May – between France and the new German Empire that had been created on 1 January of that year, France agreed to the cession of the two provinces and to pay an indemnity of five million francs. The balance of power on the continent of Europe had shifted fundamentally, and the British government had been unable – indeed, it had in large part been unwilling – to do anything about it.

One of the main reasons for the Gladstone government's failure to intervene in Franco-German relations was an added international complication introduced by the Russian government at the end of October 1870. The Russian foreign minister, Prince Gorchakoff, announced to the world that the Russians no longer accepted those terms of Treaty of Paris of 1856 which said that they could not build fortifications around the Black Sea. The British government protested to Russia, in a despatch largely drafted by Gladstone, that her actions were not justifiable: she could just not denounce parts of a treaty that she disagreed with. When the news became widely known, British public opinion was outraged and Gladstone, who was personally appalled by what the Russians had done, became concerned that the government might find itself forced into military action against them. In fact, the British government had several options. War was indeed one possibility, but another was to do nothing, or perhaps to secure Prussian help against Russia, or maybe even form an alliance with the other European powers against both Russia and Prussia. The only sensible option was the last, which was to call a European conference to discuss the question. Even that would depend on convincing the Russians that Britain meant business if negotiations were not forthcoming, and on securing the help of Bismarck.

Bismarck was quite prepared to use his influence on the Russians to persuade them to attend a conference, which duly opened in London on 17 December 1870. All of the great powers were present – except for the prostrate France, whose representative did not attend until the final meeting on 13 March 1871. Granville was pleased with the outcome: he reassured Gladstone that the Russians would be satisfied: they had got more or less what they wanted – the acceptance of their claims – but would probably not do much about them. He did not stress in his memorandum of 30 March what he and Gladstone also probably felt, that the British government had been seen to stand up to the Russians. As they had no intention of going to war over this issue, they had no real chance of persuading the Russians to change their plans: the conference made it seem as if they had scored some kind of diplomatic triumph. It was, in reality, another recognition of Britain's relative inability to influence European diplomacy and of Bismarck's new status.

Outside of Europe, Britain's relations with the United States had not been especially good. During the Civil War between 1861 and 1865 most of the British upper class had been supporters of the southern Confederacy. This had included Gladstone, who, as many northerners remembered, had gone on record as stating his support for the South. During the war the Confederates had bought weapons and ships in Britain. In July 1862, one of the latter, the CSS *Alabama*, which had been built in Liverpool, had sailed unseen from the River Mersey. She had then begun a very successful career as a commerce raider, capturing sixty-nine federal merchant ships and sinking one naval vessel and her career had only been brought to end in June 1864 when she had been sunk off Cherbourg.

The United States government, not surprisingly, wanted compensation for the damage wrought by the *Alabama* and other Confederate commerce raiders, and throughout the 1860s had called on British governments to pay up. The Americans had suggested as early as 1865 that the matter should be referred to arbitration, but this had been rejected by the then Foreign Secretary, Earl Russell. The Conservative government had proposed in 1868 that an Anglo-American commission, meeting in London, should be convened to settle all outstanding claims and, if they could not agree, a neutral third party should adjudicate between them. This was agreed to by Lord Clarendon in January 1869, but not, unfortunately, by the Americans, who began to increase their demands on Britain. It was clearly going to be difficult to strike a deal with the United States, but as time passed in 1870, Gladstone, concerned by developments in Europe and the Near East, began to become more and more convinced that one would be necessary. On 1 February 1871 he was able to tell the Queen that the United States government had at last agreed to a commission to assess the '*Alabama* claims'. But this was only the beginning of the story.

Gladstone was not especially impressed with 'all the bunkum and irrelevant trash' of the American case, which he felt was due largely to 'Americanism' and could therefore quite easily be ignored.[26] The negotiations, which took placed in neutral Geneva, began in March 1872. What particularly bothered the British was that the Americans argued they deserved payment of 'indirect claims' arising from all actions during the war, as well as the actual cost of damage caused by the *Alabama* herself. Gladstone had drafted a letter explaining and justifying his own conduct to the American government at the end of February, but the cabinet refused to let him send it. On 16 March he recorded 'laborious' discussion in the cabinet over the matter. Two days later there was 'much heavy work on the *Alabama*' and this continued into April. On the 5th Gladstone commented that there was 'much confusion' on the question, which, as he remarked three weeks later, 'bristles with difficulties'. The crisis was reached in mid-June. By this stage Gladstone was convinced it might be necessary to break off negotiations if an agreement on indirect claims could not be reached, but he was determined to find a way to strike a deal, if he could, despite the reservations of some in the cabinet.[27]

This determination helped to bring the question to a settlement. Thanks in part to the efforts of the US envoy, Charles Francis Adams, all parties agreed to abandon indirect claims. As a result of this, negotiations continued and five arbitrators – Adams, together with a Briton, an Italian, a Swiss and a Brazilian – finally gave their judgement in September 1872. The United States received fifteen million dollars (about three and a quarter million pounds) in damages. This, of course, disappointed many in Britain (and many in the United States), but overall it was a notable success for Gladstone's government. While it did not settle Anglo-American relations overnight, it did do a good deal to set them on a sounder footing.

PRIVATE LIFE

Gladstone's first term of office as prime minister was marked by considerable efforts on his part to secure the passage of his government's policies. This was reflected in his private life, as the amount of work necessary cut down drastically on his free time. He was also, of course, placed under considerable mental strain, particularly at times of crisis, and it was this which led him to get intimately involved with perhaps the most well-known of his ladies from the *demi-monde*, Laura Thistlethwayte.

During the sessions of Parliament, Gladstone regularly spent between seven and nine hours a day in the House of Commons. He usually arrived at about 2.45 p.m. and, with time off for dinner, stayed until after midnight. He stayed only occasionally at country houses, spending more time with old friends such as Robert Phillimore, at this time Judge of the High Court of the Admiralty. He also hosted political dinners for his cabinet colleagues at his house at Carlton House Terrace. He had a vast amount of correspondence to cope with, some of which consisted of begging letters that were dealt with by a team of private secretaries. Many letters, though, came from political colleagues, and to many of these Gladstone replied himself. For example, he exchanged over 1,000 letters with Lord Granville between December 1868 and December 1875, nearly all on purely political matters. (Even his country house visits, such as those to Lord Salisbury at Hatfield, were often used for political purposes.)

But he did not neglect his reading. While much of this was as back-up to his legislative proposals, he read numerous books, articles and pamphlets on religious and ecclesiastical, classical and secular subjects, such as history and taxation and fiscal policy. He read a good many works translated from German. He became particularly concerned by the Vatican Council, meeting in Rome in 1870 to discuss the future of the papacy after its secular rule over the Papal States had been brought to an end by Italian troops, and he had no time for the doctrine of papal infallibility that emerged from it. He made this view public in a pamphlet published in August 1874.

Gladstone was not really a poor man. By the time of his retirement he had assets of nearly £270,000, most of which were based on property. Over £40,000 of this was based on shares (mostly in the Metropolitan and District Railway) and also on furnishings and books and the like. But he had debts of nearly £40,000, his railway shares lost money and his estates brought in little income. With the loss of office and consequent loss of salary he found it necessary to sell 11 Carlton House Terrace in 1875.

On the whole, he remained contented with his family life. Catherine remained devoted to him, and his eldest son, Willy, elected as MP for Whitby in 1872, began to work for him as a private secretary. Two of his sons, Henry and Herbert, left home, Henry to India and his brother to University College, Oxford. His second son, Stephen, became Rector of Hawarden, a post he may well not have really wanted, but where he stayed. In December 1874, his daughter Agnes married the Revd E.C. Wickham, a Fellow of New College, Oxford and headmaster of Wellington College. Less happy events were the death of his brother-in-law, Henry Glynne, in July 1872, followed shortly afterwards by that of his niece Ida, daughter of Sir Thomas Gladstone, Catherine being particularly touched by the former death and Gladstone by the latter.

But the great event of these years was undoubtedly Gladstone's relationship with Laura Thistlethwayte. He had probably met her in 1864, but it was from 1869 that their relationship blossomed. 'Mrs T', as he often called her, had begun her career as a courtesan, but she had married in 1852 and after that had undergone a conversion to evangelical Christianity. When Gladstone lost his close friend, the Dowager Duchess of Sutherland, in October 1868, Mrs T. stepped in. Between January 1869 and June 1871, despite the other demands on his time, he had sent her 112 letters and they had met forty-five times. He received a long and rather shocking autobiography from her, but despite the revelations contained in this, and as it has been destroyed it is unclear what they were, he accepted a ring from her that he wore continually.

THE CRISIS OF THE MINISTRY

Gladstone's cabinet had tendered their resignation to the Queen on 13 March 1873. At their interview Gladstone had expressed the hope that Disraeli would be able to take office and that he himself would then be able to 'retire altogether', though the Queen doubted he would be allowed to. But Disraeli, when sent for, actually turned down the chance to become prime minister (the last time to date that anyone in his position has chosen to do this). When told, Gladstone could hardly believe his ears. He asked Colonel Ponsonby, the Queen's messenger, to request her to get Disraeli's reply in writing since he thought Dizzy was playing a dubious game:

> I thought Mr. Disraeli was endeavouring by at once throwing back on me an offer which it was impossible to me at the time and under the circumstances to accept, to get up a case of absolute necessity founded upon this refusal of mine and thus becoming an indispensable man ... to have in his hands a lever ... to overcome the reluctance and resistance of his friends who would not be able to deny that the Queen must have a government.[28]

But Disraeli refused point blank, in writing, to take office and late on 16 March Gladstone let the Queen know he would accordingly return to office. It seems clear that the Conservatives simply did not wish to once again take office as a minority government: the Liberals could hopefully get themselves into more trouble before an election was called.

But the rise in defence spending in 1871 and after, together with the brief resignation and some financial irregularities uncovered in the summer of 1873, forced Gladstone to take drastic action. By July his government had become seriously weakened, and he decided major steps would have to be taken to try and recover its position. The first of these was that Robert Lowe would have to step down as chancellor: he was duly 'transferred' to the Home Office. His replacement was Gladstone himself, who took on the post on 9 August 1873, combining it with his duties as First Lord of the Treasury. His second step was the presentation of a drastic financial reform measure. This was something he had had at heart since the 1850s, and something he had struggled to do in successive budgets since then – namely, abolition of the income tax. That, however, would result in a drastic fall in revenue, which would have to be made up for by increases in other taxes. Gladstone had been working on this idea for some time and had concluded that the best way of making up the shortfall would be by an increase in death duties. In addition, he decided duties on sugar should be abolished, but duty on spirits increased; he also wanted to cut nearly one million pounds of the local tax bill. Gladstone hoped these changes would win over many of the newly-enfranchised lower middle-classes, but the cuts would still need to be balanced by significant reductions in central government spending. Gladstone's other proposal was therefore to press for major reductions in defence spending, and it was over this issue that this ministry finally foundered.

He tried to persuade Cardwell at the War Office and Goschen at the Admiralty that these cuts in Army and Navy spending were a political necessity. As he informed Granville on 8 January: 'If we can get from ¾ of a million upwards towards a million off the Naval and Military Estimates jointly … we shall have left the country no reason to complain and may proceed cheerily with our work'. Neither of the heads of the service ministries saw it in this way. What Gladstone believed was a reasonable sum to cut from the estimates – anything between £600,000 and £1 million – was too much for them to accept. But Gladstone was well aware by this time of his government's weakness, and the need to do something:

> The signs ... multiply, and for some time have multiplied upon the Government, in the loss of controul [*sic*] over the legislative action of the House of Lords, the diminution of the majority in the House of Commons ... and the almost unbroken series of defeats at single elections in the country.[29]

On top of this was the cost of the war that had just broken out in Ashanti on the Gold Coast, making it still less likely the War Office could be brought round to agree to spending cuts. By the middle of January Gladstone had decided that he would not be able to persuade his colleagues in the service ministries to see things his way, so on the 18th he came to a conclusion – he would dissolve Parliament and go to the country. He told Bright first, and then Granville, before he went to the cabinet: 'My first thought of it was as an escape from a difficulty. I soon saw on reflection that it was the best thing in itself.'[30] A Liberal victory would be a good thing for Gladstone for several reasons. It would mean that his vision of drastic reductions in taxation and public spending was endorsed by the electorate. This in turn would mean that he would have a weapon to use against those of this own party who doubted the wisdom of cuts in defence spending, in particular. Finally, it would mean that the Conservative comeback (they had gained no less than thirty-one seats in by-elections since 1871, ten of these after May 1873) had been stopped in its tracks.

Gladstone warned the Queen on 21 January that he was going to recommend to the cabinet, when it met two days later, the dissolution of Parliament. When the cabinet met he told them his intention, stressing the present difficulties of the government and the idea of the drastic financial measures, including the abolition of the income tax, that he believed were necessary to rescue them. The cabinet, like Bright, Granville and the Queen herself, were doubtless surprised by what the prime minister proposed, but all agreed with the measure.

Gladstone believed that, while the public would be shocked by the news, 'friends will much approve our course … and the enemy will be furious'.[31] Parliament was dissolved on 26 January and on the 28th Gladstone broke the news of his policy to 5,000 of his Greenwich constituents. It was, he noted in his diary, 'An enthusiastic meeting', but he also added, rather ominously, that 'the general prospects are far from clear'.[32] While most of Gladstone's Nonconformist and radical supporters stayed loyal to the Liberal party, despite some earlier doubts over education in particular, the middle classes as a whole were not won over. The Conservatives argued that Gladstone's income tax proposals simply did not add up, that his education measures had placed the position of the Church of England in danger, that his Irish policy had placed the United Kingdom in danger, and that his foreign policy, especially his payout to the United States of the *Alabama* money, had been a humiliation for Britain. Last, but perhaps not least, the Liberals were attacked because their taxation proposals would further increase the price of beer and spirits. Against this, the Liberals could only offer their record and their proposals; most, after all, had not been expecting to have fight a general election quite so soon.

Gladstone's decision to dissolve and propose a dramatic new policy initiative was a courageous one, but it also turned out to be a disastrous one for the Liberal party. The Conservatives gained fifty-six seats in the British boroughs, including some in Wales and Scotland, which had been staunchly Liberal. In Ireland the voters swung more or less completely behind the Nationalist party, with only twelve Liberals out of 105 MPs elected. The Conservatives ended up with an overall majority of about fifty. These figures included some personal disappointments for the Liberals. Chichester Fortescue, who had sat as MP for Louth since

1847, was voted out, while Gladstone himself was beaten into second place in the two-seat constituency of Greenwich by 'Boord the distiller'. This, he wrote, 'is more like a defeat than a victory; though it places me in Parliament again'.[33] But he was never one to give up easily – certainly not to the likes of Disraeli – and initially he proposed to carry on until he had met and been defeated in the Commons. But the cabinet would not go along with this, and accordingly at their last dinner together on 16 February, Gladstone agreed to go to Windsor to see the Queen and resign office, which he did the next day. This was one of their less fraught meetings, and he thought 'nothing could be more frank, natural, and kind, than her manner throughout'.[34] (She no doubt believed she had at last seen the back of him.) Gladstone refused to accept any honour on his own behalf, but the Queen agreed to all the recommendations for honours which he advanced. He finally said his official farewell to the Queen on 20 February and on the 21st cleared out his possessions from 10 Downing Street and moved out. It seems unlikely if, at that moment, he thought he would ever see inside it again.

GLADSTONE'S FIRST MINISTRY

For many at the time, Gladstone's resignation in February 1874 must have seemed like the end of his political career. It was unlikely that a sixty-four year old man would ever be prime minister again. Historians, while obviously not seeing the ministry from 1868 to 1874 as the end of Gladstone's career, have usually seen it as the high point in it. He had worked hard to get to the post of prime minister and he worked extremely hard while he was doing the job. He was aided by a generally loyal and efficient team, over whom he exerted firm control and who he usually guided in directions he wanted to go. As a result, many of the measures passed by his government were noteworthy successes. Their education policy, and the Army reforms stand out in particular in this regard. But even some elements in his Irish policy, such as the Church disestablishment measures, were successes too. It was unfortunate that some of his other Irish policies with which he was particularly involved were either less than complete successes, such as the Land Act, or totally unsuccessful, such as the attempted reform of the Irish university system. The government's foreign policy, too, was only partially successful.

1 Gladstone, 1839, chalk drawing by Heinrich Müller, National Portrait Gallery.

2 Gladstone, 1877, photograph by William Currey, National Portrait Gallery.

3 Gladstone, 1891, photograph by Herbert Rose Barraud, National Portrait Gallery.

4 Catherine Gladstone, 1883, photograph by Bassano, National Portrait Gallery.

5 Sir Robert Peel, oil painting by Henry William Pickersgill, undated, National Portrait Gallery.

6 Viscount Palmerston, 1862, photograph by John Jabez Edwin Mayall, National Portrait Gallery.

7 Earl Granville, *c.*1883, photograph by Bassano, National Portrait Gallery.

8 Benjamin Disraeli, Earl of Beaconsfield, *c.*1881, photograph by W. and D. Downey, National Portrait Gallery.

Britain pretty much stood aside from the Franco-Prussian war, and the Russians got their way over the Black Sea question, although Gladstone's government covered their retreat on this well. The *Alabama* payout did settle a long-standing Anglo-American dispute, but politically damaged the party's standing. Economic policy, too, was not the success it might have been, while the last proposals were unrealistic and were seen to be so.

Although Gladstone's decision to dissolve Parliament may not have been a good one, it is difficult to see what else he could have done. He did not have to call an election for another year, but his party was becoming more restless and the Conservatives were steadily gaining strength through by-election victories. It may well be that if he had held on longer the final defeat would have been even more catastrophic than it was. But it was catastrophic nonetheless, and it was a deep disappointment for Gladstone: the electorate had looked at his financial vision and had decisively rejected it. It is not surprising that, given his age and his feelings at this time, he should have begun to consider his political future. In the end, he was to make the decision not to leave politics, but to step down from the leadership of the Liberal party. It would take something extraordinary to bring him back to the forefront of Liberal politics, and it was hard in 1874 to see what that might be. However, as a later prime minister has said, 'a week is a long time in politics'. The next few years of Gladstone's life were to be as eventful as any that had passed so far.

Even if Gladstone had decided to retire from politics at this time, it is almost certainly the case that historians would still view his career as a success. He had achieved personal success by making his way to the premiership. He also takes credit for the numerous achievements of his first ministry, and had not been overwhelmed by the difficulties and failures that marked his later career. On the other hand, he had not yet become the popular figure he was to be later, and he had not yet achieved the status of the 'Grand Old Man' as he was to become known. In other words, his career would have been a success in ordinary terms, but it would not have been the extraordinary career that it was to become over the next twenty years.

5

RETIREMENT AND MIDLOTHIAN, 1874–1880

The outcome of the 1874 general election was a grievous disappointment for Gladstone and the Liberal Party. 'We have been swept away, literally', he told Earl Spencer, the Irish Viceroy, 'by a torrent of beer & gin'.[1] The electorate had decisively rejected the government's licensing laws and the apparently unrealistic economic reform proposals put forward by the prime minister. What was worse, they had obviously been attracted instead by the heroic and imperialistic views of Disraeli, views with which Gladstone himself was completely out of sympathy. It is not surprising that in these circumstances he began to reflect on his political position, and came to the conclusion there was no longer a role for him at the forefront of British political life. It took some time for him to reach the decision to resign as leader of the Liberal Party, handing over power to the rather unlikely combination of 'Puss' Granville in the Lords and Hartington in the Commons.

DEFEAT AND RESIGNATION, 1874–1875

While the election result in January 1874 led to the immediate resignation of the Liberal government, it did not lead to the 64-year-old Gladstone's immediate resignation as leader of the party. In later years he declared that he had been 'most anxious to make the retirement of the ministry the occasion of my own', because he 'deeply desired an interval between parliament and the grave', partly on the grounds of his age, but he also admitted to being 'in some measure out of touch with some of the tendencies of the liberal party, especially on religious matters'.[2] It was also difficult for him, as he said at the time, to get the party to agree to 'united and vigorous action' on the economy.[3]

At the time, while it was a simple, if painful, task to resign as prime minister, Gladstone found it was less easy to leave the post of party leader. The former cabinet tried to keep him on, and he agreed on 5 March to stay on for another year. He explained his position more fully in a letter to Granville on 12 March. He had, he said, sent out a circular to Liberal MPs, in preparation for the 1874 session of Parliament, but he warned his friend that

> For a variety of reasons, personal to myself, I could not contemplate any unlimited extension of active political service. And I am anxious that it should be clearly understood ... that at my age, I must reserve my entire freedom to divest myself of all the responsibilities of leadership at no distant time.
>
> The need of rest will prevent me from giving more than occasional attendance in the House of Commons during the present Session.
>
> I should be desirous, shortly before the commencement of the Session of 1875, to consider whether there would be advantage in my placing my services for a time at the disposal of the Liberal Party, or whether I should then claim exemption from the duties I have hitherto discharged. If, however, ... it would be preferable ... for me to assume at once the place of an independent member. I should willingly adopt the latter alternative.[4]

It seems from this as if Gladstone was seeking the best of both political worlds. He did not feel as if he could be regularly in attendance at the Commons, but at the same time he would stay on as Liberal leader, at least for the time being. It is true that, if the Liberal Party wanted him to step down as leader, he was prepared to, but there was a distinct reluctance about him when it came to taking that final step. Hence, he would continue to serve as head of the party, but he would act more like a private backbench MP, attending only those debates he considered of sufficient importance. This was not, in the event, a very successful formula and, as time went by, more and more Liberal MPs came to desire his removal from the party leadership. How far Gladstone actually planned his moves over the next few months as a strategy to prove his indispensability to the Liberal Party, or how far it was simply a reflection of his inability to make up his mind what to do, is a difficult question to answer.

Whatever the reasons for the adoption of this position by Gladstone, it did not do him much good in the eyes of some eminent Liberals, or liberal sympathisers. In the Lords, the Duke of Somerset and Earl Grey both attacked him – the former over his Irish policy, the latter over what he considered to be a mistaken decision to dissolve Parliament. In the Commons, party feeling was roused against him too. Harcourt was particularly angry at the situation, thinking it ridiculous and the product of Gladstone being in 'the sulks'. The result of all this was that the Liberal Party spent a year virtually paralysed, and Disraeli's government was allowed time to prepare its policies.

Most of Gladstone's limited contributions to parliamentary debates in the 1874 session were concentrated on religious and ecclesiastical matters. These were issues closest to his own heart, but at the same time might be seen as divisive to the Liberal Party. The most important one of them was the Public Worship Regulation Bill, a measure which Disraeli's government decided to support, though it had been introduced into the House of Lords by the Archbishop of Canterbury, Archibald Campbell Tait. The Bill aimed to criminalise certain rituals that seemed to be too close to those of the Roman Catholic Church when conducted by Church of England clergymen. Gladstone, who had no liking for the discussion of this kind of thing in secular surroundings anyway, was sympathetic to the cause of 'High Church' Anglicanism and deeply disagreed with the measure. He introduced six resolutions against it, and warned the House of Commons that the archbishop was acting dangerously like the Pope in asserting an absolute and rigid control over the Church. But his speeches seemed to some to go too far on this occasion; some Liberals, including Forster and Harcourt, strongly disliked High Church Anglicanism and spoke in favour of the Bill, which also had the Queen's support. The result was a defeat for Gladstone; the Bill became law and he had managed to alienate significant sections of his own party by his attacks on it. He was particularly upset by Harcourt's 'slimy, fulsome, loathsome eulogies upon Dizzy' on this occasion. He claimed not to be annoyed by them – 'I do not respect him enough to be angry with him' – but he did 'regret it *extremely*. It is a new scandal & a new difficulty for the party'.[5]

Gladstone was not unaware of the increasing strength of feeling against him in the Liberal Party, at least if he remained in his current anomalous position. He left the country for Germany in September, while devoting more and more of his time and attention to the question of papal infallibility, rather than to any domestic political matters. Accordingly, by the end of the year he had come to the conclusion that he would have to step down as party leader. He told Granville:

> I see no public advantage in my continuing to act as the leader of the Liberal Party; and that at the age of sixty-five, and after forty-two years of a laborious public life, I think myself entitled to retire on the present opportunity. This retirement is dictated to me by my personal views as to the best method of spending the closing years of my life.[6]

In his diary, he summed up the matter rather more succinctly: 'This great affair is nearly arranged. My old colleagues all submit under protest, and I shall be free.'[7] For public consumption, most of his colleagues expressed their regrets (Bright excepted), and the Liberal press did so, too. The Queen, however, clearly felt some relief that Gladstone was at last on his way out.

His retirement did, of course, leave the Liberal Party in the difficult position of having to find a new leader. This would not be an easy job for anyone, particularly as Gladstone, though no longer party leader, was still going to be present in the Commons and was fully prepared to intervene in debates if he thought it necessary. It was also fairly clear to those who knew him that whatever he might be telling himself in January 1875, he might well soon become discontented with his modest role as a backbench MP and hope to take a more active and leading role in politics once again.

It was agreed that Granville should carry on as leader of the party in the House of Lords and joint leader of the Parliamentary Party as a whole, while there would need to be a new leader in the House of Commons. It was not that easy to find one, a fact which caused Gladstone sorrow, rather than surprise. In the end, it came down to a two-horse race between the radical W.E. Forster and Lord Hartington. Neither was particularly anxious for the job. Forster decided not to stand at the end of January, leaving the field free for Hartington, who seemed to Granville to be genuinely reluctant before he finally accepted the post on 2 February. This placed the leadership of the party firmly in the hands of the aristocratic Whigs. Hartington was the son and heir of the Duke of Devonshire, and it is often asserted that their leadership was a 'breathing space' for the party in between bouts of more radical 'Gladstonian Liberalism'.

POPERY AND PERSONAL LIFE, 1875–1878

Gladstone's personal affairs had begun to take a more prominent role in his life during the 1874 session, although, as so often, the personal and the political sometimes overlapped. This was particularly so with his concerns over the Roman Catholic Church. The removal of French forces from Rome in 1870 and the occupation of the city by Italian troops had led the papacy into a reconsideration of its place and purpose. The outcome of a Papal Council was the promulgation of a decree announcing Papal Infallibility – any doctrine laid down by the Pope must be right and whatever he said would be law for the Church. This had upset many 'old Catholics', including Gladstone's old German friend, Dr Döllinger, and, he hoped, rather than knew for sure, his sister, Helen. It had also upset Gladstone himself, who saw it as a measure which would prevent any hope of an Anglican–Roman Catholic reunion.

In September 1874 Gladstone, accompanied by his son Willy and daughter Helen set off for Germany to see his sister and Döllinger. Gladstone was upset that Döllinger had by this time been excommunicated. The visit took them first to Cologne and Helen, then to Munich and Döllinger, and then, via Salzburg, back to Cologne. When Gladstone got back to Hawarden on 26 September he was in a state of mind similar to when he returned to Britain after visiting the Neapolitan jails in 1850: this time he would have to take action about the Pope, rather than the King of Naples. The result was a 72-page anti-Papal blast, *The Vatican Decrees in Their Bearing on Civil Allegiance: A Political Expostulation*. The book put forward in forthright terms Gladstone's argument against papal pretensions: the Roman Catholic Church was now adopting a policy of violent change; all converts to Rome would have to surrender all mental and moral freedom and the Church had repudiated all modern thought and ancient history. Poor Döllinger had effectively been 'murdered'. Gladstone wasted no time; he completed the first draft by the end of September and saw the work published early in October. He had worked so hard on it he made himself ill, but it was worth it: by the end of November some 52,000 copies had been sold and another 20,500 published. The tone and argument of the work horrified Gladstone's Roman Catholic acquaintances and outraged other Catholics – and some Protestants (including the Queen). But some others approved: Bismarck, for one, who was engaged in his own *Kulturkampf* against the Catholic Church in Germany, sent his congratulations. Probably more important for Gladstone was that many Protestants, and particularly those Nonconformists whom Gladstone had offended by his spirited attacks on the Public Worship Regulation Bill, also approved. It is possible, therefore, that there was an element of political calculation in Gladstone's efforts: this work would help to reconcile some on the Liberal backbenches to him.

But purely personal matters undoubtedly occupied a more prominent position in Gladstone's life after 1874 than they had before. The saddest event of that year came on 16 June with the sudden death of Catherine's only surviving brother, Sir Stephen Glynne, though it did have its advantages for William and Catherine. It meant that Willy now became owner of Hawarden Castle, with his parents as semi-permanent house guests. (In effect, however, Gladstone senior continued to appear to the outside world as owner of Hawarden.) Other upsetting deaths occurred, too, in the 1870s. In the family, Gladstone's brother Robertson died in September 1875, leading to complications with the family firm and for Gladstone, who found this death particularly difficult to cope with. Perhaps even more shocking was the sudden death of George Lyttelton in May 1876. It seemed that he had fallen accidentally from the stairs at his London home – and Gladstone convinced himself of this – but there is no real doubt that he actually committed suicide. He had been upset by the death of his daughter May (Catherine's niece) the previous year. Gladstone was also saddened by the deaths of first, in May 1878, that of Elizabeth, Duchess of Argyll, the daughter of his old confidante, Harriet, Duchess of Sutherland, and then, in April 1879, by that of his friend and fellow scholar Sir Antony Panizzi, the librarian of the British Museum.

Gladstone, much to his wife's dismay, decided in mid-1874 to sell 11 Carlton House Terrace, as an economy measure, after a review of his financial situation (which also led him to force a 10 per cent wage reduction on the coal miners on the Hawarden estate). This sale was eventually completed in March 1875 and, after spending a few months in a house in Carlton Gardens, the Gladstones moved to the more modest address of 73 Harley Street in February 1876. This house was more suitable to upper-middle-class professionals than to a leading political figure – its previous occupant had been Sir Charles Lyell, a noted geologist – but it seems to have been in keeping with Gladstone's new wish for a more modest role in public affairs and a more active scholarly career.

Gladstone's relations with his wife were generally very good, notwithstanding their difference over the Carlton House Terrace sale. Catherine had been a keen supporter of Gladstone the politician ever since their marriage in 1839. Despite his distractions, he had found time to help his wife in the upbringing of their children and they had both followed their children's careers with interest. Catherine had taken a full role in helping Gladstone's work with prostitutes, as well as collecting money for refuges where prostitutes were sent to be educated and 'rescued', and strongly supported their activities. She had taken in women during the crisis over cotton imports to Lancashire in 1861–3, and in the 1866 cholera epidemic she established the Catherine Gladstone Home for Convalescents in Woodford, Essex. As time passed she became increasingly independent, using the railway system to travel about the country. At Christmas 1870 she was away on a mission, leaving Gladstone to enjoy the Christmas holiday at Hawarden alone. Her constant travels came to upset Gladstone somewhat, dependent as he was on her support, but she remained her own mistress and he had to adjust accordingly. Perhaps surprisingly, she knew about and tolerated her husband's close relationships with some other women – the Duchess of Sutherland from one end of the social scale, and Laura Thistlethwayte and Elizabeth Collins from the other – but it is doubtful if she realised fully the intimacy and intensity of his relationship with some of them. Some wives, with less understanding of their husband's character, might have seen things differently. Catherine supported his political career as best she could. She never became an active political hostess, like Frances, Lady Waldegrave at Strawberry Hill, but she remained a confidante, someone Gladstone could unburden himself to at times of acute political difficulty. Gladstone almost always decided for himself what to do, but there is little doubt that he was usually pleased to know that Catherine supported his actions.

Relations with their children were not always easy. Willy was in some ways a disappointment to them. It had been arranged in 1865 that he would succeed his uncle, Sir Stephen Glynne, as owner of Hawarden. Gladstone and Catherine both hoped he would become a leading politician, but following election for Whitby in 1872, he was an MP for only twelve years, and even then seems to have had outside interests. He married well, to Gertrude Stuart, daughter of Lord and Lady Blantyre, the latter a daughter of Gladstone's old friend, Harriet, Duchess of Sutherland, in July 1875, and later received the full title deeds of the Hawarden estate. Willy's political career came to a premature end when he resigned as an MP in 1885. He claimed this was to enable him to take better care of the Hawarden estate, but it is more likely it was because he objected to his father's proposed Irish policy. Unfortunately Willy died only six years later, aged forty-nine, a source of great anguish to both of his parents, at which point, his 6-year-old son William became the owner of Hawarden.

Their next child, Agnes married the Revd Edward Wickham in December 1874. Gladstone liked Wickham, and helped him into the posts of headmaster of Wellington College in 1873 and Dean of Lincoln in 1894, but unlike most of the other children Agnes saw little of her parents after her marriage and figured little in their later lives.

Stephen was something of a trouble to his parents. He seems to have had doubts about his calling into the Church of England, perhaps due to the fact that he had wanted to be a missionary abroad, but instead became Rector of Hawarden in 1872 on the death of his uncle Henry Glynne. He acted as Rural Dean of Mold between 1884 and 1892, and in 1885 married Annie Wilson from Liverpool. He remained Rector of Hawarden and, despite misgivings, stayed there until moving on, after his father's death, in 1904. Financially, at least, he was settled: his earnings as rector giving him sufficient income to be independent of his father.

Mary, like her sisters, was well-educated, mostly at home, and became a well-read and spirited young lady. Gladstone found a political use for her, too. During his second ministry from 1880 to 1885, she acted as one of his private secretaries, taking primary responsibility for matters revolving around church patronage – a fact which shows the considerable trust placed in her by her father. She eventually, in 1886, when nearly forty years old, married a clergyman, Harry Drew, an event which was to have serious repercussions for her younger sister, Helen. Mary did not disappear from her father's life altogether because of this, and continued to do some work for him. The Revd Drew was senior curate at Hawarden and, although he spent some time in South Africa on health grounds, he took a role in the work of the St Deiniols Trust, set up under Gladstone's auspices to act as an institution for religion and education in the later 1880s. In 1894 Mary and one of her own children were among those who accompanied Gladstone on his momentous visit to Biarritz. All in all, she was a strong-willed woman of great character – her decision to marry, knowing that her father did not altogether approve, being an indication of this.

Mary's younger sister, Helen, attended Newnham College, Cambridge, first as a student, then as a teacher, and in 1882 she became Vice-Principal, but her promising academic career was interrupted by Mary's marriage in 1886. She was offered, but had to turn down, the post of Principal of the Royal Holloway College of the University of London so that she could return home to take Mary's place at her father's side. Helen never married and spent the next twelve years acting as private secretary for her father. She accompanied him to Biarritz at the end of 1892, although not two years later. Following her father's death, which she registered, she became Warden of the Women's University Settlement.

Of all the children, Helen's younger brother, Henry, seems to have flown furthest from the immediate family circle, at least in middle life. From 1874 to 1889 he worked for his uncle Robertson's business in India. When Robertson died in September 1875, Gladstone had to fight hard to protect his son's position in the firm, but the young man stayed in Calcutta. In 1890 he married Maud Rendel, daughter of Stuart and Daphne Rendel – the former was a leading member of the Armstrong engineering firm, a Liberal MP, and an ardent cultivator of the Gladstone connection. From this time on, Henry was closer to his father, going with him (and Mary) on a Baltic cruise in 1895 and, when the time came, negotiating his father's funeral arrangements with the Dean of Westminster.

It was the Gladstones' last child, Herbert, who became the most eminent in his own right. Saved by his position as the youngest son from being the centre of his parents' ambitions – the fate that had befallen Willy – Herbert made his way through University College,

Oxford, graduating with a lowly third class degree in classical moderations in 1874. This did not worry his father too much, and two years later Herbert made up for it with a first class degree in modern history, obviously a subject more to his liking. In 1880, thanks to his father's patronage, Herbert became MP for Leeds, and his father's parliamentary private secretary. In March 1881, he made his maiden speech in Parliament, a strong defence of his father's Irish policy, and at the end of 1885, it was he who started the flight of the 'Hawarden Kite', which was sent up partly at least to see how far the Liberal Party would accept Gladstone's newest ideas on Irish home rule policy. Whether or not Gladstone approved of it being sent up, its ascent did not stop Herbert's own advancement. In 1886 he became financial secretary at the War Office and, in Gladstone's last cabinet, he became under-secretary to the newly-promoted Home Secretary and rising Liberal star, Herbert Asquith. His last service for his father was to accept on the family's behalf Parliament's offer of a state funeral for the 'Grand Old Man'. After his father's death he helped negotiate the pact between the Liberals and the Labour Representation Committee in time for the 1905 general election, and afterwards he became Home Secretary in the 1906 Campbell-Bannerman Liberal government. He then became first governor-general of South Africa, formed in 1910, and was ennobled as Viscount Gladstone. In 1901, after his father's death, he married Dorothy May Paget. Unlike his oldest brother, there is no doubt that Herbert was in no sense a disappointment to his parents; he had gone on to an eminent political career as an effective Liberal politician for some forty years.

William and Catherine Gladstone had presided over a large family in Victorian style. Gladstone was a stern father, although he could relax with his wife and children on occasions. Sometimes he and Catherine spent time with the children discussing issues in 'Glynnese', a language invented by the Glynne family, which Gladstone had spent years trying to learn. But he was not too relaxed with them. In later life his son Herbert remembered how things stood:

> We grew to understand that he was much occupied and must not be disturbed. We accepted that, and it was soon supported by the evidence of our senses ... We were like little dogs who never resent exclusion but are overjoyed when they are allowed in.

The result of this was that 'our affection was secured'. Daughter Mary recalled that he was a 'potentous potentate and his time, health and convenience had to be considered first'.[8] None of the children married young, and this has been seen as a tribute to their affection for their parents and as an indication of the strength of the ties binding them to each other and of parental control. While none of the children could live up totally to the eminence of their father, they were clever enough and sufficiently well-educated to make their own ways in the world in some style.

While Gladstone could spend more time with his wife and children following his retirement from the leadership of the Liberal Party, he was also able to spend more time on his literary work. These writings took several themes, as they had done throughout his life: religion and the Church, 'Homerology' (meaning writings on Homer's poetry and ancient history), and contemporary political issues, both domestic and international. His earliest productions centred on the first of these themes, and had gone as far back as his notorious first book, *The State in its Relations with the Church*, published in December 1838; this was followed by another on the same subject, defending his hypotheses, in November 1840. But he only managed a few more articles on this subject down to 1874, when the publication of *The Vatican Decrees* marked a new period of activity. He issued a defence of this pamphlet and two other articles on religious themes in 1875, and a book entitled *The Church of England and Ritualism* a year later. After his final retirement in 1896, he published an edition of *The Works of Bishop Butler* and *Studies Subsidiary to the Works of Bishop Butler*, the early eighteenth-century Anglican bishop who was a major influence on Gladstone's own theological thinking.

But articles on 'purely' religious themes were not Gladstone's main literary output. As time went by he became more and more interested in Homer. In 1857 he published two articles in the *Quarterly Review* and a three-volume work, *Studies in Homer and the Homeric Age*, a year later. He could find little time after that to publish much, although he issued some translations of classical works which he and his brother-in-law, Lord Lyttelton, had made in 1861. In August 1869 he managed to publish *Juventus Mundi: The Gods and Men of the Heroic Age*, a popularised version of his earlier *Studies in Homer*. In 1874 he published four articles around this subject in the *Contemporary Review*, and two years later another five appeared, together with another book, this one entitled *Homeric Synchronism: An Inquiry into the Time and Place of Homer*. Even in the 1880s he was contributing articles to the *Contemporary Review* on the Greek gods.

It is not especially easy to get to grips with Gladstone's views on Homer and Homeric society, but one thing is very clear. His views were considered by contemporaries to be at best eccentric; at worst they were felt to be almost blasphemous. Gladstone was particularly anxious to show there was a direct and discernible relationship between the civilisation of ancient Greece and the revelations of the Bible. Homer, according to him, was the precursor of the Bible. The ancient Greeks did not have the benefit of Christian values, but, as an ancient society relatively uncorrupted by the world, they could be seen as closer to God than many more recent ones. They should be studied as a supplement to the Bible and Christian theological works. The very idea that people outside the Jewish–Christian tradition could contribute to modern values was outrageous to some. Perhaps the best summary of the establishment's views on Gladstone and Homer was that of Professor F. Muller of Oxford University: 'So great a man, so imperfect a scholar!'[9]

Gladstone also wrote numerous works on contemporary politics. The first of these was an anonymous article, 'The Course of Commercial Policy at Home and Abroad', published in 1843 while Gladstone was at the Board of Trade, which served as a defence of the Peel government's commercial and economic policy. His first concentrated outpouring of this type of work followed his resignation from Palmerston's ministry in 1855. The following two years, 1856 and 1857, saw a series of articles in the *Quarterly Review*, including 'The declining efficiency of Parliament' and 'Prospects political and financial', both overt and increasingly strident attacks on Palmerston's government. He reflected on the circumstances and consequences of 'The fall of the late ministry' in April 1858 and on the effects of 'The war in Italy' in April 1859.

While prime minister, he could do less in this respect, but in opposition in 1876 the Balkan crisis led to the publication of his single most famous pamphlet, *Bulgarian Horrors and the Question of the East*, a fervent attack on the Turkish oppressors. He also wrote articles discussing Beaconsfield's (Disraeli had become Earl of Beaconsfield in August 1876) Egyptian policy in August 1877, looking at 'Aggression on Egypt and freedom in the East' in *The Nineteenth Century*, and at the

Treaty of Berlin in June 1879. Once again, his output declined while in office, but after the resignation of his third ministry, he offered, in August 1886, some reflections on *The Irish Question*. He continued to write during the last ten years of his life. In 1896 his last published article appeared in *The Nineteenth Century*. Perhaps appropriately, given Gladstone's earlier publishing triumphs, it was entitled 'The massacres in Turkey'. His last published piece was an interview on his long-dead friend, Arthur Hallam, printed in the *Daily Telegraph* on 5 January 1898, only five months before his own death. In the midst of all his other work and writings, Gladstone found time, in November 1868, to publish *A Chapter of Autobiography*, before the responsibilities of office overtook him. Though he started work on an autobiography in 1892, he never completed it.

Gladstone's output of written works, given his other commitments, is truly staggering. Colin Matthew calculated that between 1874 and 1880 Gladstone published nearly sixty articles and two books of new material, as well as seven volumes of *Gleanings of Past Years*, a collection of selected articles. He estimated that by 1880 Gladstone had earned over £10,000 from his writings, almost half of that in the years from 1876 to 1880 – and most of that for the *Bulgarian Horrors* pamphlet of 1876. His depth of reading was equally great: in June 1879 it comprised twenty-eight books and seven periodical articles, on a wide range of subjects, covering books on British history and, for example, a pamphlet on *The Chinese Question in Australia*. All in all, this displays a remarkable energy. However, he never completed another major work of the scale of the *Studies in Homer*, partly because other things intervened to prevent him devoting the necessary time to it, and partly because, as a result of the criticism of his books on Homer, he grew more cautious and more aware of his limitations as an author.

GLADSTONE AND THE DISRAELI GOVERNMENT, 1875–1878

Following his resignation from the Liberal leadership, Gladstone rather stepped back from the political limelight. It was not that he abandoned political life altogether, it was rather that it would take very particular things to bring him back into the fray in the Commons. The first few years of Disraeli's government saw it bring in a series of reform measures about which he had relatively little to say. Most of these can be credited to Disraeli's active Home Secretary, Richard Assheton Cross.

The importance of Cross's legislation has recently come under scrutiny and doubt has been cast on its value. Among the first of his measures was the repeal of Gladstone's 1871 Trade Union Act. This Act had been greeted with anger by the Trade Unions, and Cross replaced it with a Conspiracy and Protection of Property Act. This made peaceful picketing legal and stated that a group of people engaged in an industrial dispute could do anything that it was legal for an individual to do. This therefore legalised collective bargaining. Given the effects of the trade depression, however, it did not do the unions a great deal of good, at least in the short term. Strikes by workers in Wales in 1873 and 1875 were both unsuccessful and unions in some areas were almost completely crushed.

Another measure was the Artisans' Dwellings Act. This enabled councils to draw up improvement schemes for areas of towns that seemed unhealthy and gave them loans to do the necessary work. But taking action would incur expense, and by 1881 only ten out of eighty-seven English and Welsh towns that were eligible to do so had taken up any loans. A second Act, developing aspects of this one, was passed in 1879, but many working in the area of housing in the 1880s thought these Acts, by encouraging the demolition of slums but not insisting on the construction of replacement housing, had had disastrous consequences for the poorer urban workers.

A third was the Sale of Food and Drugs Act. Given the support the brewers had granted the Conservatives in the 1874 election campaign, it is not surprising that Cross acted early to reward them by repealing Bruce's Licensing Act. He introduced a more wide-ranging Act, covering the adulteration of all kinds of food and drink. This, while effective – it lasted until 1928 – did have a loophole for brewers, however, because it did not specifically forbid the placing of salt in beer to encourage thirst.

Another measure was the Public Health Act, a consolidating Act bringing together previous legislation. It empowered local authorities to set local rates on property and use the money received to build and run hospitals, to purchase land for local parks, and even, if they wished, to own gas and water supplies. It also dealt with a wide range of drainage and sewerage matters. The Duke of Richmond introduced the

Agricultural Holdings Act in the Lords. This was modelled on Gladstone's Irish Land Act and it offered to tenants who had been evicted compensation for improvements they had made. Lord Chancellor Cairns' Land Transfer Act laid down long-lasting rules on this subject.

Probably the most famous incident of the 1875 session, though, involved the 'Sailor's Friend', Samuel Plimsoll. It was not unknown at this time for ships to be sent to sea overloaded, often with disastrous results. Nor was it unknown for ships to be sent out over-insured, with the intention they should be lost and the owners claim compensation. When in July 1875 it appeared that a bill to prevent this was going to be postponed, Plimsoll created a scene in the Commons, and secured the passage of a temporary measure. This was made permanent in the 1876 Merchant Shipping Act, which ordered that shipowners should not overload their ships and recommended, though it did not compel, owners to paint a line on the ship's hull to indicate full loading level (what became known as the 'Plimsoll Line').

Reforms on this scale did not appear after 1875, however. The one measure of any significance to pass in 1876 was Lord Sandon's Education Act. This developed the Liberal Act of 1870 by making it compulsory for all children between the ages of five and ten years to attend school and, if they failed to reach certain standards, to stay at school until they were fourteen years old. The Act also stated that local authorities had to appoint attendance committees, whose job was to ensure that parents did send their children to school. Boards of Guardians were to pay the fees for very poor parents. Few other reforms were enacted, mainly because the government was preoccupied with foreign policy. One other measure that the government did bring in in the 1876 session was the Imperial Titles Act, by which Queen Victoria was able to add to her list of titles that of Empress of India, something which pleased her greatly, and her devotion to Disraeli accordingly increased.

The most obvious point to make in a biography of Gladstone in connection with these measures is his limited involvement with them. The only one he made any serious comment on was the last. On 9 March 1876, and at its final reading on the 23rd, he spoke out against the Imperial Titles Bill, thereby offending further the Queen and upsetting many of his own aristocratic connections. At least, with this he was in sympathy with the bulk of the Liberal Party and some of the Liberal leadership. He also, not surprisingly, attacked the budgets of the Chancellor of the Exchequer, Sir Stafford Northcote, though without any great effect. But it was foreign affairs that increasingly came to dominate Disraeli's government from 1875, and it was these that attracted Gladstone's attention.

Perhaps the most famous action of Disraeli's government – or, rather, of Disraeli himself – was the purchase, in the summer of 1875, of the shares which the Egyptian Khedive, Ismail, held in the Suez Canal Company. The Suez Canal, which had been built by a French engineer and a company owned partly by French capitalists and partly by the Egyptian government, was opened, despite British opposition, in 1869. It cut the time needed to sail between Britain and India by several weeks and therefore made Egypt a vital strategic point for the British. It was built as part of Ismail's modernising drive: he hoped to use the tolls from ships passing through it to finance developments in his country. Unfortunately, his spending continued to outrun his income, and in desperation he tried to sell his shares in the Suez Canal Company to the British government. In November 1870 Granville had turned him down, but Disraeli saw the importance of the Canal. Five years later, in a brilliant stroke of publicity, he borrowed four million pounds from the Rothschilds and bought Ismail's shares. Gladstone greeted the news with some dismay: 'I am aware of no cause that could warrant or excuse it, except its being necessary to prevent the closure of the Canal. But that cause I apprehend could not possibly exist.' By early in the new year he seems to have been less bothered by the purchase: 'What is the harm that has attended or is likely to attend private proprietorship in this case?'[10] His main underlying complaint was surely that it was Disraeli who had done it, and this, together with his dislike of borrowing money, meant he could not possibly approve. The purchase of the Canal shares was to come back and haunt Gladstone himself within a very few years.

These Egyptian events paled into insignificance when compared with the enormous explosion that shook the Balkans in 1875 when the beginning of one of the periodic revolts by Balkan Christians against their Ottoman Turkish rulers occurred – this time in Serbia. It soon spread to the area that eventually became Bulgaria. The Turks were not unaccustomed to dealing with this sort of thing, and began to repress the Bulgars with fearsome brutality. To a significant number of Victorian British Christians tales of rape and infanticide carried out by Muslims on Christians aroused horror and anger. What was worse was the fact that the British government, aware that the Russians might intervene to help their fellow Orthodox Christians and Slavs and worried as always by the spread of Russian power in the Balkans, seemed to be siding with the Turks.

Gladstone began to feel he ought to do something. In September 1876 he published his most influential pamphlet ever, *Bulgarian Horrors and the Question of the East*, which in a month sold 200,000 copies. The movement against the government's pro-Ottoman policy at this stage was strongest in the Nonconformist areas such as south-west and northern England and Wales, and it is fairly clear that Gladstone saw that harnessing himself to this movement would serve as a way of reconciliation with those Nonconformist elements he had so recently angered.

Gladstone's pamphlet stands as a fine example of his writing skills and his power to move his readers:

> But I return to, and end with, that which is the omega as well as the alpha of this great and mournful case. An old servant of crown and state, I entreat my countrymen, upon whom far more than perhaps any other people of Europe it depends, to require and to insist that our government which has been working in one direction shall work in the other, and shall apply all its vigour to concur with other states of Europe in obtaining the extinction of the Turkish executive power in Bulgaria. Let the Turks now carry away their abuses in the only possible manner, namely by carrying off themselves. Their Zaptiehs and their Mudirs, their Bimbashis and their Yugbashis, their Kaimakams and their Pashas, one and all, bag and baggage, shall I hope clear out from the province they have desolated and profaned.[11]

Clearly, Gladstone's pamphlet is calling for the Turkish government to be removed 'bag and baggage' only from Bulgaria, not from Europe as a whole. But this qualification was submerged by the power of the narrative and Gladstone's pamphlet was taken as a call to the Turks to remove themselves altogether from the Balkans, and he was applauded or attacked for that reason.

His campaign was not immediately successful. For one thing, in April 1877 the Russians declared war on Turkey. This increased anxiety about Russia and gave more support to the government's pro-Turkish policy. For another, when Gladstone introduced, a month later, a series of five resolutions calling for action by the great powers to force the Turks to grant concessions to their Christian subjects, this implied active intervention by the British. Not all Liberals – among them John Bright and his pacifist allies – were prepared to go along with this. Finally, the movement seemed exclusively Liberal, orchestrated by, among other organisations, Joseph Chamberlain's National Liberal Federation. Gladstone's failure to achieve a great deal in 1877 was summed up by the rejection of his resolutions, after a five-day debate and strenuous efforts on his part, by 253 votes to 354.

But he still had some allies. At the end of May he visited Birmingham and stayed with Chamberlain. Here, he received 'a triumphant reception', and made a 45-minute speech to 'A most intelligent and duly appreciative audience – but they were 25,000 and the building I think of no acoustic merits, so that the strain was excessive.'[12] In October he spent some three weeks in Ireland, his first and only visit, where he had some conversation with both Catholics and Protestants and was awarded the freedom of the City of Dublin. But he did not go much beyond there.

The following year, 1878, was to be what Gladstone himself described as 'a tumultuous year'. In January, the government, faced with Russian successes in the Balkans, asked Parliament for an extra six million pounds for the defence budget, and ordered the Mediterranean fleet through the Dardanelles to Constantinople, as a warning to the Russians. In March, the Russians imposed on the Turks the Treaty of San Stefano. This would have almost completely dismantled the Ottoman Empire in Europe and created a 'Big Bulgaria', effectively a client state of Russia, enormously increasing Russian influence in the area. This assertion of Russian power prompted Beaconsfield's government – not without some dissension – to call out Britain's reserves in April. Britain did not want to fight but 'by jingo' she was ready to if necessary. What gave the Russians more pause for thought was that the advances had also provoked concern in Vienna, home of the Austro-Hungarian government and Russia's rival in the Balkans. The danger of a European conflict increased markedly. Bismarck was anxious to avoid war between his two friends, Russia and Austria-Hungary, and agreed to summon an international conference, or congress, in Berlin, where he would act as an 'honest broker'.

The Congress of Berlin, which took place between 13 June and 13 July 1878, was Beaconsfield's last triumph. Many of the details had been settled in private beforehand, but it still took threats from the Earl of Beaconsfield and pressure from Bismarck to persuade the Russians to accept the final settlement. It did not favour them, or the Turks. 'Big Bulgaria' was divided, and the Austrians secured control of Bosnia and Herzegovina. Britain received guaranteed Asiatic Turkish lands against Russian encroachment and in return received Cyprus, which she could use as a naval base to support the Turks, should the need arise. Whatever the Ottomans thought about this agreement they had no choice but to accept it; it did seem a little curious though that the power offering to protect the Empire was helping itself to some of its territory. In the short term this was a victory for Beaconsfield; he brought back, as he said, 'peace with honour' from Berlin. But in the longer term its consequences were not so good. Austro-Russian rivalry was reinforced, and the Austro-Hungarian government reflected on the value of its British connection. Britain was a naval power, but any war with Russia would be a land war, so Austria-Hungary needed an ally with an army. Hence she came closer to Germany, and in October 1879 the two powers signed a defensive alliance. The possibility of an Austro-Russian conflict involving Germany therefore increased – and, in 1914, became reality.

The prime minister had the support of the British people, as Gladstone found out. On 24 February 1878 a stone-throwing crowd broke some of the windows of the Gladstones' London house. When the government decision to call out reserves was discussed, Bright and his allies – Gladstone included – voted against it. But other Liberal MPs threatened to vote for the government if they did so, and Hartington's line was that the Party should abstain – but even then some Liberals voted for the motion. None of this made Gladstone hold his fire. On 30 July he launched a strong attack on the government and its conduct of the negotiations in Berlin:

> I do affirm that it was their part to take the side of liberty; and I do also affirm that as a matter of fact they took the side of servitude.

> I think we have lost greatly by the conclusion of this convention; I think we have lost very greatly indeed the sympathy and respect of the nations of Europe ... This setting up of our own interests, out of place, in an exaggerated form ... has greatly diminished, not, as I have said, the regard for our material strength, but the estimation of our moral standard of action, and consequently our moral position in the world.[13]

It is easy enough to see from this how far from Beaconsfield's (or Bismarck's) views on foreign policy Gladstone's were. In the short term, Gladstone was overwhelmed by public feeling in favour of Beaconsfield, but he told one correspondent in November, 'My opinion is that this government is moving to its doom and I hope the day of Lord Granville's succession to it may be within a twelvemonth'.[14] The government did not last much longer than that, but it was not Granville who was to succeed it.

MIDLOTHIAN AND RE-ELECTION, 1879–1880

Beaconsfield's government may have conducted a triumphant foreign policy in 1878, but towards the end of that year and during 1879 it was to stumble badly. This was due to two wars in very different parts of the world, Afghanistan and South Africa. One of Britain's main security concerns over her Indian Empire was the protection of its north-western frontier from attacks from Afghanistan. As the Russian Empire expanded to the south-east, the chances of a successful Russian invasion of Afghanistan increased, and the danger was that, rather than Afghan tribesmen invading India, it would be the Russian army. Britain therefore had to watch developments in Afghanistan carefully. During the nineteenth century she evolved two policies to counter the Russian threat. One was the so-called 'forward policy', which meant placing Anglo-Indian forces in Afghanistan and ensuring the country had a pro-British (and therefore anti-Russian) ruler. This had been tried in 1839 and had resulted in the disastrous first Afghan war, with the destruction of a British force in the Khyber Pass in the winter of 1841–42. Though this had been avenged and Kabul occupied in 1842, the Army was soon withdrawn and a second policy, known as 'masterly inactivity', was developed. This meant simply watching developments in Afghanistan and waiting for the Russians, should they come, on the bank of the River Indus.

Whatever the merits of the two policies – and the second seems in many ways the better, because it would cause the Russians to face problems of supply and unfriendly Afghans to their rear – it was the shock of the 1841–42 disaster that drove the British to adopt the second for over thirty years. But in 1876 Beaconsfield's government sent the flamboyant Lord Lytton out to India as Viceroy. Lytton demanded that Sher Ali, Amir of Afghanistan, should accept a British mission and British agents to watch his frontiers. But Sher Ali refused, and what was worse, in July 1878 a Russian mission arrived at Kabul. The result of this was a full-scale British invasion of Afghanistan at the end of the year, and in early January 1879 the British occupied Kandahar. Sher Ali died and in May his son and successor agreed to a treaty allowing the British mission in Kabul. This looked like a success for Beaconsfield, but in early September Afghan troops attacked and massacred the mission. The British once again invaded, this time it seemed successfully, but the damage to Beaconsfield's government had been done. In fact they had not really been in favour of Lytton's policy, but the strength of feeling against imperialism, which Gladstone was keen to exploit, had increased accordingly.

While these events occurred to the north-west of the Indian Empire, others were unfolding in southern Africa. The situation there had developed since 1815 when Britain had annexed the Cape Colony. The Dutch had begun to settle in the Cape in the seventeenth century, and their assertive policies had driven the local inhabitants further inland. These Europeans – or Boers, as they became known – developed a sense of racial superiority over the local inhabitants. The British, however, followed policies the Boers found unacceptable: the abolition of slavery in 1833 had caused many of them to migrate further inland in the Great Trek between 1835 and 1837. In doing so they encountered other African tribes, foremost among them the warlike Zulus. In 1836 at the battle of Blood River the Boers had inflicted a major defeat on the Zulus. The British, who had several times found themselves engaged in wars against local tribes to preserve their power, did not prevent their departure. They were, however, aware of the risks posed by having independent Boer territories on their frontiers and in the 1840s decided to annex them. They soon regretted this extension of their responsibilities and increase in costs. In January 1852, by the Sand River Convention, the Boer territory to the north of the Vaal River (the Transvaal) was declared independent on condition it did not allow slavery in its territories. In 1854 the Boer territory between the Orange and Vaal Rivers (the Orange Free State) was granted its independence on similar terms by the Bloemfontein Convention. The British, however, kept control of the coastal area of Natal. By the mid-1870s, however, the Boer republic of the Transvaal was in dire financial straits and practically defenceless. Accordingly, in April 1877, it was declared annexed to the British Empire once again. The Earl of Carnarvon, Beaconsfield's colonial secretary, decided the best way to deal with the problem of southern Africa once and for all would be for all the territories in the region – the Cape Colony, the Transvaal, the Orange Free State and Natal – to be brought together in one confederation under British overlordship.

The new British High Commissioner for South Africa, Sir Bartle Frere was appointed only in April 1877 to bring about the policy of confederation. While he felt he could do nothing about it at that time, he thought he could do something about the threat of the Zulus, now fully recovered from their earlier defeat. He asked London for troop reinforcements, but Beaconsfield's government, with its attention focused on Afghanistan, refused to send them and ordered Frere to follow a cautious policy: the last thing they wanted was another war. This did not stop Frere, who in November 1878, issued the Zulus with an ultimatum, knowing they could not accept it. When the ultimatum duly expired in January 1879 without a Zulu response, British forces invaded Zululand. This should have been a straightforward operation: the Zulus did not possess firearms, while British troops were armed with the latest rifles. However, thanks to a display of incompetence almost unmatched in British military history, on 22 January a British and allied force of over 1,500 men was attacked and massacred at Isandhlwana. The heroic defence of Rorke's Drift over the next night did little to make up for it, nor, did the successful execution of a retreat from Zululand. Reinforcements, rushed to the spot, helped the British secure an overwhelming victory over the Zulus in July, but by then Beaconsfield's enthusiastic imperialist policy had suffered another serious check.

While the Liberal leadership had been caught on the horns of a dilemma over Beaconsfield's Turkish policy, it was easier for it to find common ground in the party against the Conservatives' Afghan and South African policies. As early as December 1878 Hartington had launched a strong attack on the government over its actions in Afghanistan, knowing this would please both his own radical back-benchers and Liberal Nonconformist supporters in the country. Over the next year Hartington's publicly pronounced policy became both distinctly more radical and more decisive; it became increasingly likely that, should the Liberals win the next general election, he, rather than Granville, would become prime minister.

But, whatever the effect of these policies on Hartington and his position, their effect on Gladstone was even greater. In January 1879 he was approached by a group from the Scottish Midlothian constituency asking that he accept their nomination as Liberal candidate for the seat. After some thought, he accepted and, as a consequence, began one of the most famous speaking tours in British political history. This was not the first time a British politician had spoken to large crowds – Lord Palmerston had done as much; nor was it the first time Gladstone had done so. But it was the scale of the 'Midlothian Campaign' that sets it apart. Between his departure from Hawarden on 24 November 1879 to his return on 8 December, Gladstone made thirty speeches, lasting from less than ten minutes to one and three-quarter hours, to over 85,000 people. Their numbers ranged from the 20,000 or so at Edinburgh Waverley Market to thirty at 'Sir J. Watson's, after dinner'. He spoke at the railway stations on the way; he made five speeches on 1 December alone, and spoke in all for about fifteen and a half hours. His last was to the procession of 3,000 that had escorted him from Chester railway station to Hawarden on his return.[15] For a 69-year-old man this was a formidable achievement. All the speeches were noted down for publication in the daily press, for Gladstone was not only speaking to the voters of the Midlothian constituency, he was preaching to a national audience.

In the campaign Gladstone denounced 'Beaconsfieldism', which he said had not only led to unnecessary wars and unnecessary expenditure and taxation, but had also presented a perverted view of British interests. He argued that Britain's foreign policy should be directed by a desire to preserve peace, to keep out of dangerous alliances with foreign powers that might pull Britain into war, and to accept the doctrine of equal rights for all nations. He also contended that British policy should always be inspired by a love of freedom, hence Britain should still take an active role in world affairs when it was necessary for her to do so. Finally, Gladstone expressed an optimistic view of the world, as he told one of his audiences in Edinburgh:

> Whatever we may say amidst the clash of arms and the midst of din of preparation for warfare in time of peace – amidst all this yet there is going on a profound mysterious movement, that, whether we will or not, is bringing the nations of the civilised world, as well as the uncivilised, morally as well as physically nearer to one another, and making them more and more responsible before God for one another's welfare.[16]

Gladstone had no doubt that he was fighting a battle for 'justice, humanity, freedom, law … on a gigantic scale', and doing so 'for millions who themselves cannot speak'. He also believed he had been 'morally forced into this work as a great and high election of God'.[17]

The whole character and conduct of this first Midlothian campaign certainly touched a chord with some elements of the Victorian public, and it seemed like some of the great religious revivalist meetings that periodically shook the Victorian world. It made Gladstone extremely popular in some quarters, well away from Midlothian. Gladstone, in the opinion of one stationer in London, was now 'the man for England'. As, just a year before, anyone daring to criticise Beaconsfield's eastern policy had been howled down by jingoist mobs, so now it was the Gladstonian call for peace (and retrenchment) that seemed so popular. The question facing the Liberal leadership was to know how popular it really made their party. On 16 December the Liberal elder statesmen – Granville, Hartington, Cardwell and Harcourt – held a meeting to discuss party strategy. They decided that Gladstone was still too much an object of suspicion to elements in the party to be asked to lead it. It might well be, in any case, that his triumph was only 'a flash in the pan'. In February 1880 Liberal candidates were defeated in by-elections held at Southwark and Liverpool, and it looked as if the Conservatives might, after all, have recovered from his onslaught. Even so, it caused general surprise when on 8 March 1880, Beaconsfield announced the dissolution of Parliament.

Two months earlier, before Gladstone could embark on an election campaign, he had a melancholy duty to perform. On 12 January,

Gladstone, his brother Thomas and his sister-in-law, Lady Louisa, set off for Holland, where their sister Helen lay desperately ill. She died four days later on the 16th. Gladstone brought her body home, and she was buried at Fasque 'with the Anglican rite'. He convinced himself that, despite Helen's announced conversion to Roman Catholicism in 1842, she would have wanted this, justifying it in a long memorandum penned early in February.[18] He felt she could not have accepted the latest developments in the Roman Catholic Church and therefore would have been happiest to be buried in a Catholic, but not Roman, manner. He was genuinely upset when his sister died, but it would not be unfair to suggest he was taking a lot on to do what he did. In reality he had no real justification for his assertion that Helen would not have wanted a fully Roman Catholic burial service, but the whole affair shows his desperate desire to believe that she really wanted to return to the Anglican Church and, as so often, the emotional force that underlay his 'logic'. Many of his decisions, both personal and political, were made on emotional grounds, and the logical justification for them was arrived at only afterwards, and served to allay public and quite possibly private fears as well.

In the political world, the Liberal party leadership had moved swiftly when the dissolution of Parliament was announced. Only two days later, on 10 March, Hartington arranged a meeting at Devonshire House, his London residence, inviting Gladstone to confer with him. Shortly afterwards, Gladstone set off for Edinburgh to begin his 'Second Midlothian Campaign'. He issued his election manifesto on 11 March, and followed this up with a number of speeches on a variety of domestic and international affairs, including the government's record on domestic legislation (or rather its recent lack of it) and the latest developments in the eastern question. Once again, he followed an exhausting schedule. On the afternoon of 22 March, for example, he made five speeches in three different parts of Edinburgh, although these were very short by his standards, the longest lasting only some fifty minutes. He told his audiences, that as Liberals:

> We cannot reckon on the wealth of the country, nor upon the influence which wealth and rank usually brings. In the main these powers are against us, for wherever there is a close corporation, wherever there is a spirit of organised monopoly, wherever there is a narrow and sectional interest apart from that of the country, and desirous to

> be set up above the interest of the public, there, gentlemen, we, the Liberal party, have no friendship and no tolerance to expect.

But, he argued, the nation was now behind the Liberal party, and the nation, while it was difficult to rouse, 'when roused [was] harder still and more hopeless to resist'.[19]

The nation, in some places, was certainly behind Gladstone. As in 1868, he had been nominated as a candidate for more than one seat, the second in this case being the three-member constituency of Leeds. Gladstone had always been rather cautious about this, as Leeds had a strong Nonconformist element among its electors. Even so, in 1880 he was elected top of the poll there without even visiting the constituency. What was more important for him, though, was the result in Edinburgh, declared on 5 April. He was elected by a majority of just over 200, which he thought was a 'quite satisfactory' result. He was stirred more by the estimated 15,000 people who came to congratulate him: 'Wonderful, & nothing less, has been the guiding hand of God in all this matter.[20] As a result of this, Gladstone politely declined the Leeds seat, and later in the year his son Herbert was elected to the vacancy.

The results in the country as a whole reflected Gladstone's personal success: the Liberals won 353 seats, a clear majority over the 238 for the Conservatives and 61 for Irish home rulers. The Liberals gained ground significantly, everywhere, except in London and the home counties. In Lancashire, thanks to Hartington's own emulation of Gladstone's Midlothian strategy, they gained twelve seats, and outside England Conservative representation was reduced to a mere seven seats in Scotland (compared with the Liberals' fifty) and only two in Wales (compared with the Liberals' twenty-eight).

Quite why the Liberal Party had emerged so successfully is difficult to say and various factors contributed to it. For some people, it was the moderation of Hartington and the Whig leadership of the party that appealed; certainly some of Gladstone's radical rhetoric did not attract them very much. But for large numbers of Nonconformist radicals Gladstone's speeches had made him once again their champion. Gladstone also put into words the thoughts of many who were out of sympathy with the jaded imperialism of Beaconsfield's government. It would seem clear that, important as Hartington's efforts were, it was the

'Grand Old Man' who made the difference in this election. While there was no doubt that the Liberals should form the next government, however – and Beaconsfield resigned on 21 April – there was considerable doubt about who should be the next prime minister.

On the face of it the choice was between the two leaders of the Liberal party, Granville and Hartington, and the Queen would have to summon one of them to try and form a government. Hartington had plenty of friends to encourage him to take the job, among whom was Victoria herself. The day after Beaconsfield resigned, she summoned him to Windsor. Whatever his theoretical position, Hartington knew that, even if the Queen did ask him, he could not take the post of prime minister without the agreement of Gladstone, and immediately after his journey to Windsor he went to call on him. At their meeting, Gladstone expressed himself surprised that it was Hartington, rather than the man he considered to be '*the* leader of the party', Granville, who had been sent for, but the Queen had told Hartington that his moderation made him the more attractive proposition. Hartington had already told the Queen his belief that Gladstone 'would not take any office or post in the government except that of First Minister', and he had accordingly advised her to send for Gladstone. The Queen had sent Hartington back to see Gladstone in the hope he could persuade his former leader to serve in a Hartington cabinet, but Gladstone bluntly informed him he should tell the Queen 'that I adhere to my reply as you have already conveyed it' to her. He went on to explain that he would support any Hartington government from the backbenches as far as he could, but 'promises of this kind I said stood on slipping ground and must always be understood with the limits which might be prescribed by conviction'.[21] Gladstone, therefore, would stay on the backbenches and oppose any Hartington government when he thought it necessary. It is not surprising that, faced with this rather half-hearted backing, Hartington went back to the Queen and told her she simply would have to send for Gladstone. Even so, it was not easy for his and Granville's combined efforts to persuade her that she should take this step. However, she finally gave way and on 23 April Gladstone was duly called to Windsor, though before he went, he made sure that Hartington and Granville would accept offices in his new government. Gladstone's meeting with the Queen left him 'All things considered … much pleased'.[22] The Queen did not hide her disquiet at his return, though the discussion generally concerned almost entirely the distribution of offices and not questions of policy. But Gladstone had now, once again, become undisputed Liberal leader and prime minister.

The years from 1874 to 1880 were therefore crucial to Gladstone's career. There is no doubt that he had intended to retire after his defeat at the polls in 1874, but the prospect of it had not pleased him. After some time on the back benches he found there were too many things happening for him to ignore. He could not sit idly by while the unfortunate Bulgarians were slaughtered; he could not allow British forces to be deployed unjustly against less fortunate peoples; he could not tolerate Beaconsfield's triumphs. The result was a revival almost second-to-none in British political history. His pamphlets sold well, but to see him in person became the desire of more and more English men and women, and Gladstone obliged. His monumental tour of Midlothian was one result and the Liberal triumph in the 1880 elections was another. But it was now necessary for him to return to the post he had given up in 1874. His first ministry had been, in many respects, a success; it remained to be seen whether his second would be able to keep up the record.

6

THE SECOND AND THIRD MINISTRIES, 1880–1886

In 1880 Gladstone returned to the post of prime minister. He had the support of the Liberal majority in the House of Commons, and even of the two erstwhile leaders of the party, Granville and Hartington. His task now was to construct a ministerial team that would enable him to continue the work he had left unfinished in 1874, as well as to undo what he saw as the harmful effects of the six years of Conservative rule and deal with any unforeseen events that might yet occur. Even without any of these problems, he knew he still had a lot to do.

THE FORMATION OF THE CABINET

In 1880, as in 1874, Gladstone had once again to create a cabinet which would reflect the make-up of the Parliamentary Liberal Party. Even before he had seen the Queen to accept office, he had had a talk with Granville and Hartington, to prepare the ground. He recorded that Granville immediately accepted his offer that he should once again become Foreign Secretary:

> but modestly and not as of right. I proposed the India Office ... perhaps the most difficult of all at this time, to Hartington, which he desired time to consider. I named Childers as the most proper person for the War Office.[1]

Both Hartington and Childers eventually agreed to take the posts offered, even though the Queen, remembering that Childers had not been very popular while First Lord of the Admiralty in the early 1870s, was rather reluctant to see him at the War Office.

Other ministerial positions were filled without too much trouble. Sir William Harcourt became Home Secretary, and the Earl of Kimberley, Secretary of State for the Colonies. The Earl of Northbrook became First Lord of the Admiralty. But, so far, the more radical wing of the Liberal Party had not found a seat in the cabinet and there were two of them who thought they deserved a place: Sir Charles Dilke and Joseph Chamberlain. The Queen thought Gladstone had assured her that no radicals would be in the cabinet, and, whatever he had said, the Prime Minister knew persuading her to accept even one was going to be difficult. In the case of Dilke, well known for his (former) republicanism, it would be almost impossible. But Dilke and Chamberlain had already decided they would act in concert on this matter, and that one of them at least should get a cabinet place. Gladstone decided to make Dilke under-secretary at the Foreign Office, which was not a cabinet office – that proved hard enough – and bring Chamberlain into the cabinet as President of the Board of Trade. That was acceptable to them, but there were many on the radical wing of the Party who thought both men should have been in the cabinet, and they often said so. Chamberlain's appointment is somewhat surprising. After all, he came from the provinces (Birmingham), he was a Nonconformist, he had not been to Oxford, Cambridge, or any other university, and he owed his reputation to work he had done entirely out of Parliament – as reforming Lord Mayor of Birmingham in the earlier 1870s and leader of the National Liberal Federation from 1877.

Two other important cabinet posts remained to be filled – those of Chief Secretary for Ireland and Chancellor of the Exchequer. One man who had yet to find a job was W.E. Forster, one of the leading lights of the 1868–74 ministry, and this was not least because he had offended many radicals by his handling of the education question and they had still to be reconciled to him. But, as Gladstone knew, Forster was a strong man, both mentally and physically, and so should make a good Irish Chief Secretary, if he could be persuaded to accept the position. He was brought round to it by the offer of a seat in the cabinet to accompany it.

As for the Exchequer, Gladstone felt the only likely candidates were himself and Robert Lowe, but Lowe had left office under a cloud in 1873, and the Queen had no liking for him either. The result was that Lowe was pushed upstairs to the House of Lords with a viscountcy (the Queen would have preferred the more usual and more modest barony offered to ministers on retirement, but Gladstone stood firm on this). Gladstone himself, therefore, took on the additional burden of the Exchequer.

It had not, however, been an especially easy task to construct this cabinet. One eminent figure – the Earl of Derby – turned down the offer of a post on the grounds that it would make his abandonment of the Conservatives in 1878 appear more from selfish motives than out of genuine aversion to their policies. Gladstone would particularly have liked to attract Derby into the government, from both political and personal motives. He was well aware of the grandeur of Knowsley and of the great position occupied by the Stanley family in the north-west of England, so attracting a Stanley into his cabinet would be a great coup indeed. Others, too, for various reasons declined to work for the government in different capacities. One man offered his own services in the cabinet but was rebuffed by Gladstone, and Morley lists four other (anonymous) individuals who, with varying degrees of bitterness, turned down offers from the new prime minister.

Gladstone managed to get the new cabinet together before the end of April 1880. He was quite satisfied with it, and believed he had successfully balanced the Whig and the more radical wings of the Liberal Party. His main anxiety was that the Queen would find fault, but, as he found out on the 28th, when he and his colleagues went to Windsor Castle to be sworn in, he need not have worried on that score – at least, so he thought: 'Much popular feeling at all points of arrival and departure. Audience of H.M. 3–31/2 [p.m.]. I think H.M. was completely satisfied and relieved.'[2] However, Conservatives around the court thought differently. Lady Salisbury consoled Lord Beaconsfield with the thought: 'Depend upon it the Great Lady is right. It will not last long.'[3]

Gladstone, in fact, faced several problems. If anything, his cabinet was rather too Whig in composition: most of its members were aristocrats or their connections, with only Bright, Chamberlain and Forster (and possibly Gladstone himself) representatives of radical opinion. This may, in part, have been because he wanted to console the Whigs at his own elevation and the consequent demotion of Granville and Hartington. It was, however, a brave attempt by Gladstone to ensure that the Party stayed together, but that would depend more on the policies the new government adopted.

DOMESTIC LEGISLATION, 1880–1885

There are two preliminary points that need to be made with regard to the domestic legislation of Gladstone's second ministry. First, the legislative measures passed by this ministry seem to be relatively less important than those passed by his first, although this point is open to debate. The second is that the domestic legislation of Gladstone's second ministry was often impinged on, if not overwhelmed by, successive crises in foreign and imperial affairs, and of this there is no doubt. There were, nevertheless, several Acts of Parliament concerning domestic issues passed during this time in office that warrant their due share of attention.

Even leaving aside questions relating to the Transvaal, Egypt and Ireland, Gladstone had plenty to do. There was one initial problem he found difficult to deal with and which would not go away. A successful candidate in the 1880 election was Charles Bradlaugh, elected MP for Northampton. Bradlaugh was a defiant freethinker, republican and, worse still, an atheist. When called for, he refused to swear the oath of allegiance demanded of all MPs on their arrival at the Commons and wished instead to affirm (as witnesses could do in court, thanks to Bradlaugh). The Speaker refused to allow this, and a House of Commons committee decided, by one vote, that Bradlaugh should not be allowed to take his seat and called for a by-election to be held. Thus a struggle began between the Commons and the electors of Northampton, who continued to re-elect Bradlaugh, which lasted until 1885 when he at last agreed to take the oath; six years later, in February 1891, a Religious Disabilities Removal Act was finally passed allowing new MPs to affirm.

It is, perhaps, difficult to grasp now how much heat the Bradlaugh case generated. Many Liberal MPs spoke out strongly against any measure that would allow affirmation; but there was one who did not. Gladstone, from the first, addressed the House in Bradlaugh's favour, even though he openly disagreed with his opinions. It is correct to see this as an example of his increasingly 'liberal' world view: forty-five years earlier he had said anyone who was not a Christian was unfit to govern the country and should not, therefore, be allowed into Parliament.

In 1880 the Gladstone government passed the Employers' Liability Act. In itself this was a modest measure, but it did make it somewhat easier for employees to sue their employers, and it showed that the state was now prepared to interfere, at least to an extent, with the absolute freedom of contract. In part, to show the government was not just anti-industrialist, an Act was passed directed against the rural landowners. The Ground Game Act allowed tenants certain rights to kill rabbits and other nuisances on their land. Additionally, as part of his June budget, Gladstone removed the malt tax, placing instead a duty on beer, a step which benefited farmers while attacking brewers – a group for whom Gladstone, remembering Bruce's Licensing Act and the backlash against it experienced in the 1874 election, had no particular love. The budget itself was generally seen as a success, even though, as one of its proposals, Gladstone added 1d to the income tax. As a reward to Liberal Nonconformists, Gladstone also saw through the Burials Acts: now, at last, Nonconformists could be buried in proper, consecrated, ground alongside members of the Church of England.

Taken together the domestic legislation of the 1880 session marked a promising start for the new government; unfortunately, it was not to be continued in 1881, when imperial and Irish matters came to the fore. In 1882 Lord Selborne, the Lord Chancellor, secured the passage of the Married Women's Property Act, an extension of an Act of 1870. By this Act, married women were allowed rights regarding earnings and property (they were now allowed to keep both in their own names) that were already granted to single women. In the 1883 session the Corrupt and Illegal Practices Act was passed. This Act, the significance of which has been increasingly appreciated recently, put firm limits on electioneering practices: the amount of money candidates could spend was restricted, and unpaid volunteers, rather than professional agents, were to undertake canvassing. These measures still hold good.

Gladstone himself had little direct role in the framing of this legislation, though of course he played his part in seeing it through. Even so, now in his seventies, he was still a busy man. However, the death of Beaconsfield in April 1881 had given him pause for thought, and the effort of getting controversial Irish legislation through and dealing with the Egyptian crisis kept him in the Commons for longer and longer periods of time – no less than 148 hours in July 1882, for example. It is not surprising therefore that in December of that year he retreated a little and handed the Exchequer to Hugh Childers. Nor is it surprising he was beginning to tell his colleagues with increasing frequency that probably fairly soon he would have to retire. What is unexpected perhaps is that he did not retire, and that he remained leader of the Liberal Party until well into the 1890s. Quite why he did not step down earlier is a matter for debate. His own reasons varied: he would have to stay on to ensure the unity of the Party, and, as time went on, he felt he had to stay on to see the Irish legislation through. But Gladstone was adept at finding reasons for staying in office: he had done so in 1861, even though he had opposed Palmerston's defence policy, so he stayed on in 1881 too. The underlying reason was probably the same: Gladstone was a politician and he liked being prime minister, despite the burdens of the job. He stayed on because he wanted to.

By the autumn of 1883 Gladstone had come to the conclusion that the time had come to revisit the question of popular representation. In doing so he was to run up against opposition, and not only from the Conservatives, but also from Hartington and the Whigs. What precipitated his decision at this point is difficult to say: there were no popular cries for this kind of reform, and socialist pressure groups (such as the Social Democratic Federation of H.M. Hyndman, founded in 1881) were of insignificant importance. It may be, as Crosby suggests, that some of Joseph Chamberlain's comments over the summer had prompted him into action. There was some force behind Chamberlain's demands. As one of the leaders of the radical elements in the Party, he began, in August 1881, to co-ordinate the publication of a series of articles on a Radical Programme in the *Fortnightly Review*. These articles, which covered matters like religious equality, the distribution of taxation, and attacks on landlords and the evils of slum housing, were to have a long-term impact on Liberal thinking – after, indeed, Chamberlain had left the Party – but in 1885 their effect was lessened by the reform acts. It may be, therefore, that Gladstone decided to take on parliamentary reform to outbid Chamberlain and divert attention from some other issues of social reform he did not really want to tackle.

A rather different point, made by Matthew, is that Gladstone had for some time had plans for further parliamentary reform and had already as early as 1881 thought it would be a good idea to leave a year, like 1884, 'free' for legislation about it. Either way, Gladstone spent much time on his September 1883 cruise to Scandinavia reflecting on the future of British politics. When he returned to England he had a wide-ranging vision of what was needed in the way of parliamentary reform, and proposed a measure that was to consist of three elements: first, that there was to be a new franchise qualification – essentially, the householder franchise introduced into English towns in 1867 was to be extended to the counties; second, that there was to be a redistribution of seats; and, third, that the measure was to be enacted in the whole of the United Kingdom, which would therefore, for the first time, include Ireland. Gladstone was determined one bill should be introduced which would cover all of these aspects of the reform question. When the matter came up for discussion in the cabinet on 22 November, there was a furious row between Chamberlain and Hartington, the Secretary for War, which Gladstone found difficult to calm; Hartington was calling for the abandonment of the combined franchise reform and redistribution measure, and for not including Ireland in the proposal. By the end of the year the matter had still not been definitely settled, and on 31 December Gladstone and Hartington had a meeting about it that lasted for some two and a half hours. At the meeting, Gladstone warned Hartington that he would have to resign if agreement could not be reached. He went on to tell the Secretary for War what he thought the effects would be if Hartington's ideas were adopted.

> I urged principally
>
> a) The ruin of the party, immediately, or else in a short time hence, and the prospect of its re-forming hereafter under extreme [he meant Chamberlain's] auspices,
> b) the fearful evil of branding Ireland with political inequality – the only way which could make her really dangerous.[4]

In the end, a compromise was reached. It was agreed at a cabinet meeting on 3 January 1884 that the proposed Bill would include the extension of the franchise and be extended to Ireland, but that the redistribution part of it would be left out, to be included in a measure to be brought in later in the 1884 session. So far, so good: now all the government had to do was draft the Bill and get it passed by the Commons, the Lords and the Queen. It was not going to be an easy ride.

The passage of the reform measures in the 1884–5 sessions became increasingly mixed up with events in the Sudan – though it is best to treat them separately here, as the story is complicated enough. The Representation of the People Bill was introduced in February 1884 and passed the Commons without difficulty, although it caused Gladstone to go on record as an opponent of women's suffrage; he claimed this, if it was included, would give the Lords an excuse to reject the whole measure. But, on 8 July, the Lords duly rejected it anyway. In an astute move, knowing full well the turmoil the question had already caused in the cabinet, the peers declared they would only be able to accept it if it was combined with a Redistribution Bill. Gladstone was furious: by blocking the Representation of the People Bill the Lords had blocked the will of 'the nation'; but he would not dissolve Parliament: he would see a Reform measure through, come what may.

Over the summer recess Chamberlain organised a 'Peers versus People' campaign. He managed to get some 100,000 people to a reform meeting in Hyde Park, and, for the first time in several years, Gladstone found the opportunity to address 'the people'. Compared with the tumults of 1831–2 and 1866–7, however, this was all pretty tame. Armed with this degree of popular support, Gladstone, on 24 October, reintroduced the Representation Bill in the Commons. But in November he began behind-the-scenes negotiations with the Conservatives' nominal head, Sir Stafford Northcote. Northcote told Salisbury that Gladstone's furtive approach suggested he was anxious for a settlement to be reached which he could then put to his own party. Salisbury proved amenable, and on 17 November Granville and Gladstone told their respective Houses that, if the Lords passed the Representation Bill, redistribution would be discussed as a separate issue by the two parties.

Some radicals were displeased; it seemed that the Commons had been humiliated by the Lords – but Sir Charles Dilke, for one, was not. He accompanied Gladstone, Salisbury and Northcote to meetings in Downing Street in the week after 19 November. Curiously enough, in this instance, it seemed Salisbury was the more radical, his calls for redistribution on the grand scale being accepted by the Liberal leadership. The agreed measure was presented to the Commons on 1 December and, five days later, the Lords passed the third reading of the Representation Bill. Those Liberals in the Commons who were unhappy about the bargain kept it pretty much to themselves, and, after quiet debates in both Houses, the Redistribution Bill became law on 25 June 1885, after Gladstone had resigned office.

Taken together, these two Acts represented a radical reform of the British electoral system. The number of voters increased in one bound from just over two and a half million to over five and a half million – a remarkable increase that far outstrips both the 'Great Reform Act' of 1832 and the Conservative Reform Act of 1867, though still a long way short of democracy. As a percentage the figure had more or less doubled: from 30.3% to 61% (in 1891) of the male population. It meant that in England at least, agricultural labourers and smallholders now had the vote, while in Ireland farmers with medium-sized land holdings were allowed to register. Gladstone no doubt hoped that those newly-enfranchised electors would reward the Liberal Party – but the example of what happened to Disraeli's Conservatives in 1868 might have stood as a warning.

The redistribution of seats, too, was not necessarily going to operate in the Liberals' favour (something of which Salisbury was well aware). Overall, 132 seats were made available for redistribution, thanks mainly to the reduction of the number of seats in many boroughs from two to one. The Greater London area gained forty, up to sixty-two seats, and extra ones were added to many of the northern industrial towns – in both cases, significantly enough, areas where Conservatives were gaining ground among the 'white-collar' workers.

Gladstone's efforts in these matters have been carefully studied. With knowledge of the election results of 1885, it is easy for historians to argue he had been outmanoeuvred by the Conservatives playing on the Grand Old Man's anxieties about a clash with the Lords. The settlement also, of course, still left many men, and all women, without the vote, and they would have no reason to be content with it. On the other hand, as an act of statesmanship it had considerable merits, amending the parliamentary system in a way that recognised the changing shifts of population and working patterns. It was unfortunate that these changes were not working in favour of the Liberal Party, and that, even as early as this, some of the seeds of the destruction of that great Victorian institution were already being sown.

FOREIGN AND IMPERIAL POLICY: 1880–1885

It was questions of foreign and imperial policy as much as anything that had brought Gladstone back to power. His criticisms of what he called 'Beaconsfieldism' revolved around the flamboyant and disastrous foreign policy of the previous administration – Isandhlwana was remembered. But his second term as prime minister was almost fatally undermined by its own overseas policy and difficulties, especially in Southern Africa, and in Egypt and the Sudan; and if Beaconsfield's Afghan and Zululand involvement had caused him problems, Gladstone's problems over Khartoum were no less serious.

Granville returned to the Foreign Office in April 1880. The first thing he and Gladstone had to do was to deal finally with the Treaty of Berlin. One matter connected with it was the occupation of the island of Cyprus, which Salisbury and Beaconsfield – rather curiously for a supposed pro-Ottoman government – had taken from the Ottomans as the price for their support against the Russians. Gladstone, Granville and their backbenchers, not being very pro-Ottoman themselves, had no problems with this policy, and the occupation of Cyprus was to be of considerable use later on when things developed in Egypt.

In Afghanistan, the ruler favoured by the British, Abdul Rahman, a nephew of Sher Ali, was recognised as Emir, but in July 1880 Ayub Khan, another claimant, marched against Kandahar. The British force sent against him was badly defeated at Maiwand on 27 July and the British garrison in Kandahar besieged. Fortunately for the British, their senior commander in Afghanistan, General Sir Frederick Roberts, successfully marched to its relief and defeated Ayub Khan. This restored British prestige, but confirmed a decision already taken in London that British troops should be withdrawn from Afghanistan, leaving Abdul Rahman in control.

In South Africa, one thing had not changed with the new government in Britain – Sir Bartle Frere, the mastermind behind the Zulu war, stayed in post. Gladstone himself did not want to remove Frere. He thought he would be the best man to carry forward the preferred policy of Confederation that Carnarvon had embarked on in 1877.

Besides, as the Queen herself reminded Gladstone, he had promised her he would not be making changes in personnel like this. But at the end of July 1880 news was received that the most pro-British of the provincial assemblies, the Cape Parliament, had, in Gladstone's words: 'Put confederation wholly out of view, for a time quite indefinite, and almost certainly considerable'.[5] With this knowledge and a growing awareness that the Liberal backbenchers would be pleased if they did something, the Gladstone cabinet recalled Frere. Beyond that, they did nothing, leaving the confederation policy as their only option, but knowing that the Boer inhabitants of the Transvaal and Orange Free State wanted their independence from the British Empire, rather than annexation to it.

In December 1880 a large Boer force gathered at Parderkraal in the Orange Free State. News that something was wrong – very wrong, indeed – did not reach London until the 30th of that month and Gladstone and the cabinet took little notice, having Ireland very much on their minds. It was assumed the British Army, and their highly-rated commander, General Sir George Pomeroy Colley, could deal with the situation. Attempts in London to find a political solution were undermined by the general's activities on the spot to find a military one. But, as Colley and the British Army were to learn to their cost – although they seem to have forgotten their lesson from some eighteen years later – the Boers were not easy opponents. Colley was instructed to call on the Boers to suspend hostilities and wait for a British Commission of Inquiry. He sent the message to the Boers, but before receiving any answer, he and his men occupied Majuba Hill on 26 February 1881. The next morning the Boers attacked and, in a battle that has gone down as one of the British Army's least successful, they defeated the British force and killed its general. Gladstone learned of the disaster three days later, as he lay in bed recovering from a head injury received when he slipped in snow on leaving a dinner with the Prince and Princess of Wales. He was devastated. Now he would have to put South Africa at the top of his political agenda.

What should he do? Many, including the Queen and most Conservatives, thought the war should be carried on and the defeat at Majuba 'avenged'. It might then be possible, as an act of both kindness and generosity, to grant the Boers what they wanted. Gladstone thought otherwise; even before the defeat, the British had already started negotiations with the Boers, and now, he thought, these should be brought to a conclusion. He told the Commons in July that:

> It would have been most unjust and cruel, it would have been cowardly and mean, if on account of these defensive operations we had refused to go forward with the negotiations which, before the first of these miscarriages had occurred, we had already declared that we were willing to promote and undertake.[6]

General Wood, Colley's successor, thought he could defeat the Boers easily enough, but this time the British government refused to allow itself to be dictated to by one of its generals. As a result, an armistice was signed, a commission sent out and in August a convention was 'negotiated' with the Boers at Pretoria. By this it was agreed that the Transvaal and Orange Free State were independent states, subject only to British 'suzerainty', though no one defined exactly what that meant. The Boers were not particularly happy with the agreement, feeling they had not really had any say in its negotiation and that it was imposed on them, but, for the moment, they accepted it.

With the problems in Afghanistan and southern Africa out of the way, at least for the time being, the Gladstone government soon found itself involved in an even bigger difficulty in Egypt. The recent history of Egypt had not been an especially happy one. In particular, the financial state of the country had not improved despite the selling of the government's Suez Canal shares in 1874, and two years later the Khedive Ismail had suspended his debt payments. As a result, an Anglo-French Dual Control Commission was installed, to put Egypt to financial rights, or, as its enemies said, to arrange things so that Egypt's considerable foreign debt could be paid. This meant two things for Egyptians: increases in taxes and cuts in government expenditure. Neither expedient made the foreign Control Commissioners popular. As with the Boers, the Gladstone government's accession to power made no real difference to Egypt, where the high-handed British Commissioner, Sir Evelyn Baring, carried on as before.

In 1881 grievances in the Egyptian army, caused by the cuts imposed resulted in mutiny and the ruling Khedive (installed by the Europeans in place of his father in 1878) made no attempts to crush it – perhaps because of his inadequacy or, as is more likely, because he recognised it for what it was, a genuine national revolt, and sympathised with it. The story which then unfolded is, so it appears, straightforward and easily told. In the course of 1881 a new nationalist leader, Colonel Ahmed Arabi, effectively seized power in Egypt, forcing the Khedive in January 1882 to dismiss the prime minister and making himself minister of war. This was followed by negotiations and failed attempts to interest the Ottoman government in restoring order in what was still nominally their province. After riots in Alexandria on 11–12 June, when the Egyptians killed some fifty foreigners, the Control Commissioners requested help from their home governments.

In response, by the beginning of July, Admiral Sir Beauchamp Seymour RN, with ten battleships and other gunboats and a French naval squadron, had anchored off Alexandria. But the French government, distracted by one of the domestic crises to which the Third Republic was so prone, ordered their vessels away, and so it was left to the Royal Navy to deal with the increasingly threatening situation. The Egyptians, far from being overawed by the warships, had begun to add to the fortifications at Alexandria, and Seymour asked the British government what to do. He was told to tell the Egyptians to stop work on the forts and, if they did not, to use force to make them. When his ultimatum was rejected on 11 July, Seymour's ships opened fire in a terrific bombardment that achieved very little, but it was enough to persuade the Egyptians to abandon their defence.

As a result of this, Gladstone's government decided law and order and the Khedive's authority would have to be restored, and the only way this could be done was by using the British Army. Accordingly, one of the country's leading generals, Sir Garnet Wolseley, was despatched to Egypt, and, in a model operation that climaxed in the battle of Tel-el-Kebir on 13 September and the capture of Arabi the following day, ended the mutiny. Gladstone was pleased: Arabi, whom he saw as a military dictator of the worst sort, was in custody and all would soon be well. Then the British could leave Egypt to her own devices. The British government therefore found it easy to promise the other powers (especially the French, who felt aggrieved that Egypt, Napoleon's old stamping ground, was now effectively a British possession) they would leave – a promise they repeated sixty-six times before finally withdrawing in 1920.

The story, then, is simple. This was a typical imperial peacekeeping operation which Gladstone, though no friend of imperialism, was able to approve. Unfortunately, it is not so straightforward, as there is considerable debate about exactly why the British got themselves so involved in Egypt. The traditionally accepted view is that they did so because they perceived a threat to the Suez Canal, a vital stage on the route to India, and acted to safeguard the waterway. Even Gladstone had confessed to Granville on 7 July that, 'we were bound to protect the Suez Canal',[7] was music to the ears of Hartington, to whom Granville was writing, and who was one of the interventionists in the cabinet. Add to that the danger posed to European life and property in Egypt, and Gladstone's belief that Britain was undertaking an act on behalf of Europe, and the explanation for British intervention is clear.

But still the question must be asked whether the Suez Canal was actually in danger. To at least one witness in Egypt, Wilfred Scawen Blunt, it was not. Blunt knew Arabi and was himself a liberal, and he supplied Gladstone and his colleagues with evidence that Arabi was not an unthinking military despot, and that law and order was not completely disappearing in Egypt. However, a lot of other people were prepared to say quite the opposite, painting a picture of Egypt's descent into anarchy with the canal under real threat. Their testimony has lately come under scrutiny and it has been convincingly argued that it cannot be relied upon: it was in their interest to argue the canal was under threat and thus involve Britain in Egypt to safeguard their holdings in Egyptian government stocks and share holdings in the Suez Canal Company – if an Egyptian nationalist such as Arabi took power in Egypt he might stop the payment of debts to Europeans, and so he would have to be removed. Gladstone's government, therefore, was misled by 'the men on the spot' into taking action. Interestingly enough, among those holding Egyptian bonds – worth £19,400 – was the Prime Minister himself.

It seems too much to suggest that Gladstone sanctioned the intervention in Egypt in a blatant act to safeguard his own investments. He convinced himself of the reality of the threat to the canal – after all, he was hearing from every side it was threatened, and of the wickedness of Arabi. It still seems ironic, however, that it was an apparently anti-imperialist government, led by one of the firmest of all anti-imperialist prime ministers, which should have taken the step which, if Robinson and Gallagher are correct, began the sequence of events that are called the 'Scramble for Africa'.

The occupation of Egypt in September 1882 was far from being the end of the Gladstone government's involvement in north-east Africa. When the British became the de facto rulers of Egypt – the Khedive's authority, though apparently restored, now clearly rested on the British garrison – they also took on some of the country's other difficulties. One of these problems, and a contribution to the domestic financial plight of the Egyptian government, was events further south in the Nile valley, in the Sudan. Ever since the days of Mehemet Ali in the 1830s, the Egyptian government had tried to retain control of this region, which was a source both of raw materials and prestige. Egyptian rule in the Sudan was not noted for its efficiency or its benevolence, however, and in 1881 a charismatic individual from Dongola, Mohammed Ahmed, declared himself the 'Mahdi', or 'expected one', who, at the very least, would rid the Sudan of the hated Egyptian rulers. He began a campaign against outlying Egyptian garrisons, and Egyptian authority to the south began to totter.

From the start, Gladstone was determined that his government would have as little as possible to do with the Sudan. As early as 2 November, just six weeks after Tel-el-Kebir, he said so, publicly:

> It is no part of the duty incumbent upon us to restore order in the Sudan. It is politically connected with Egypt in consequence of its very recent conquest; but it has not been included in the sphere of our operations, and we are by no means disposed to admit without qualification that it is within the sphere of our responsibility.[8]

But things went from bad to worse. The British could not stop the Egyptian government's despatch of an army southwards in September 1883 to restore their 'authority' in the Sudan, even though it was commanded by a British officer, Colonel William Hicks. Initially successful, Hicks's army was defeated at Berber on 5 November and he himself was killed. Now Gladstone could act: the cabinet came to a decision that the Egyptians should evacuate the Sudan. This was a decision the Egyptian government did not like and it accordingly resigned, but it was one the British would not allow to be overturned. It had the support of Sir Evelyn Baring in Cairo, but sections of the increasingly imperialist

British press were not altogether happy, seeing it as a British, rather than an Egyptian, retreat. Gladstone, though, was determined: the Sudan was a useless drain on Egyptian resources and for that reason alone would be best left. But he also had another reason for wanting the Egyptians out, and he was not afraid to communicate it to the House of Commons when he declared in May 1884 that the Sudanese were 'people struggling to be free, and they are struggling rightly to be free'. It was a pronouncement he was to regret later.

One of the problems with the withdrawal was there remained several Egyptian garrisons scattered around the Sudan, including that in the regional capital, Khartoum. If withdrawal was to be successful these troops (and possibly their families) would have to be collected together in Khartoum and taken back down the Nile. To organise and oversee this operation would take someone exceptional. As it happened, there was such a man who had the appropriate military experience; he had fought against rebels in China in the 1850s, and he even had experience of working in the Sudan, where he had spent time in the 1870s working for the Khedive. Unfortunately, he was about to take up a post for the king of the Belgians, Leopold II, in his so-called 'Congo Free State' and so, if he was to be appointed, it would have to be done quickly. His name was Lieutenant General Charles George Gordon.

The decision to send Gordon to the Sudan was not Gladstone's, since he was out of London when Granville, Hartington, Northbrook and Dilke met in a room at the War Office to interview him. Gladstone warned Granville to be sure Gordon would not exceed his instructions and involve Britain in the affairs of the Sudan. Many people wanted Gordon to go. They included Wolseley, the crusading Liberal journalist W.T. Stead, and much of 'public opinion' as reflected in the newspapers, and so the decision to send him was taken. It was a mistake, because of all the men who could have been sent to evacuate the Sudan, Gordon was the least suitable.

Charles Gordon had an unusual, and in some ways impractical, personality. When his travel arrangements had been made and he arrived at Charing Cross station to begin his journey, he had neither a watch – his friend Wolseley had to give him one – nor money: Granville had to buy his ticket. Gordon also believed he had a mission – he was sent by the Almighty. This mission, as he saw it, was not to evacuate the Sudan and leave the population to Islam: he was going to make sure the Sudan was not abandoned. Once he reached Khartoum, he began to organise the evacuation of the Egyptian garrisons to the city, but there he stopped. Rather than evacuate the Sudan, Gordon remained in Khartoum until surrounded by the forces of the Mahdi. This meant he could not leave – the British Army would have to come to his rescue.

Now began a struggle of wills between two of the strongest personalities of the age: Gordon had only to stay where he was, Gladstone would have to reverse the policy of evacuation and send a British 'relief expedition' to Khartoum. This, he was very reluctant to do, and things moved slowly. As early as the middle of February 1884, the need to 'relieve' Gordon was becoming apparent and by 21 April most of the cabinet, according to Dilke, felt 'an October expedition is certain'.[9] But Gladstone did not think so. The danger was that any British force in the Sudan might effectively make the country a British province. The other point was that Gladstone would not be dictated to. It was only on 8 August that Hartington, who had succeeded Childers at the War Office in December 1882, warned Wolseley to start making preparations for an advance on Khartoum and, at about the same time, the House of Commons was asked for a vote of credit to pay for an expedition. Gladstone was, and still is, the archetypal 'Victorian', and, notwithstanding his 'failures', there can be no doubt that he was a great politician and a truly liberal statesman.

The cabinet had not found it easy to come to a conclusion on what to do about the Sudan question, but Whig pressure played one of several roles in getting Gladstone finally to accept the idea of a 'Gordon relief expedition', which began after Wolseley reached Cairo on 9 September. The story of this expedition is well known, dramatic and unfortunate. Wolseley's advance up the Nile was hindered by rapids, and he sent a detachment – the desert column – overland to try and speed things up. This part of the expedition struggled on against fierce opposition and heat, and two of its commanders were successively killed. On 21 January 1885 four of Gordon's steamers sent down from Khartoum met the desert column, which, on the morning of the 24th, boarded them and set sail for Khartoum. But they arrived too late, because the city had fallen and, although they were not aware of this, Gordon had been killed two days before. On 5 February 1885 Gladstone, who was staying with Hartington at his country house, recorded:

> After 11 am I heard the sad news of the fall or betrayal of Khartoum ... went off by the first train and reached D[owning] Street after 8.15. The circumstances are sad & trying: it is one of the least points about them that they may put an end to this gov't.[10]

The horror and outrage with which the news was greeted was shared in some very high quarters in Britain. The Queen herself sent a telegram – for once, not in code – to Gladstone: 'These news from Khartoum are frightful and to think that all this might have been prevented and many precious lives saved by earlier action is too fearful.[11] This message caused him, for once, to lose his temper with the Queen:

> Mr. Gladstone has had the honor to receive your Majesty's telegram *en clair* relating to the deplorable intelligence received this day from Lord Wolseley ... Mr. Gladstone does not presume to estimate the means of judgment possessed by your Majesty, but so far as his intelligence and recollection at the moment go, he is not altogether able to follow the conclusion which your Majesty has been pleased thus to announce.

Gladstone went on at length to explain to the Queen that there were difficulties in deciding what to do and when to send the troops in the first place, and of climate and terrain in which they operated that led to the failure of the expedition. But, he concluded, of all the difficult questions to answer, perhaps the most difficult were those about

> the reproach of those who might argue that our proper business was the protection of Egypt, that it never was in military danger from the Mahdi, and that the most prudent course would have been to provide it with adequate frontier defences, and to assume no responsibility for the lands beyond the desert.[12]

When the crisis broke, Gladstone could have handled it better. The night Gordon's death was confirmed saw him at the theatre; not a tactful manoeuvre. When he addressed the Commons on the situation, he did not pay tribute to Gordon or to the efforts of Wolseley's troops. On 27 February his ministry survived a vote of censure in the Commons by a majority of only fourteen. Nor was it the only problem in foreign affairs to be faced by the government at this time. On 30 March a Russian force defeated the Afghans at Pendjeh, and a major crisis on India's north-west frontier blew up. In Berlin, a West Africa conference was being held to discuss the future of colonial commitments in that continent, while the Boers of southern Africa were in London to renegotiate the Convention governing Anglo-Boer relations. On top of this, in September 1884, public concern over the state of the Navy surfaced in the so-called 'Navy scare', orchestrated by W.T. Stead and the *Pall Mall Gazette*. All of these developments would cost the government effort and money and popularity. It is not surprising that Gladstone, seeing how unpopular his ministry appeared to be, should have contemplated resignation after the February 1885 vote of censure.

Of all these events, it was those in the Sudan and Afghanistan that did most to hurt the government when they combined together in early 1885. While Gladstone may have had doubts about the Sudanese policy, he had none about that to be followed in Afghanistan. As he put it himself, 'We must do our best to have right done in the matter'.[13] In this case, it meant giving the Afghans British support against Russian encroachment. To pay the costs of war in the Sudan and to cover developments in Afghanistan (the two areas were not distinguished), the government asked for a vote of credit of eleven million pounds, the largest ever peacetime vote for military expenditure. Most Conservatives and many Liberals were happy to support this.

Interestingly, policy in the Sudan soon changed. At first, Wolseley was ordered to 'smash the Mahdi', but in May he was told to evacuate the Sudan – greater things were at stake further east. While reluctant, Wolseley could at least obey orders, and British withdrawal from the interior of the Sudan began. The Russians, taking advantage of Britain's difficulties in the Sudan, had determined to continue their expansion into territory claimed by Afghanistan. Britain, watchful as ever of Russian movements on the north-west frontier of India, viewed with anxiety this development and when the Russians inflicted a defeat on Afghan forces at Pendjeh, moved to support Afghanistan and stand firm against the Russians. They decided, however, to try to put pressure on the Russians in the Black Sea. They failed in this, as the Ottomans refused to let British warships enter the Black Sea. This, however, convinced the Russians that they had no need to worry about British pressure nearer home so that they could afford to be more conciliatory further afield; they had no need to threaten the British in Afghanistan. Accordingly, the British and the Russians agreed to arbitration on 4 May and a new Russo-Afghan boundary was established in September.

Once seen as itself firing the 'starting pistol' for the 'Scramble for Africa', the Berlin West Africa Conference, which opened in November 1884, is now seen as of less significance, and Gladstone himself was not especially involved in it. It seems to have been one way for Bismarck to signal the involvement of the German Empire in imperial diplomacy in Africa. In February 1884 Dilke had negotiated a convention with Portugal that recognised Portuguese claims over the Congo estuary. This, unsurprisingly, upset King Leopold, Bismarck and the French. Since Britain needed German support in Cairo, they abandoned the Dilke Convention in July, and four months later went to Berlin together with the representatives of fourteen other governments. The final treaty of Berlin recognised the anomalous status of Leopold's Congo 'Free State' and laid down rules of 'effective occupation' before territories could be claimed. Immediately after the conference closed, Bismarck, bowing to domestic pressure, annexed four territories in Africa to the German Empire.

Over the next few years European forces 'effectively occupied' nearly all of tropical Africa. This, the most obvious manifestation of the 'new imperialism', was something with which Gladstone was completely out of sympathy, and it was something he believed all Liberals would agree with him about. However, he was to be sadly disappointed where Chamberlain and Rosebery were concerned.

What to do in southern Africa was a special case. President Kruger of the Transvaal visited London to renegotiate the Pretoria Convention of 1881. He wanted the abandonment by Britain of her claims to suzerainty over the Boer Republics. Gladstone had been unhappy with the South African situation for years, and was probably quite pleased that in the London Convention, which was duly agreed in 1884, all reference to British suzerainty was omitted. So far as he was concerned, and so far as Kruger was concerned, it meant the British no longer lay claim to it; it was not how Joseph Chamberlain understood it some fifteen years later. From this uncertainty, another Boer war, lasting longer and doing far more damage than the first, arose.

Gladstone's second ministry survived its foreign difficulties, but they did it severe damage, and Gladstone himself was not immune from the repercussions. In particular, the death of Gordon damaged his reputation, irreparably in some quarters – including with the Queen, not that she liked him anyway. Gladstone did not forgive Gordon, some five years later writing that he was a 'hero', but one who claimed 'the hero's privilege of turning upside down and inside out every idea and intention with which he had left England, and for which he had obtained our approval'.[14] Gordon's death, however, was just the peak of disasters that had started in South Africa in 1881, and particularly in Egypt in 1882. Gladstone's government found itself pursuing a policy in Africa that, while it was more in keeping with the times, was more imperialist even than Beaconsfield's and less in sympathy with the Prime Minister's own views on the imperialist question. It was also to cause him problems in the future.

IRISH POLICY AND THE DEFEAT OF THE GOVERNMENT

The Irish question had played a dominant role in the life of Gladstone's first ministry and, not surprisingly, it was to play a very important one in the second ministry too. By the time he returned to office, Ireland was once more in a state of turmoil. In 1878, a year after his first visit to Ireland, an agricultural depression hit the country, as well as large parts of mainland Britain and Europe. But in Ireland, where many tenants still lived in great insecurity, it was felt keenly very early on, especially in County Mayo. There, relations between landlord and tenant deteriorated to such an extent that a 'land war' broke out. In October 1879 the Irish National Land League was funded under the presidency of the leader of the Irish Home Rule party, Charles Stewart Parnell. Parnell, himself, was in many ways a good Liberal who was out of sympathy with those radicals who had set up the Land League, but he realised that, if properly directed, the League could help him to achieve his ambition of securing a government for Ireland, based in Dublin. His public pronouncements were themselves radical, however, and their effect on the Conservative government profound. In September 1879 Parnell made his position crystal clear: 'The land of this country cannot be cultivated unless the people of the country own it'. Two months later he urged his supporters to keep 'within the law', but that, he said, could include paying no rent if such rent was unjustly high.[15] The landlords and the British government responded aggressively and when Gladstone took office the 'land war' in Ireland was in full swing.

The 1880 elections had done Parnell no harm at all. Nineteen of the twenty-one newly-elected Nationalist MPs were his supporters and he was able to secure undisputed leadership of the party. In October he made public his aim to place Irish government into Irish hands, out of those of the 'English Parliament'. It was clear to Gladstone, therefore, with whom and with what he would have to deal. The fact that it would not be easy for him was soon made apparent by the difficulties surrounding his first Irish measure, the Compensation for Disturbance (Ireland) Bill. This Bill, which was designed to reduce the number of evictions for non-payment of rent, was the brainchild of Forster and was introduced into the cabinet with Chamberlain's support. Getting it through the cabinet, however, was difficult enough with Whig elements, in particular, displaying their hostility to it. It was eventually introduced into the Commons and passed, but was decisively defeated in the Lords on 3 August. Gladstone seems to have felt enough was enough, and decided to let the matter lie.

Rural Ireland was still disturbed, however, and so in November, rather against his better judgement, Gladstone accepted Forster's call for a measure of coercion. This involved the use of imprisonment without trial, and was viewed by Gladstone as one of his Irish Secretary's 'perverted ideas'. The reason he accepted, he later declared, was that his refusal would have 'broken up the government' at a time when its 'mission' – to reconstruct 'the whole spirit and effect' of Britain's foreign policy 'had not yet been fully accomplished'.[16] But Gladstone insisted, if coercion was introduced, it would have to be in conjunction with the opposite policy of 'conciliation'. What this involved was a new, improved version of the 1870 Land Act.

Neither policy was going to be easy to enact. With the opening of the 1881 session of Parliament the Irish Nationalists adopted their own policy of obstruction; they would talk incessantly in the Commons and block any and every measure proposed by the government. The first of these was the Protection of Person and Property Bill, introduced by Gladstone on 31 January. He had decided this would be forced through without an adjournment. After over twenty-four hours' debate the Speaker began to doubt whether this course of action would work, and he eventually agreed with Gladstone to introduce the 'guillotine', or time limit, on debates. Even so, it was over forty-eight hours before this particular debate was brought to a close, and the measure went through. The Lords, not surprisingly, were less concerned by this Bill and by the beginning of March it had become law with Forster and the authorities enforcing it rigorously in Ireland.

Gladstone began serious drafting of a Land Bill in March, and it soon ran into trouble. On the 31st the Duke of Argyll, a friend of Gladstone's (they had been in cabinets together since 1852) resigned in protest against it. Argyll could not accept a measure which, he said, had been brought in only in response to a campaign of terrorism and one which would interfere with the rights of landlords. Gladstone was inflexible; Commissions of Enquiry under the Duke of Richmond and Lord Bessborough had supplied him with ideas of what to do, and he intended to act. The Bill, as eventually put forward, granted to Irish tenants the 'three Fs' they had been demanding throughout the 1870s: tenants should now only have to pay 'fair rents', to be settled by an independent tribunal; they should have 'fixity of tenure' – the right to remain tenants so long as they paid their rents; and they should be allowed the right to 'free sale', selling their tenancy to anyone, at any time they wished.

None of these proposals were particularly outrageous. Landlords would still receive rental payments and if they did not would still be able to find tenants who would pay. They would not, however, be able to demand unreasonable rents that their impoverished tenantry could not afford and then simply expel them and replace them with wealthier people. To contemporaries, though, they were far from reasonable. First, and not least, it was an interference with the hallowed rights of property, with the complete freedom of landlords to do what they wished with their own property. Second, it was drafted in such a way as to render its meaning almost unintelligible to many. When to these sources of hostility is added the ill-feeling borne to Gladstone by the Irish Nationalists because of the Protection of Person and Property Act, it is no surprise that it took one of Gladstone's greatest efforts to see this measure through the Commons. In the end, it needed fifty-eight sittings to secure the passage of the Bill and Gladstone told the Queen that its Committee stage had lasted longer than any bill since the First Reform Bill of 1830. He himself was 'radiant' after it passed. The Lords took less time to deal with it; it seems as if Salisbury simply could not find enough support once the Commons' front line had been broken and Irish landlords themselves seemed prepared to accept it.

Parnell was uncertain what to do. He had criticised the Bill in the Commons, but calculated that, after all, it might help his tenant supporters. He decided they should 'test' the Bill, but even this was enough to convince Forster that Parnell should be arrested under the terms of the Protection of Person and Property Act. His arrest confirmed his popularity with the Irish Nationalist Party, but it was also popular, though for different reasons, in England, as Gladstone discovered when he announced it at the Lord Mayor's banquet in London on 13 October. By the end of the year the Irish government had detained over 800 suspects, including Parnell who was confined in Kilmainham Gaol.

Gladstone spent a lot of time after the 1881 session discussing and reflecting on the possibility of retirement, but, as he was well aware, he still had plenty to do. For one thing, Ireland remained a problem. He had vague notions of dealing with Irish local government in the 1882 session, but this soon aroused sufficient hostility for him to abandon the idea even before Parliament met. However, early in the session he made one of those occasional statements that caused both amazement and horror. He declared that, if the Empire remained intact and imperial matters were decided at Westminster, he did not think there could be any objection to 'an Irish body to deal with Irish legislative affairs'. He then went on, in effect, to invite the Irish Nationalists to come up with some concrete proposals for an Irish assembly. The Queen strongly objected, but Gladstone assured her he was not, nor would he be, proposing 'Home Rule' for Ireland. As he remarked, though, times might change, so it would be helpful to know what exactly the Nationalists wanted.

Quite what Gladstone was doing at this point is hard to say. It might have been that he was 'testing the waters' himself to see how much opposition even a limited 'Home Rule' measure would meet. In other words, it might have been that this was a prelude to the great developments of 1886. On the other hand, it could also have been an occasion when Gladstone had got somewhat 'carried away' and said more than he intended. After all, he was busily telling a lot of people he was soon going to retire, so that there was no chance he would be able to get an Irish Home Rule measure through Parliament. Whichever it was, the pronouncement was soon overwhelmed by other developments relating to Ireland.

The first of these was the opening of cabinet discussions with the detained Parnell. Chamberlain had begun to discuss the future with Captain William O'Shea, who had contacts with Parnell (closer than he might have realised, since O'Shea's wife, Katherine, was Parnell's lover). The result was a letter from Parnell to O'Shea in which he declared that, if the government took steps to amend the Land Act so that tenants in arrears of rent could be helped to pay off their debts before they were evicted, the Nationalists would become full public supporters of law and order. This Gladstone was prepared to do, and the cabinet would go further. On 2 May they agreed to the immediate release of Parnell and two other MPs from Kilmainham gaol, the review of all other cases of detainees and the lapse of the Coercion Acts. Gladstone insisted in the House of Commons that Parnell's release was not the result of a 'deal' between him and the government, but the agreement soon became known as the 'Kilmainham Treaty'.

The whole thing came as a surprise to the Commons and to Forster, who promptly resigned, declaring publicly his opposition to it. Gladstone gave some thought to who should succeed him and decided on a family member and favourite, Lord Frederick Cavendish. It is somewhat strange he did not appoint Chamberlain, who had been involved in the negotiations and who declared he would have felt obliged to accept the offer if made, but he apparently simply did not think of Chamberlain as a possibility.

The Kilmainham Treaty might have marked a new phase in the development of the Irish question, but it was soon undermined. While Parnell was still in prison, other, more desperate characters than he, decided to act, violently, to rid themselves of the unpopular T.H. Burke, Under-Secretary at Dublin Castle. On 6 May they intercepted him in Phoenix Park, Dublin and stabbed him to death. His companion, who happened to be Lord Frederick Cavendish, was murdered with him. Gladstone arrived home from a Saturday evening social round and was told the news by his secretary, Edward Hamilton. His anguish was clear, and he and Catherine soon visited Lady Frederick, but it seems most unlikely he then went back to work, a story that is often reported.

Parnell was appalled and outraged, but he could not undo the damage caused. The extent of this was made apparent on 10 May when the cabinet – after a four-hour debate – agreed to introduce a Bill renewing the suspension of the right to trial by jury. It did not, however, prevent the dejected Gladstone from introducing, five days later, the Arrears of Rent (Ireland) Bill, diverting money from surplus revenues of the Church of Ireland to help pay off arrears. This proposal caused outrage in the Conservative ranks and Balfour went on record with his description of the proposal, based as it was on a deal made with Parnell and his supporters and drafted immediately after the Phoenix Park murders, as a deal which 'stood alone in its infamy'. Gladstone was deeply hurt by this, and made it known to his daughter Helen, hoping no doubt the news would find its way to Balfour. (Helen was Vice Principal of Newnham College and the principal was Balfour's sister.) It did not, however, prevent the measure from going through, and in time it did a good deal to help bring matters in rural Ireland under control.

By the end of the year Gladstone celebrated the fiftieth anniversary of his entry into the House of Commons. Those who supported him greeted the occasion with suitable celebration; those who did not with something less than congratulations. The Irish MPs were among those who had limited reason to be grateful to him. He did not follow up the Arrears Act with any further Irish legislation during the 1883 session and disappointed those in both the Irish and Liberal parties who had hoped for more reforming measures. The idea of an Elective Council Bill which would have allowed regions the smallest degree of 'home rule' in local matters, was not proceeded with. The hope now was that 1884 would produce something more.

It did. The big domestic issue of the 1884 session related to parliamentary reform, to which question Gladstone had given considerable thought in the previous year. From the start he was convinced that any measure should be inclusive, both in what it covered (the franchise and the redistribution of seats) and in where it covered. It would, 'I think', he told Hartington, 'be impolitic and inequitable to exclude Ireland … I believe too that the exclusion would ensure failure.'[17] He decided the Irish franchise should be amended, to be on the same terms as that in the rest of Britain, and therefore Irish counties and boroughs should receive household suffrage. This, the Irish government hoped, might reduce somewhat the influence of the tenant farmers.

The Irish Nationalist MPs seem to have appreciated that the Franchise Bill, as initially proposed, would give some advantages and (like most Liberals) did not oppose it. They had good reason not to, in

Gladstone's own opinion. Combined with the changes under the redistribution measure, he thought it would enable the Nationalist Party to almost double its seats in the Commons. Parnell himself seems to have been of the same opinion, so the Irish stood aside as the Liberal and Conservative struggle over the Bill raged on. Once it was passed, however, Parnell and his supporters would once again feel themselves free to act as they wished.

Early in 1885 a new proposal entered the arena. This was something brought forward in the cabinet by the radicals, Dilke and Chamberlain, having originated with Parnell. The idea was that there should be locally-elected county councils in Ireland, each one of which would send representatives to a 'Central Board' that would have the responsibility of overseeing the Irish central government departments. The heads of the Irish government in Dublin Castle did not like the idea at all since it represented a reduction of their more or less autocratic power (though they found more palatable reasons for opposition to present to the cabinet – in particular, the measure left the position of Irish MPs uncertain). Gladstone himself was broadly sympathetic to it, though he did not come out strongly in support of it, and did not pay much attention to its passage in cabinet. Chamberlain fell out with Parnell – not the best way of supporting a proposal based on his ideas. The result of these factors was that on 9 May 1885 the cabinet nervously voted against bringing the proposal forward.

The failure of the radicals to carry the Central Board proposal was to have grave repercussions. Chamberlain, in particular, was furious with Gladstone. He was convinced that the lackadaisical attitude of the 'Grand Old Man' had done most to defeat the measure; had he supported it more strongly it would have got through. In future, the Birmingham Radical would find it more difficult to co-operate with the Liverpudlian Liberal. Why Gladstone had not supported it strongly seems fairly obvious. The efforts of securing the passage of the Reform and Redistribution Bills had been so great that Gladstone was tired. He was probably thinking quite seriously about retirement. The preoccupations of events in the Sudan continued to press heavily on him as well, and he simply did not have the energy to give the proposal his full attention. But he was aware of its importance. As he told Lord Spencer, the Viceroy in Dublin, the scheme was as 'dead as mutton for the present, though as I believe for the present only. It will quickly rise again

& as I think perhaps in larger dimensions.'[18] That prediction was to come true within the year.

Gladstone's second ministry was brought to an end very suddenly on 8 June 1885. But there were severe strains in the cabinet before this. Calculations showed there was a likely budget deficit of four million pounds for 1885–6, while a note of credit for eleven million pounds would be needed to cover Afghan and Sudanese operations. Added to this was Parnell's increasing awareness that the Liberals would do nothing for him and therefore he should look elsewhere for support. Gladstone warned his colleagues on 8 June that there was a possibility the government might be defeated on the budget. Sure enough, they were defeated that evening by a combined body of 264 Conservative and Irish Nationalist votes to 252 Liberal. Some seventy-six Liberal MPs had not turned up to vote. Gladstone adjourned the House and telegraphed the Queen the news she was no doubt pleased to hear – that he intended to resign.

Salisbury was understandably cautious about taking office. He could not call an election until the question of redistribution had been dealt with and his party therefore remained a minority in the House of Commons. Without some assurances from Gladstone that the Liberals would not oppose necessary measures such as financial supplies, it would not be able to do anything. (There may also have been anxieties about divisions in his own party, which being in office was likely to bring out into the open.) Behind-the-scenes negotiations involving the Queen and her staff and Salisbury's nephew, A.J. Balfour, lasted until 23 June, before he finally agreed to form a government and Gladstone's second ministry came to an end.

Gladstone may not have been altogether upset by his defeat. Ireland was only one of a number of problems. Not all Liberals had been happy with the reform measures, and many were angered by the death of Gordon and developments in the Sudan and South Africa. But it was Ireland that had also been the cause of the most serious divisions in the party and in the cabinet, which Gladstone had been unable to heal. It might be better to let the Conservatives into office for a while, until an election could be held under the new franchise, to give the Liberals the chance to reflect on the future. Hopefully, after an election, they would once more be back in office with a secure majority.

Gladstone's second ministry had lasted through five tumultuous years. Of its domestic legislation, there can be no doubt that the Reform and Redistribution Acts of 1885 were the most important measures. Though these did not introduce universal manhood suffrage, they did significantly increase the voting population. Whether or not these new voters would support the Liberals would have to be seen. In terms of foreign policy, however, it had not been a success. Far from reversing the Beaconsfield government's policy of expansion of the Empire, Gladstone's government had actually continued it with the occupation of Egypt. Withdrawal in South Africa and from the Sudan was countered by attendance at the Berlin West Africa Conference and a stridently anti-Russian policy over Pendjeh. The fact was that Europe, as a whole, was becoming a more imperialist-minded place, with Paris seeking compensation for its 1871 humiliation and Berlin its 'rightful' place in the 'sun'. These feelings would spread and become even more intense over the remainder of the century, but they were feelings with which Gladstone had less and less sympathy. The defeat in 1885 was not, therefore, an unmixed disaster for him: now he would have time to plan for the future.

LEADER OF THE OPPOSITION, JUNE 1885–JANUARY 1886

The months between the defeat of Gladstone's second ministry and the formation of his third were to witness one of the greatest and most controversial developments in his political career. There were some hopes that his second defeat would mark the end of Gladstone's public life. One who particularly shared this hope was the Queen, who on 13 June wrote to him to offer him an earldom. It would be, she said, 'very gratifying to her' if he would accept the offer – as no doubt it would have been because it would have removed Gladstone from activity in the Commons. But Gladstone, grateful as he was, politely declined on the main grounds that he could still render the Queen more valuable service in the Commons than in the Lords.[19] To quash any idea that he might stand down from the leadership of the Liberal Party in the Commons, he told his ex-cabinet colleagues in a circular that he was going to take up his 'usual' seat on the opposition front bench.

Gladstone was not, at seventy-five, a young man, and his health, unsurprisingly, began to cause him problems. He had started to be concerned about his speaking powers in June 1885, and, when he was relieved of the cares of office, his voice deteriorated badly. A visit to Oxford in early July made things worse, but did not stop him speaking in the Commons for an hour. His medical advisers told him bluntly he must not attend the Commons and sent for a specialist, Dr Felix Semon. Dr. Semon diagnosed 'chronic laryngeal catarrh' and prescribed drastic treatment for it. It was, the specialist declared, caused by Gladstone's continued public speaking and the strain on his throat. Between 18 July and 8 August, Gladstone had to take medicine and be treated with 'interior applications to the vocal chords as well as by galvanism outside'. These 'applications' continued throughout the summer, and prevented Gladstone from repeating the triumphs of his 1879 Midlothian election campaign.

This rather dubious medical treatment may have been beneficial, but what probably did Gladstone more good was a period of rest and a summer cruise. On 8 August he and Catherine began a three-week cruise with Sir Thomas and Lady Brassey in their yacht *Sunbeam*. This took them on a very restful visit to Norway, where, unlike in Denmark in 1883, there was no royalty to meet or entertain. Gladstone recovered his health very quickly, despite some residual difficulties with his voice, and returned from the trip revitalised and ready for action.

He would need to be. Salisbury's government was not really in office long enough to achieve much in domestic or imperial policy, but they did have plans for Ireland. One thing they wanted was to keep the support of their new-found ally, Parnell. To this end they announced they would not renew the 1882 Coercion Act, thus overturning their previous hard-line policy on Irish law and order and denouncing Spencer as too severe, when they had before argued he was not severe enough. They also passed the 'Ashbourne Act', which, by offering tenants loans at a low rate of interest, enabled them to buy their property – a more effective measure in this respect than Gladstone's 1870 and 1881 Land Acts. The Conservative Lord Carnarvon arranged to meet Parnell – in private – so the two could discuss what it was Parnell wanted of them. Whatever it was, the Conservatives seemed to offer enough – or the Liberals too little – since, when the election campaign began in earnest in November, Parnell urged Irish voters in Britain to vote Conservative.

Gladstone spent a lot of his time in opposition devising a definite policy for the future of Ireland. As early as July he began writing and discussing Irish policy with leading Liberal figures. The key to this policy, he had decided by November 1885, was a measure of Home Rule. In fact, Gladstone had been in contact himself with Parnell, through the intermediacy of Mrs O'Shea, to see exactly what he had in mind. When Gladstone received Parnell's 'proposed constitution for Ireland', he reflected on it and then, on 14 November, 'sketched' his own ideas:

1. Irish Chamber for Irish affairs.
2. Irish representation to remain as now for Imperial affairs.
3. Equitable division of imperial charges by fixed proportions.
4. Protection of minority.
5. Suspension of imperial authority for all civil purposes whatsoever.[20]

What Gladstone meant was there should be an Irish parliament to deal with all Irish affairs under the same royal prerogatives as the Parliament at Westminster, but that the burdens of the national debt should be shared. He also intended that subjects such as defence and foreign policy should be deemed as 'imperial' and discussed only at Westminster. In essence, this proposal is similar to the powers granted to the newly federated Canadian colonies by the British North America Act of 1867. It is noteworthy that he showed some awareness of an 'Ulster problem' even at this rather early date.

It was one thing to draw up a Home Rule proposal such as this, but quite another to see it into law. Gladstone would have to 'sell it' to his former cabinet colleagues, to the Liberal party as a whole, to the British and Irish public and, most difficult of all, to the Conservative-dominated House of Lords. He was well aware of all of this and very anxious not to appear to go too far, too soon. Lord Rosebery, who was his host at the time he received Parnell's message and drafted his own sketch, did not get a sight of either Parnell's or Gladstone's ideas. The furthest Gladstone would go, even to his closest cabinet colleagues, was that no plan for Ireland should be publicly produced – although, by omission, he now admitted to having one himself.

Given the tremendous uproar the Home Rule issue caused, and the extent to which the issue dominated the last years of Gladstone's (political) life, the matter of how he came to the decision to support the proposal has received considerable attention from historians. All kinds of questions are raised by it, such as what brought Gladstone round to it, whether it was a sudden change of mind on his part and whether he realised quite how much trouble it was going to cause. It may be, as Richard Shannon suggests, Gladstone wanted a justification to keep him in politics and leader of the Liberal Party and an heroic cause to sell to the public, a view largely shared by Lord Jenkins and Derek Hamer. Colin Matthew's case is that Gladstone saw Ireland in Peelite terms: a problem only he could solve, and he could do so by administrative action, dragging the Liberal Party with him. James Loughlin, after a detailed study of the question, concludes Gladstone simply came to share sympathy for Ireland because of the 'inherent injustice' of Britain's treatment of the country. Travis Crosby accepts all these explanations and stresses they were all a part of Gladstone's constant desire to control events and the situations in which he found himself. Morley paints a more heroic picture: Gladstone's range of experience and his mastery of European history gave him a unique and broad vision of possibilities and necessities, compared with other politicians, and it was this which propelled him in the direction of Home Rule.

It is perhaps significant that his diary does little to help the historian answer any of the questions connected with Gladstone and Home Rule. There is no evidence of a sudden conversion, and nothing to show he was acting from politically selfish motives; in fact, the reverse would seem to be true – Gladstone came to the conclusion Home Rule would have to be enacted, but exactly when he did so will never be known. It would not appear to have been the result of an abrupt change of mind, but more the consequence of reflection over a period of months, if not of years. As for his perception of the effects it would have on the Liberal Party, it is, once again, very difficult to be certain. What seems to be the case is that this was a manoeuvre fairly typical of Gladstone. He had decided on a policy, which he knew was the correct and just one, and he was going to see it enacted. Whether the Liberals accepted it or not was, if not irrelevant, at least a secondary consideration. He wanted them to follow him and he hoped they would. He had no doubt most of them would see its inherent justice, and therefore they would follow it; if they did not, then they would have to consider their own future. If Gladstone adopted the policy of Home Rule for Ireland as a device for consolidating his grip on the

Liberal Party – at least as it was in 1885 – it was one that would more likely cause it to break up. In the longer term, it would tie the remainder – those who stayed loyal to Gladstone – firmly in his camp. But, in the last analysis, it is likely that Gladstone took up the policy because he believed in it, and more or less irrespective of its political consequences.

Gladstone, however, remained a politician, always careful to mind his step in the public view. Hence he remained guarded about his Irish Home Rule policy, although he was prepared to mention it in his electoral address – until a minor earthquake shook the political stage. Quite out of the blue, on 17 December there appeared over Hawarden a 'kite', flown by Gladstone's son Herbert, who was both a convinced Home Ruler and aware of his father's plans. The 'Hawarden kite', an article on Gladstone's 'Authentic Plan' for Home Rule, was published in the *Standard* on the last but one day of the general election, which had begun some three weeks earlier. Its appearance caused a storm in both Liberal and Conservative circles.

Why the 'kite' was flown at all was, and remains, something of a mystery. It has been suggested that Herbert misunderstood his father's intentions and therefore released it 'accidentally'. It has also been suggested that Gladstone wanted it flown in order to gauge public opinion on the Home Rule question and to reassure the Irish Nationalists of his policy towards it. Whatever the reason, it caused outrage amongst his Liberal colleagues. Whether they approved of the policy or not, all were in agreement that Gladstone should have discussed it openly with them before 'going public' with it. It was particularly annoying to the anti-Home Rulers. During the autumn, the Whigs, particularly Hartington, and the radicals, Dilke and Chamberlain, had begun to be increasingly suspicious of what Gladstone was up to. Chamberlain, while he obviously accepted the idea of a Central Board, was especially furious because he believed Gladstone had not supported his policy, but had now proposed one that was far more radical. He had outbid Chamberlain for the support of the radical wing of the party.

Whatever the reason the kite was flown, Gladstone, faced with an outburst of hostility to it, hastily hauled it down. He had not yet, he said, committed himself to a definite plan for Home Rule, nor for the separation of Ireland from the rest of the United Kingdom. But by then, it might be argued, it had done its job. In particular, it had shown the Nationalists that Gladstone, unlike the Conservatives, whose government had no intention of doing anything of this kind for Ireland, looked on the idea of Home Rule in a friendly manner. As the results came in, it became ever more clear what the Irish Nationalists thought was going to be of particular significance.

The Liberals won the general election of 1885 with 334 MPs returned, compared with 250 Conservatives, but not by a particularly convincing margin. Parnell's Irish Nationalists, as expected, increased their representation to eighty-six members, and they therefore held the balance of power in the Commons. The Liberals could rid themselves of the Conservative government only if the Irish did not vote for it. At the same time, if the Liberals became the government themselves, they would depend on Irish Nationalist support, and Parnell would expect to be paid for that support. Gladstone, for one, was prepared to pay the price demanded, a Home Rule measure, but he would have to pay it quickly; and, as he was well aware, not all of his own party shared his views.

There were some interesting and, for the Liberals, worrying factors in the election results. First, after 1885 there were no Liberals returned for Irish constituencies; the Irish electorate either voted Nationalist, or Conservative in the case of Ulster and Dublin University. Secondly, the Liberal vote in the towns declined spectacularly. In London, where the number of constituencies had been vastly increased, the Conservatives gained thirty-six seats. In the counties, for once, the Liberals did well, but whether they would continue to do so was uncertain and, as the urban population increased and the number of rural constituencies declined, this would not necessarily help them. It is generally agreed that the Conservative negotiations over redistribution had been of considerable benefit to them and would continue to be for the rest of the century.

When the new parliamentary session began Gladstone was keen to defeat the government. He did not, however, want to do so over the Irish question, which he rightly feared was too sensitive for his own party. One of the standard ways to oust a government is to pass an amendment on the Queen's speech, in which she outlines the ministry's policy proposals for the session. Victoria's speech in 1886 made no mention of Ireland, but the motion that defeated the government related to a different issue: the omission of any proposed measure to help the depressed agricultural population in the United Kingdom, and was proposed by a radical MP and 'henchman' of Joseph Chamberlain, Jesse Collings. In the vote that followed, which was really a vote of confidence in the government, the ministry was defeated by 329 votes to 250. But the figures do not by themselves tell the whole story, since the majority included the Irish Nationalists, but not seventy-odd Liberals (including the elderly John Bright) who abstained, while the minority vote actually included eighteen Liberals, among them Lord Hartington. It was an ominous victory, therefore, for the Liberal Party, but sufficient to cause the resignation of the Conservative Prime Minister, Lord Salisbury.

GLADSTONE'S THIRD MINISTRY, JANUARY–JUNE 1886

Gladstone took on the task of forming his third ministry after receiving a summons from the Queen, delivered at about midnight on 29/30 January 1886. Edward Hamilton nicely summed up his problems.

> The composition of the Cabinet will be a most difficult task, what with the awkwardness of dealing with the foreign secretaryship, Dilke's temporary disability, the mood of Chamberlain and Harcourt, and the doubtful attitude of others besides Hartington. Rosebery was to be Foreign Secretary. The only question is – will he face the great responsibility of the office.[21]

Gladstone spent much time on 30 and 31 January, and on 3, 4, and 5 February, meeting and writing to people and attempting to construct his cabinet. (On 2 February he had given away his daughter Mary when she had married Revd Harry Drew at St Margaret's, Westminster, a welcome break from the pressures of ministry-building, though he was not best pleased about the event.) The Queen had caused the difficulty over the foreign secretaryship: she had not made many conditions, but one of them was that Granville, of whose foreign policy she disapproved, should not return to the post. Dilke could not be appointed as he had got himself involved in a squalid divorce case; even though he was found innocent of any impropriety, Gladstone felt he could never appoint him again and his ministerial career was finished. Chamberlain and Harcourt had joined with Dilke and Hartington at the beginning of the new year to try and bring Gladstone into line on the Irish question, although of the four only Hartington had gone so far as to refuse any post under Gladstone. Chamberlain had hoped that he could be appointed Colonial Secretary, but Gladstone had only offered him the Admiralty, and in the end he had secured the even less prestigious post of President of the Local Government Board. It is not surprising that his relations with Gladstone remained uncertain and his patience would soon be exhausted. Rosebery, the Queen's choice as Foreign Secretary, did, at least, accept office, while the unhappy Granville accepted the less important Colonial Office, Childers the Home Office, and Harcourt, despite his apparent reservations, became Chancellor of the Exchequer. But Gladstone could not persuade Derby, Northbrook, Goschen or Bright, all staunch opponents of Home Rule, to accept any position in the government.

Gladstone took office in February 1886 in the hope that he would be able to solve the Irish question. Those who took office with him did not necessarily realise quite how far he was prepared to go to do it. It was symbolic that his appointment of Chief Secretary for Ireland was the radical and outspoken Home Ruler John Morley. There were also other issues that affected the country at this time, such as riots in the West End of London by the unemployed, but, to Gladstone, compared with the great question of Ireland, these were of no real significance. He began working on two measures relating to Ireland, the details of both of which were kept under wraps for as long as possible. The first was a definite measure for Home Rule, on which he had started serious work in February, even before Parliament met, and the proposals for which were based closely on the initial sketches Gladstone had made in November 1885. The second was another Land Purchase Bill, this one involving the state underwriting loans to enable Irish landlords to sell, and tenants to buy, their land. As events were to show, it was the first of these measures that meant most to Gladstone.

Work on the two bills was closely connected. Initial drafting of the Home Rule Bill began first, but its details and those of the Land Purchase Bill were completed in tandem. It is possible that Gladstone was using the latter as a smokescreen to shield discussion of the major issues of the Home Rule proposal until it was finalised. It seems as if the Land Purchase Bill was designed to help secure the passage of the Home Rule measure.

Actually getting either proposal to Parliament proved difficult, and Gladstone exhausted himself grappling with the details and discussing various issues with colleagues and the Queen. The crisis arrived on 13 March 1886. In cabinet on that day Chamberlain, still angry over his treatment, demanded to see the full details of the Home Rule proposal. It took a full week for Gladstone to get the new Government of Ireland Bill printed, but it took a day less than that for Chamberlain (and George Otto Trevelyan, the Scottish Secretary) to submit their resignations. The two men had been especially angered at the degree of authority to be vested in a new Irish assembly, which was to be set up under the terms of the Bill. This was to consist of two separate 'orders'. The first order would comprise the twenty-eight Irish Peers who sat in the House of Lords at Westminster and seventy-five other members, elected for a ten-year term, all of whom were to have a respectable income. The second order would be made up of the 103 Irish MPs at Westminster and another 101 representatives elected on a similar basis to them, all for a five-year term. An Irish executive authority would be created from the assembly, which could set levels of taxation and control Ireland's domestic policy; while the assembly could discuss and vote on these matters, those relating to 'imperial' questions – which were deemed to include defence and foreign policy – were kept out of their control and remained the responsibility of the parliament at Westminster. Ireland would also have to pay its share of the national debt of the United Kingdom. After a long dispute with Parnell it was agreed this should be one-fifteenth of the total. The compromises to imperial sentiment were more than counterbalanced by the decision made by Gladstone, after considerable hesitation, to exclude all of the Irish MPs from Westminster, which imperialists saw as far too much of a concession to Irish Nationalist sentiment. A Bill incorporating these proposals was nevertheless presented to Parliament on 8 April 1886.

Gladstone introduced the measure in one of his great parliamentary performances, a speech lasting, he calculated, some three and a half hours. The loyal Hamilton believed, such was the reaction to it, that it 'was indeed a notable day – the most notable day in the annals of the present Houses of Parliament. It was moreover a great day in a great career.' There was 'never anything like the excitement'. There was, he remembered, 'a storm of applause' when the 'Grand Old Man', finally, sat down.[22] But he was being over-optimistic if he thought this piece of

Gladstonian oratory would secure the passage of the Bill. Leaving aside for the moment the vexing question of the House of Lords, Gladstone knew he had major difficulties to contend with in the Commons, even among his own Party. There were concerns about Home Rule on principle, as well as anxieties about the security of Ulster Protestants. There was always the possibility – mooted by the embittered Chamberlain – that Gladstone was adopting the policy simply as a means of diverting the Party away from his own programme of social reform. Gladstone believed he had been directed by a higher power, but the plain fact was that he had decided the time had come to act, and he acted, as so often, in a decisive fashion. In response, Lord Morley (the Chairman of the Board of Works) resigned even before the Land Purchase Bill was introduced, and on the day before its presentation, 15 April, there was a meeting of nearly fifty disgruntled Peers and others, including Hartington, at Derby House.

The Land Purchase (Ireland) Bill was a complex proposal drafted by John Morley with the hope of persuading a class of Irish landowners to stay in the country even after a Home Rule measure was enacted. It was also intended to establish a new class of Irish peasant landowners. Any landowner who wished to sell his property, however, would be compensated out of the British Treasury. This was the part of the Bill that caused the greatest anger. The sum set aside to allow this in the final version of the Bill was fifty million pounds (even this was a reduction from the £120 million initially suggested), which was an enormous sum to come from government revenues, and it was one that many radicals were quite unprepared for from Gladstone, of all men. The Government of Ireland Bill had caused Gladstone enough trouble: this one, it seemed, was going to cause him even more. He now decided he had had enough to do with the earlier proposals, so this Bill, about which he had at one time such high hopes, was quietly dropped.

Gladstone became concerned with the establishment, on 22 April, of an office for dissident 'Liberal Unionist' MPs and was no doubt relieved to take an Easter break at Hawarden. This did something to reassure him, however, as large crowds of supporters gathered to see him there. But by the time another bad-tempered cabinet was held on 4 May, over sixty Liberal MPs had come out openly opposed to the proposal. Gladstone, as usual, stuck to his guns.

He opened the debate on the crucial second reading of the Government of Ireland Bill on 10 May and it continued for nearly a month, until 8 June. As he became increasingly aware of the strength of the Liberal Party opposition to it and more concerned at its consequences, he began, for once, to waver. On 27 May over 200 Liberal MPs attended a Party meeting at the Foreign Office, and to this he offered a compromise. If the second reading of the Bill was agreed and Home Rule accepted in principle, he offered to withdraw the measure as it stood, rework it (or some aspects of it, at least) and resubmit it to a new session of Parliament in the autumn. The MPs present loudly cheered him for this – and it looked for a moment as if a Liberal Party split might be avoided. But some Liberals remained irreconcilable, holding their own meeting in opposition, while Gladstone himself seemed to pull back from the offer he made to the Foreign Office meeting when he was back in the Commons. The debate went on.

On the last night Gladstone made another of his great speeches, though it was not one that went down well with Unionist or Conservative – or even some Liberal – ears. It was, declared the Prime Minister:

> one of the golden moments of our history – one of those opportunities which may come and may go, but which rarely return, or, if they do, return at long intervals, and under circumstances which no man can forecast.[23]

In this speech Gladstone proceeded to tell the 'dreadful story of the Union' since 1801, which he 'unfolded in all its hideous features'. When it came to a vote, only thirteen MPs were absent: of those present, 311 voted for the government, but 341 voted against it. Of these, most disastrous of all for the Party, were ninety-four Liberals. The cabinet had no hesitation in deciding what to do, and on the same night agreed on resignation and calling for a dissolution of Parliament. Gladstone's third ministry was over.

Gladstone's brief third premiership was dominated from first to last by the question of Ireland. This is certainly because he let it be dominated in this way, and other matters were downplayed or ignored. But the Home Rule Bill he came up with was complicated, and has recently been judged as almost certainly unworkable, even if it had been passed.

The fact that it did not pass represented a disaster, perhaps for Ireland, certainly for the Liberal Party. The split, with dissident Liberals beginning to group together as Liberal Unionists, was developing into a major problem. It may be, however, that a division such as this in the Liberal Party was on the cards in any case. The Whig elements, led by Hartington and tied to the aristocracy, were becoming more and more disillusioned with Gladstone and what, to them, were his increasingly radical policies, and they had been since the later 1860s. Many radicals under the wing of Joseph Chamberlain were also becoming unsettled with him. He was not radical enough for them, and Irish Home Rule was simply a cover for his inherent conservatism. In view of their different outlooks, it comes as something of a surprise that both of these groups could ally together against Gladstone, and then join with the Conservative Party. But Lord Salisbury was prepared to give Chamberlain what he wanted, the post of Colonial Secretary, which Gladstone could not, or would not, do.

For Gladstone, personally, the collapse of his third ministry seems almost to have rejuvenated him. He how had a cause to fight for, and it was one in which he genuinely believed – Home Rule for Ireland – and he would lead a loyal Liberal Party into the election campaign, with no intention of retirement. It remained to be seen, however, what the British electorate thought of his policies. Not for the first time, Gladstone stood ready to be judged by the people.

7

OPPOSITION, THE FOURTH MINISTRY AND RETIREMENT, 1886–1898

The defeat over the Irish Home Rule Bill in the House of Commons on 8 June 1886 marked the end of Gladstone's third ministry and brought about the dissolution of Parliament. It meant that Gladstone's immediate task was to present his Irish policy to the electors and secure their support for it so that he could put pressure on the Lords. Unfortunately, it was not to be: instead of returning the 'Grand Old Man' to the House of Commons in triumph, the voters reduced the Liberal party to a shadow of its former self and condemned him to years of opposition.

THE ELECTION OF JULY 1886 AND THE SPLIT IN THE LIBERAL PARTY

Gladstone was unopposed for his Midlothian seat on this occasion, and so his election campaign was directed at the electors throughout the country and it was, as might be expected, a prodigious effort. He explained to one audience in Liverpool how things stood: he 'went in bitterness, in the heat of the spirit, but the hand of the Lord was strong on me'.[1] Gladstone reminded his audience of his views, declared in Edinburgh in 1880, of the problems faced by all Liberals. The 'classes', by which he meant 'the dukes … the squires … the Established clergy … the officers of the army, or … a number of other bodies of very respectable people', were against the 'masses', the remainder of the population. His point was that in all matters:

> where the leading and determining consideration that ought to lead to a conclusion are truth, justice, and humanity, there, gentlemen, all the world over, I will back the masses against the classes.[2]

But Gladstone faced an uphill task for all kinds of reasons were causing many of the previously Liberal voters to abstain or even to turn out and vote against them. Memories of Gordon and anti-Catholic prejudice erupted throughout the country, while his fiery rhetoric, as in Liverpool, might have scared off as many electors as it encouraged.

The main problem for Gladstone and his friends was that there were two Liberal parties to vote for in 1886. The MPs who had opposed Gladstone in the Commons made no secret of their opposition to him in public, and these 'Liberal Unionists' actually formed an electoral pact with the Conservatives; by the time the elections were over there were seventy-eight of them in the House of Commons. The Conservative Party itself did very well, securing 314 seats, while the Gladstonian Liberals trailed well behind them, being reduced to just 181 MPs. Not even Parnell's Irish Nationalists, with eighty-five seats, could make a difference to the overall balance of power in this Parliament. 'The defeat', Gladstone ruefully recorded in his diary 'is a smash'.[3] On 30 July he tendered his resignation to the Queen.

The underlying cause of this disastrous split in the Liberal Party has been long debated. Gladstone himself believed, and historians have long maintained, that it represented a ' revolt of the Whigs'. In general terms it is fair to say that most of the aristocratic 'Whig' elements in the party deserted Gladstone at this point over the Irish question, while the majority of the middle-class Radicals stayed loyal to him in spite of it. But it has more recently been stressed that many better-off 'Whig' members of the Liberal Party had been showing signs of disillusionment with it since the time of Gladstone's first ministry. It is also true that some 'moderate' Liberals, including some of those who might be considered 'better off', remained loyal to Gladstone even at this time, while, on the other hand, one of the leaders of the revolt was Joseph Chamberlain, the personification of middle-class radicalism. In any case, it does not seem to matter very much: enough voters had deserted Gladstone to give the Conservatives an overall majority in the Commons and put Lord Salisbury back into office, even without the Liberal Unionists' support.

It was the Conservatives who were to dominate British politics until the twentieth century.

When Gladstone resigned as prime minister in 1886 he had no intention of resigning as leader of the Liberal Party, unlike in 1874: this time, he would stay on, return to office and see a Home Rule measure through. He went, with Lord Acton, on a brief visit to Bavaria in August, to see Döllinger (for the last time, as it turned out), but then he returned home and by 20 September was back once more in the Commons. At the end of the year the Liberal Party's position seemed to improve somewhat when, on 22 December, Lord Randolph Churchill, Salisbury's Chancellor of the Exchequer, resigned. On the same day Chamberlain made a speech that was taken to hold out an 'olive branch' to his former Liberal colleagues. The result of this was a 'Round Table' conference, comprising Chamberlain and Harcourt, Lord Herschell, Sir George Trevelyan and John Morley, all former members of Gladstone's cabinet, convened in an attempt to reconcile Chamberlain and his followers with the main body of the Liberal Party. Gladstone expressed his general approval of the idea but carefully kept his distance from it, allowing it a free hand, as much as he could, in case it failed. He was not too worried if it did: all Chamberlain had to do, as far as Gladstone was concerned, was to admit he was wrong and then rejoin the Party.

The conference appeared to go well at first, but then Chamberlain published an article in the *Baptist* calling for the disestablishment of the Welsh church and accusing Gladstone of preventing this by his obsession with the primacy of Irish Home Rule over all other Liberal policies. This outright assault on the Grand Old Man appeared to the other Liberal conference members to contain arguments which contradicted what Chamberlain had been saying to them in private. The conference adjourned for two weeks, but never resumed: it seemed Chamberlain had after all decided to throw in his lot with the Conservatives. Further evidence that the Liberal Unionists were becoming more closely tied to the Conservatives was shown by the appointment of G.J. Goschen, who had been Gladstone's First Lord of the Admiralty from 1871 to 1874, as Churchill's successor as Chancellor of the Exchequer in January 1887.

Chamberlain was, in fact, correct: as far as Gladstone was concerned, the main cause to dominate his last years in active politics was that of Irish Home Rule. In the period between his third and fourth ministries his speeches were dominated by the question to the exclusion of most other matters, including those like Welsh church disestablishment, which were attracting more and more attention within the Liberal Party itself. But Lord Salisbury's second ministry was also dominated to a large extent by the Home Rule question. In March 1887 the prime minister's nephew, A.J. Balfour, became Irish Secretary, and 'Bloody Balfour' began to stand firm against the demands of Irish tenants.

By August 1887 Parnell had become convinced that tenant farmers in Ireland would not be able to afford their rents over the winter and so introduced a Tenants Relief Bill in Westminster to try to ease their difficulties. The government, however, refused to accept it. This was followed by the so-called 'Plan of Campaign' in Ireland, when Irish radicals William O'Brien and John Dillon called on tenants on every estate to organise and pay an agreed rent to their landlord: if he did not accept the sum offered, they should pay the money into a campaign fund instead. The government's response was a Crimes Act, steered by Balfour through the Commons and helped on the way by the use of the parliamentary 'guillotine'. This meant a time limit could be placed on the discussion of all clauses of a bill when in Committee, at the end of which they would have to be voted on. The result was a three-year 'Land War' in Ireland, beginning at Mitchelstown, County Cork, on 9 September, when a crowd was shot at by a body of policemen whom they had trapped in their own police station. Other violence followed this affair. As far as Balfour was concerned, his aim throughout was to enforce the law: the 'Plan of Campaign' was illegal and tenants would have to pay their rents, or face the consequences.

This attack on the Irish population gave Gladstone the cause for which he could fight. He began on 19 August 1886 by publishing a pamphlet on *The Irish Question, I: The History of an Idea, II: Lessons of the Election*. In it he outlined how his Irish policy had evolved and explained why Irish Home Rule was an obvious one for him to adopt. He also explained how the Conservatives would at first resist the policy, as they had resisted Catholic Emancipation and Corn Law Repeal, but they would then give in to it. He followed this in January and February 1887 with a series of speeches against the government's policy in Ireland and that summer he made another triumphant tour, this time to Wales, making numerous speeches, both public and private, seeing a procession of some 60,000 people in Swansea. 'It has really been a "progress", and an extraordinary one', he concluded.[4] In December, however, he took himself and Catherine off to Florence for a holiday, as had been recommended by his doctor.

In 1888 he kept up the offensive on the government and in June he launched a full-scale attack on the new Crimes Act. He announced that there was now an unprecedented division between the British Government and the Irish people which was the direct result of this. It had not reduced crime, but then, he declared, it was not intended that it should: what it was intended to do was to prevent the Irish people from expressing their legitimate grievances. He concluded in striking tones: 'Ireland is perhaps the most conspicuous country in the world where law has been on one side and justice on the other.'[5]

On 7 November, in Chamberlain's Birmingham stronghold, Gladstone gave another rousing address, this time to some 20,000 people attending the National Liberal Federation Conference. He supported the Irish, he said, because justice was on their side. The Conservative Government was not on the side of right, but then it was a 'Government of unequal laws'. Ireland could not be governed as it was at present, 'by perpetual coercion' and even the Union itself could not be defended: after all, it had only been brought into existence by the 'foulest and wickedest means'.[6] This kind of oratory, upsetting though it was to the Queen and some Liberal leaders such as Harcourt and even John Morley, was perfectly acceptable to many of the party rank and file.

Irish political developments continued to dominate Gladstone's political life in 1890 and 1891, but in a new way. He had come closer to Parnell over the years, and the Irish leader spent 18 and 19 December 1889 at Hawarden. But the Irish leader's private life was soon to become more public, causing a broad rift between the two men and within the Irish Home Rule Party. For many years Parnell had been the lover of Mrs Katherine O'Shea, with the knowledge and acquiescence of her husband, Captain William O'Shea. As early as April 1881, Captain O'Shea had acted as go-between for Parnell with the Liberal cabinet, and he had stayed in contact with the government throughout its existence, though it was his wife who had done most to bring Parnell and Gladstone together. Five days after Parnell left Hawarden, Captain O'Shea, now more an ally of Joseph Chamberlain than of Gladstone, filed a petition for divorce. This would lead to a trial before the Divorce Court.

On 17 November 1890 the case came to Court. Initially Gladstone was prepared to wait and see what happened, but on receipt of a large number of letters, 'all one way', on the case, by 21 November he came to a conclusion:

> I agree with a newspaper ... that the dominant question, now properly before Mr. Parnell for his consideration, is what is the best course for him to adopt with a view to the furtherance of the interests of Home Rule in Great Britain. And, with deep pain but without any doubt, I judge that those interests require his retirement at the present time from the leadership ... I have no right spontaneously to pronounce this opinion. But I should certainly give it if called upon from a quarter entitled to make the demand.[7]

Gladstone, armed with this opinion, held a meeting with senior colleagues (Granville, Harcourt, John Morley and the chief whip, Arnold Morley). A meeting with Justin McCarthy, a Home Rule MP and journalist, followed, in which Gladstone told him his opinion was clear: Parnell should go. But Parnell refused to leave quietly. McCarthy could not bring him to step down and John Morley could not find him to show him a copy of the letter Gladstone had sent to him, outlining his views of what Parnell should do. Gladstone seems to have been furious with the Irish leader: he insisted his letter should be published, and was determined Parnell should not defy his wishes. Parnell published his own counter to Gladstone's letter, but when the Irish Home Rule Party held a meeting on 5 December, McCarthy led forty-five MPs from the room, leaving him with only twenty-eight supporters. Parnell's public position was ruined, and he died the following year. In Gladstone's opinion the cause of Irish Home Rule was damaged by these events, but he did not think it was beyond repair: he also saw that he was now its undisputed champion and when he was next prime minister he would have to deal with it properly, once and for all.

Despite Gladstone's pre-eminent concern with Ireland, others in the Liberal Party and the government had other things on their mind during these years. In the Liberal Party itself some of the younger members were beginning to develop their own ideas about the future of Liberalism. Gladstone had no great sympathy for 'progressive' ideas, such as Welsh or Scottish Church disestablishment, and he was not an outspoken supporter of temperance. When James Keir Hardie, a future Labour Party leader, led a deputation of coal miners to the 1889 Liberal Party conference to petition Gladstone for his support for their campaign for an eight-hour working day, he was not in favour of their call.

But at the 1891 National Conference of the Liberal Federation to be held in Newcastle, it was another matter. It was important for the Liberals to develop something approaching a coherent party policy since everyone knew Lord Salisbury would have to dissolve Parliament during or at the end of the next session, which marked the end of his term of office. In addition to this, the appearance of 'Socialist' groups, such as the Fabian Society and the Social Democratic Federation, gave warning of the fact that the left wing of the party might lose ground unless some action was taken on working conditions and other social matters. The result of these tensions was the promulgation of what became the 'Newcastle Programme' of the Liberal Party. A whole range of social questions were covered in this programme, including church disestablishment, the inclusion of all men in the electorate, payment for MPs (this had been a Chartist demand in 1838), elected parish councils, and employers' liability, the limitation of working hours and restrictions on the powers of the House of Lords.

Gladstone presented his major speech to the conference on 2 October. It made some mention of all of the points in the Newcastle Programme, but it also, as was to be expected, gave precedence to the Irish Home Rule question and the withdrawal of British forces from Egypt. Some things (such as the issue of votes for women, of which Gladstone did not approve) were left out of the speech altogether. He did not put forward any concrete details of his own regarding the elements of the programme and, as an endorsement of it, it was all somewhat vague. Even so, it was a success as a speech, reminding at least one of his hearers of his visits to the north-east of England some thirty years before, when Chancellor of the Exchequer in Palmerston's ministry, and it roused many of the party faithful for the electoral fray. Even at the time, however, it was severely criticised by some, and historians since have not always been kind to it. In particular, some hearers got the impression that Gladstone did not entirely believe in what he was saying: in other words, he was accepting some of the views of some of the party so that they would continue to support him to achieve what he most wanted. Other things could wait, but for Gladstone Irish Home

Rule could not. Historians argue that his devotion to this cause, and his commitment to it, acted as a millstone on the development of the party. Perhaps the Newcastle Programme, if wholeheartedly adopted could have helped to secure an electoral triumph, but Gladstone was going to use it only as means of returning to office and subsequently carrying through what he really wanted. It is not surprising that the Liberals did not do especially well in the 1892 general election given their leader's rather blinkered political outlook. Gladstone clearly believed Home Rule must take precedence; until it was passed, the Liberal Party could not adopt any other policies.

Lord Salisbury's Conservative government had, outside of Ireland, pursued a relatively quiet domestic policy, while the prime minister, who also acted as foreign secretary, had preoccupied himself with foreign policy questions. Most interest in this sphere concerned Africa, though there were also some important developments in European diplomatic relationships. Salisbury's most important achievement in Africa in these years concerned Portuguese pretensions in southern Africa and the East African Sultanate of Zanzibar (which included much of the East African coast as well as the island itself and was the target of German ambitions).

In southern Africa the Portuguese had occupied land along the coast to the north of Natal, in Mozambique, and claimed territory inland from there. But the British had plans of their own for this area, situated as it was to the north of the Boer Republics of the Orange Free State and Transvaal. In 1890, forces of the British South Africa Company had occupied the area of Matabeleland (now Zimbabwe) and Mashonaland.

This company, owned by Cecil Rhodes, an ardent imperialist, had been granted a Royal Charter in 1889, which allowed it to administer territory on behalf of the Crown. It could collect tax revenues and use those to pay employees to act as civil servants and soldiers, as well as trade with the locals, and it appeared to be a cheap way of expanding the empire. In 1891 Salisbury was able to bully the Portuguese – who were dependent on British diplomatic and financial support – into accepting a deal limiting their claims and allowing the British to settle in Matabeleland. These developments were watched with increasing anxiety by the Boers.

Things were less easily settled further north. A German East Africa Company, led by Dr Karl Peters, had been securing influence in the interior for several years in the south of the region, in what is now Tanzania. They were countered by the Imperial British East Africa Company of Sir William Mackinnon, which was active in what is now Kenya and Uganda. This company had been granted a Royal Charter in 1888. A final settlement was made between the British government and the new German Kaiser, Wilhelm II, in July 1890. Wilhelm was anxious to come to a striking diplomatic deal with Britain to show his people what he could do (he had just brought about Bismarck's resignation), and he and Salisbury reached an agreement. The British did well out of it in Africa, securing the rights to a Protectorate over the Sultanate of Zanzibar with a boundary line keeping German territorial claims away from the headwaters of the Nile. The Germans did well out of it in Europe: they secured the island of Heligoland, which had been British since 1807, and which would dominate the western exit to the new Kiel Canal. The Kaiser, who was Queen Victoria's grandson, was an enthusiast for warships and viewed this canal as a necessity for the new, enlarged German navy.

In Europe, however, Salisbury could do very little to prevent one of the great diplomatic revolutions. While Bismarck was in office one of his chief desires was to keep Germany on good terms with Russia since the alternative would place Russia alongside Germany's mortal enemy, France, and put Germany in between two less than friendly powers. But the deaths of the elderly Kaiser Wilhelm I and of his son, Friedrich I, both in 1888, led to the accession of the young and impetuous Wilhelm II. After two years Wilhelm II had had enough of Bismarck; nor had he any particular love for Russia either, any more than the Russian Tsar Alexander III had for him. The Russians and the French also had need of each other: the French could make good use of Russia's grain, Russia could make good use of French money to finance her ongoing industrialisation programme. It did not take long for the two sides to reach agreement: in August 1892 a military convention was signed, which in January 1894 was turned into a full political alliance. By this, some twenty years before the outbreak of the First World War, the powers that would face each other across continental Europe in August 1914 were set up, although Britain had yet to decide which, if any, side she would take.

Gladstone's response to these various diplomatic developments was not especially marked, but it is easy to see what he felt about them. When news of Bismarck's fall reached him he had little to say about him: the two men simply did not share same outlook. Bismarck himself had no love at all for Gladstone and he made this plain on more than one occasion, but the Grand Old Man did not really think he was worthy of much notice.

As far as the 'Scramble for Africa' was concerned, Gladstone was quite out of sympathy with it, as events in his last ministry were to show. He maintained his calls for a British withdrawal from Egypt, all too aware of the damage the occupation was doing to Anglo-French relations, as well as the injustice inflicted on the people of Egypt. He claimed not to know where some of the places in Africa that were under discussion actually were. He seemed less worried about his old areas of interest, the Balkans and other parts of Europe, which appeared relatively quiet anyway. But he was very clear where he wanted Britain to stand in world affairs: on the side of right, of free trade, and of (Christian) civilisation – exactly where, as he said in an article in the *North American Review* in January 1890, the new great power, the United States of America, should stand in the future.[8]

Salisbury's government also carried through a number of domestic reforms in the period from 1887 to 1892. Most important perhaps was the Local Government Act of 1888. By this means, sixty-two elected county councils came into existence based on the old shires, and, independent of these, also created were county borough councils. These were in towns of over 50,000 inhabitants, each of which was now given an elected local authority with the powers of a county council. Each new county council, or county borough council was granted direct control of roads and bridges and local police forces. In London, a new county council (the London County Council) was established, which took over the responsibilities of the old Metropolitan Board of Works; included in the council's responsibilities were roads and sewage disposal, but not the Metropolitan Police, which stayed independent of the London County Council and remained (as it still is) under the direct control of the Home Secretary. Most notably, perhaps, the county and borough council electors included women, if they were unmarried and paid rates on their properties, though they could not stand for election. The whole scheme made a good start, and in London the first Chairman of the London County Council, was none other than the eminent Liberal peer, Lord Rosebery.

The Conservatives also provided some measures of educational and factory reform. In the first case, by the 1891 Education Act, the payment of all elementary school fees was abolished. In the second, a Factory Act raised the minimum age for the employment of children in factories to eleven and fixed women's daily hours of work at a maximum of twelve. The year of 1889 was marked by a dock workers' strike by which they were able to raise their wage to 6d (2.5p) per hour, and in which the government had not intervened.

The Liberal Party as a whole had watched these developments with some anxiety. The reform of local government was something Gladstone's second ministry had repeatedly set out to achieve, but had not managed, and now the Conservatives had. The Education Act, granting free education to all children, was also something that many members of the Liberal Party had looked on favourably. By their measures of factory reform and standing aside from strikers, the Conservatives had begun to appear as the friends of the working classes. It is not difficult to see where at least some of the inspiration for the Newcastle Programme had come from: the Liberals, after all, had to be more radical than their Conservative opponents and had to win over the newly-enfranchised lower-class voters.

There was, however, one other thing about which Gladstone had strong objections, but which the world of the late 1880s and 1890s was becoming dangerously preoccupied by: namely, the increased levels of military and naval estimates. In 1888, one of the periodic 'naval scares' swept the Admiralty. A report by three admirals on the 1888 naval manoeuvres came to the conclusion that the battle fleet was no longer up to the desired 'two-power standard' (which meant the Royal Navy should have more battleships than the two navies of France and Russia added together); in fact, they declared, it was not strong enough to fight even one great power. To make up the deficiency it would be necessary to build, as a matter of urgency, ten new battleships, as well as forty-two cruisers and eighteen 'torpedo gunboats'; the cost for all this was estimated at some £21.5 million, which would be provided over a rolling programme, something to which Gladstone usually expressed strong objections. But the Naval Defence Act was voted through without too much opposition and certainly none to speak of from Gladstone, who confined himself to attacking the principle of the 'rolling programme'. This is surprising, given Gladstone's strong opposition to the proposed increases in naval spending in 1893–4, but there may be explanations for this. Gladstone seems to have been lacking in energy at this time. His son Willy lay mortally ill with a stroke, while his eldest brother, Sir Thomas, had died on 26 March, so that, due to such family concerns, perhaps questions of finance and politics appeared somewhat less important.

Gladstone's private life in these years of opposition was not especially happy: Sir Thomas and Willy were not the only ones to die around this time. In September 1887 Laura Thistlethwayte's husband died of an 'accidental' gunshot wound. At the end of March 1891, Earl Granville, one of Gladstone's closest friends and oldest political allies, died – this prompted a sombre reflection from the Liberal leader: 'His is a loss that can never be replaced. And it always seems to me, when persons sensibly younger than myself are taken away, as if my surviving them were a kind of fraud.'[9]

But there were also some happier events. The most notable came in 1889, when on 25 July he and Catherine celebrated their golden wedding anniversary (the year also marked the fifty-fifth anniversary of his entry into Parliament). This was followed by a visit to Hawarden in August, where the inhabitants of the village paid for the construction of a drinking fountain in commemoration of the event, and the castle was provided with a new entrance porch at the expense of the Gladstones' children, one which was big enough to accommodate his ever larger collection of axes. In September a visit to Paris turned into a remarkable occasion for the elderly couple. When they arrived at the Hippodrome, activities ceased and the orchestra played 'God Save the Queen'. At the opera, Gladstone and party were seated in the presidential box and he even braved the heights of the Eiffel Tower (though Catherine was unable to because of 'indisposition').

This was not the Gladstones' only foreign visit during this period. Earlier, at the end of 1886, they had set off for Florence via Paris on the outward journey and Cannes on the return leg. While in Florence, Gladstone planted a tree and prepared an article for the *North American Review*, attacking an American agnostic. At the end of 1887 they had made their way as far south as Naples as guests of the Stuart Rendels. Rendel, a rich associate of the Armstrong firm, was anxious to cultivate Gladstone at this time, and there was soon to be a family connection. Henry Gladstone became engaged to Rendel's daughter Maud. But the

Gladstones did not go to Rome at this time as he did not wish to meet the King of Italy or the high-ranking politicians who had just brought Italy into a closer alliance with Germany.

The Gladstones also moved house again in London, first in 1888, to James Street, Buckingham Gate, and then, two years later, to 10 St James's Square. This was far more at the centre of things than the more remote address they had been using in north-west London and there is little doubt that Catherine would have been pleased by this move.

THE 1892 GENERAL ELECTION AND THE FORMATION OF THE FOURTH MINISTRY

Parliament was dissolved in June, and on the 24th of the month Gladstone issued his address to the electors of Midlothian. In it he called first of all for the passage of Home Rule for Ireland, on lines laid down over the previous six years. In addition, he hinted at changes in the Scottish and Welsh church establishments, doing to their 'national churches' what he had done to the Anglican Church of Ireland nearly thirty years before. He also wanted franchise registration amended, with the principle of 'one man, one vote' adopted, and limitations put on miners' working hours. All in all, this amounted to a radical programme, something along the lines of that adopted at Newcastle the previous year. For Gladstone, however, it is fairly clear that his main aim, overreaching all others, remained the settlement of the Irish issue. With that out of way he might well retire and leave the field for his younger colleagues to force through the other measures.

Gladstone's view was that for Irish Home Rule to have any chance of success, it would have to be passed by a large majority of the House of Commons: only then would he feel able to bring real pressure to bear on the House of Lords. But for that he needed a Liberal majority of at least one hundred seats in the lower house. Gladstone, largely immobilised by an injury received in Chester, where he had been hit in the eye by a missile thrown by an old woman, spent the election period at Lord Rosebery's house of Dalmeny. He believed he would have a majority of between three and four thousand votes in Midlothian, while his agent warned him it might only be two thousand, but when the result was announced on 13 July the margin of victory was a mere 690. This weak performance was matched by that of the Liberal Party as a whole. It appears the electors did not find what Gladstone's Liberal Party had to offer attractive enough to vote for it. They either stayed at home or, worse still, turned out and voted for their opponents, the Conservatives, or, in the case of West Ham in East London, for James Keir Hardie, a representative of the Independent Labour Party. Gladstone's stress on Irish Home Rule had simply overshadowed the other declared Liberal policies based on the Newcastle Programme, but Home Rule was a policy that lacked relevance for many of the British electorate. The result was that instead of the overwhelming majority hoped for, and half-expected, the Liberal and Home Rule parties together had a majority of only forty seats (353 Liberals and Home Rulers to 314 Conservatives and Unionists). It was clear that Gladstone would find it hard to force any measure past the House of Commons and almost certainly impossible to overcome the hostility of the House of Lords.

But he did have a majority, albeit a small one, and he immediately began to form his fourth cabinet, which was made up of an interesting mix of politicians. Five out of seventeen were peers (compared with six out of fourteen in 1880) and seven were non-Anglicans (compared with two in 1880). Gladstone himself had served in Palmerston's government of 1860, while two of the cabinet, Herbert Asquith and John Morley, would still be active Liberal politicians after 1918. Sir William Harcourt once again accepted the post of Chancellor of the Exchequer, while the touchy and pro-imperialist Lord Rosebery, encouraged by his friend Edward Hamilton and the support of the Queen, was persuaded into accepting the Foreign Office for a second time. Morley returned to the post of Chief Secretary for Ireland and Henry Campbell-Bannerman, who was to lead the Liberal Party to its great election victory in 1905, returned as Secretary for War. Asquith, Liberal prime minister from 1908 to 1915, entered the cabinet for the first time as Home Secretary, and Earl Spencer took the post of First Lord of the Admiralty, probably not realising just how important this task was going to become in the life of the ministry.

THE FOURTH MINISTRY, AUGUST 1892–MARCH 1894

Gladstone was eighty-two years of age when he became prime minister in 1892. Not surprisingly, his health became a serious factor in the life of the government. At the end of 1893 he noted various problems with his digestion, but his deafness and loss of eyesight caused him greater difficulties. When one of the increasingly infrequent cabinets was held Gladstone made sure the ministers sat round a writing table, with himself in the centre. When relations between Rosebery and the Prime Minister became more strained because they communicated in writing more than speaking, Gladstone's private secretary, Algernon West, suggested they should meet more often. Rosebery did not think this was a good idea; he explained that he would have to shout so Gladstone could hear him, but then Gladstone would shout a reply, and the result of this would be that an argument would soon develop out of what had been a perfectly calm exchange of views. When they had an audience, the Queen found Gladstone placed himself ever closer to her, and he himself felt that he heard less than half of what passed in the Commons.

He also found it increasingly difficult to read; he could hardly cope with the print on official documents and had to tell a private secretary to write in darker ink. The final difficulty was the development of cataracts in both eyes. The first, in the right eye, was later successfully removed in an operation on 24 May 1894, some ten weeks after his resignation. Unfortunately, a second developed in his left eye, and it was felt it would not be advisable to operate on it. When to these problems are added some of the other physical difficulties Gladstone faced – neuralgia, shortness of breath and exhaustion – it is no surprise he had doubts himself about once again leading the country. He recorded on 15 July 1892 his own assessment of his capabilities: 'Frankly; from the condition (*now*) of my senses, I am no longer fit for public life: yet bidden to walk in it.'[10] In his letter of resignation, some two years later, he explained to the Queen why he could not go on:

> he is sensible of a diminished capacity for prolonged labour ... his deafness has become in parliament, and even in the cabinet, a serious inconvenience, of which he must reckon on more progressive increase. More grave than this, and more rapid in its growth, is the obstruction of vision which arises from cataract in both his eyes. It has cut him off in substance from the newspapers, and from all except the best types in the best lights.[11]

This would certainly suffice as cause to go, as far as the public needed to know, but it was far from being the whole story.

His declining health meant that Gladstone spent time abroad during these sixteen months. On 21 December 1892 he and daughter Helen set of for Biarritz (Catherine stayed at home this time). He evidently found the rest reinvigorating, for when he left there on 9 January 1893 he had put on weight, and on his return Edward Hamilton found him (and Catherine) in good and lively spirits, ready to face the rigours of the new session. This, however, turned out to be a major trial and by the time he went once more to Biarritz at the beginning of 1894, he was under siege in the cabinet. He did not bow to calls, orchestrated by Rosebery, to declare his intentions over his future before he left: that decision would have to wait until his return. A large party, headed by Gladstone and his wife and including Mrs Mary Drew and one of her children, together with Herbert Gladstone and Algernon West, left London on 13 January 1894, returning on 10 February. But this was hardly a holiday. Gladstone was in low spirits and spent most of his time while away discussing the vexed question of the navy estimates, while the cabinet, who had been told they should not meet in his absence, waited anxiously for his return and his now hoped-for resignation. They did not have long to wait.

Whatever the state of Gladstone's health by the time of his resignation, when he took office two years earlier his desire to see the Irish question through helped to give him the strength to take an active role in the struggle. His work on the drafting of the Government of Ireland Bill and its defence provides the story of the last great public struggle in his career. It was, as Colin Matthew points out, 'a straightforward proposal for constitutional amendment'.[12] It proposed the establishment in Ireland of a two-house legislature, with a government based in it, exactly on the Westminster model. Full authority, however, would come to it only gradually, so that power over the judiciary and police force, land legislation and finance, would be taken up over a period of time, rather than immediately the bill was passed. This made sense, since there were as yet no office buildings available for the administration in Ireland.

There were, however, two major problems with the proposal. The first of these concerned the future place of Irish MPs at Westminster. Gladstone had set up a six-man committee of the cabinet to look into this. They concluded that eighty Irish MPs should attend Westminster and vote on what were deemed 'Irish' or 'Imperial' questions, but not on those that were felt to be 'British' ones; however, no one specified exactly what these questions were supposed to be.

The second point at issue, and one that was more difficult to settle, concerned financial arrangements. It was agreed that Ireland should contribute a certain sum of money to the Imperial Treasury, which would come from Ireland's customs duties. Unfortunately, due to a miscalculation arising from faulty arithmetic in the Treasury and at Dublin Castle, the amount raised by these duties was overestimated. The error was such that the amount it was believed Ireland could afford to donate to the Imperial Treasury was so great that, if taken, there would not be sufficient left for the new Irish government to administer the country. The mistake, however, whether deliberate or not (some said it was a Unionist attempt to wreck the whole thing) was not uncovered until after the Bill had been introduced, and, like that section relating to the MP question, this part of the Bill had to be amended during the Committee stage of the debate.

Gladstone himself introduced the Government of Ireland Bill to the Commons on 13 February 1893 and this marked the beginning of an arduous 82-day-long debate. The Conservative and Unionist opposition fought the measure clause by clause. In all, they spoke for 152 hours and made 938 speeches; the government managed to speak for 'only' fifty-seven hours and gave 459 speeches. The Liberal Party had agreed, at a meeting held at the Foreign Office on 27 March, that they would leave most of the work of defence to the Prime Minister, just as Gladstone wished. The second reading of the bill began on 6 April, followed by the crucial Committee stage, during which the problems relating to Irish MPs and finances were revealed and had to be dealt with. It was agreed that Irish MPs should sit at Westminster without any restrictions, while the financial question was settled so that one-third of Ireland's current revenue, whatever that might be, would be devoted to the Imperial exchequer.

Attempting to secure the passage of the Bill exhausted the elderly Gladstone, but his efforts thrilled his supporters. As one of them remarked on 11 May: 'I have never seen Mr. Gladstone so dramatic, so prolific of all the resources of the actor's art. The courage, the authority, and the melodrama of it were irresistible.' But it could be difficult:

> For ten minutes Mr. Gladstone spoke, holding his audience spellbound by his force. Then came a sudden change, and it seemed that

> he was about to collapse from sheer physical exhaustion. His voice failed, huskiness and indistinctness took the place of clearness and lucidity ... By sheer strength of enthusiasm and an overflowing wealth of eloquence, Mr. Gladstone literally conquered every physical weakness, and secured an effect electric in its influence even on seasoned 'old hands'.[13]

It was a remarkable effort, and the debate itself was violent – on one occasion literally so. Tempers frayed in a summer heat-wave and when, on 27 July, the guillotine was invoked to bring an end to the discussion of the Committee, a fight broke out in the Commons because the Unionists refused to take part in the vote. The Bill finally passed its third reading on 1 September by a majority of thirty-four, but by then it had run out of steam. The House of Lords took very little notice of it, dismissing it on 8 September, after only four days of debate, by a massive 419 votes to forty-one. Gladstone's reaction was muted: he appears to have been exhausted by the effort of getting the Bill through the Commons. He had left London and was in Scotland by the day of the Lords' vote, and did not return until 1 November. He did not call a cabinet to discuss the Bill's failure, and his somewhat half-hearted suggestion that the measure should be reintroduced in 1894 and that he would dissolve the Commons if the Lords rejected it again was not taken up. He did not press the point. The Liberal and Nationalist parties in the Commons simply did not have the strength to force the Lords to compromise on the Home Rule issue, and neither did the Prime Minister. The question of Irish Home Rule was to rest for another twenty years, and it was a reformed House of Lords that allowed a bill to pass in 1914; however, the outbreak of the First World War prevented its enactment.

While Irish Home Rule was the question which dominated the first year of Gladstone's fourth ministry, it was not the only issue facing the government. Another was the Local Government (or 'Parish Councils') Bill. As usual Gladstone took little interest in this local government measure, the passage of which was finally secured on 1 March 1894, two days before his resignation, by H.H. Fowler, the President of the Local Government Board. Seeing this through was no small achievement on Fowler's part: he spoke on it over 800 times. As finally passed, it established nearly 7,000 elected parish councils, with responsibility for local affairs in villages and towns of over 300 inhabitants. Perhaps the most significant thing about it was that it allowed all women, even those who were married and therefore did not pay rates, not only to vote but also to stand for election. It can be seen as a small step towards political enfranchisement for women – but this was something Gladstone did not favour.

If the Local Government Bill was a kind of subtext in the life of Gladstone's last ministry, there was another issue at the very heart of its existence, and this one did not go away – it concerned the future of Uganda. The situation in Uganda had reached a crisis by 1892. A three-way power struggle had erupted there between Protestants (supported by the Imperial British East Africa Company), Catholics (under French influence) and those who retained their traditional beliefs. The company, far from making a profit out of its investment, had run into severe financial difficulties and, without an injection of government funds, would either face insolvency or have to withdraw. To Rosebery, the newly-appointed foreign secretary, British withdrawal from Uganda was unthinkable. Rosebery was in favour of a policy of 'continuity' with that of his Conservative predecessor, Salisbury. Uganda could serve as a base from which to send a force northwards, into the Nile valley, helping to keep the French clear of the headwaters of the Nile, an area the British could not let fall into hostile hands as it would threaten their position in Egypt. In any case, one did not abandon part of the British Empire, and certainly not to bloodthirsty natives.

As far as the Foreign Secretary was concerned the retention of Uganda was not just a question of expediency: since the Imperial British East Africa Company had been given a Royal Charter it was the duty of the government to back it up. If the company could not continue to administer the area, it was the British government who now had the responsibility for 'the territory, the inhabitants and the missionaries'.[14] Gladstone, like many others in the Liberal Party, was not convinced by Rosebery's arguments: on 26 September 1892 he told Spencer: 'Rosebery has I think been carried quite off his legs by the Jingoes at the Foreign Office and its agents'.[15] To an extent, he was right: the Foreign Office was gathering all the support it could from missionary organisations and the press for the policy of retention. The result of this disagreement was a serious rift between the Prime Minister and the Foreign Secretary.

Gladstone was determined to defeat Rosebery without causing a major crisis in the government. He knew how sensitive Rosebery was, so this would not be an easy task, but he did not fully grasp the degree of Rosebery's commitment to Uganda. Throughout September and October the two men exchanged letters, with Rosebery pressing for a cabinet meeting and Gladstone trying to delay one. When a meeting was held at the beginning of October, Rosebery and his only two allies in the cabinet, Fowler and the President of the Board of Trade, A.J. Mundella, defied Gladstone and the majority. Gladstone and his friends, like Harcourt, were furious. In the event, all that could be agreed, and it took until November to reach even this limited agreement, was to send out a commissioner to investigate how things really were in Uganda and what it would be best to do with the country. So far, so good; but the commissioner chosen to go was Sir Gerald Portal, who had previously served in Egypt as Lord Cromer's secretary. Portal was informed by Rosebery that he was to report as his conscience dictated – but to say that Britain should retain possession of Uganda. He found this easy enough to do, and on the basis of his report, Rosebery, in March 1894, shortly after Gladstone's resignation, announced that the proposed policy of withdrawal had been abandoned. Uganda became a British protectorate on 19 June 1894.

The whole Uganda episode was a sorry one for Gladstone. His own view had been consistent: the Liberal government had no business expanding the British Empire, Uganda itself was of no use and was only an expense. It was true it might help Britain in her quest to retain control over Egypt, but then he felt Britain should abandon her occupation of Egypt anyway. In this, he had the support of most of the cabinet, but despite this, it was Rosebery who had won the argument. He had withstood all Gladstone's pressure, enlisted the support of the missionaries and the media (as well as of the Conservative Party) and done enough to see his policy carried out. He also did enough to succeed Gladstone as prime minister, even though one thing this Uganda policy had done was to turn Gladstone very much against the idea.

Elsewhere in the African empire, the expansion into Matabeleland and Mashonaland by the British South Africa Company had led to war with the local native powers. But Gladstone had more to do than concern himself with events so far away and not, apparently, to do with the British government. In any case, he seemed to quite like Rhodes, whom he had met on two occasions and, rather curiously, did not see the extent of his imperialist ambitions. (Rhodes believed in an 'all red route' from the Cape to Cairo and wanted to build a railway between the two places, totally on British land). Rhodes gave money to the Liberal Party, so he was left alone to do as he wished by the Liberal government, and the power of the chartered company grew as a result. Unfortunately, no one saw the increasing anxiety of the Boer settlers, who felt more threatened than ever by British involvement in their territory.

If Gladstone was generally out of sympathy with imperial expansion, he was also out of sympathy with expenditure on 'defence'. Ever since the days of Palmerston's ministry in the 1860s he had stood out against increasing spending on the navy and army. It was, perhaps ironically, this question that was to bring about his final retirement from public life. From the summer of 1893 the First Lord of the Admiralty, Lord Spencer, had begun to press for an increase in the navy estimates. Several factors had led to this. First, there was the new Franco-Russian military agreement, which brought Europe's two largest naval powers (after Britain) together and posed a distinct threat to Britain's position in the Mediterranean. Second, the expenditure agreed by the 1888 Naval Defence Act had nearly run out. Third, the German government's naval plans were beginning to come to fruition. Added to these factors was pressure from both the Conservative leaders and even the Queen, together with the loss of two Royal Navy battleships in a collision in the Mediterranean in broad daylight.

In December 1893 the cabinet met to discuss the Admiralty's navy estimates for 1894–5. By this date large sectors of influential public opinion had become alarmed at French shipbuilding and were calling loudly for expansion. The naval officers on the Board of Admiralty declared to Spencer that they would resign if the government did not agree to their proposals. The full building programme put forward called for the construction of seven large and two smaller battleships, some twenty cruisers, over 110 destroyers and torpedo boats, and other vessels. Worse than the size of the proposed navy, however, was its probable cost – it was estimated at no less than £31 million to be spread over five years.

Gladstone was not impressed. When Lord George Hamilton, a former Conservative First Lord of the Admiralty, moved a motion calling for increased estimates, Gladstone made it a motion of no confidence in the government. He told Hamilton on 17 November 1893 that 'neither the House nor the country need entertain the smallest apprehension of the distinct naval superiority of Great Britain'.[16] The government won by thirty-six votes, and, while Gladstone was pleased with this, he realised the difficulties of his situation. It was, he noted, 'almost hopeless when a large minority allows itself [to] panic and joining hands with the professional elements works on the susceptibilities of a portion of the people to alarm them'.[17] This, however, 'was simply one of those periodic invasion scares' which Gladstone had witnessed since the 1840s, none of which had come to anything; he was not worried now.

But many people were. The Queen, the First Lord and Naval Lords of the Admiralty, Rosebery and the Foreign Office, nearly all of the cabinet, many members of the Liberal Party, the Conservative Party, the press and many members of the public were all ranged against him. At this point, Gladstone felt the full weight of his declining physical powers, especially his loss of vision. The cabinet became more convinced he would resign at any time, but on 8 January 1894 he addressed them for no less than fifty minutes, attacking the Spencer programme and putting forward his own plan for gradual naval expansion. He could not yet bring himself to resign, clearly feeling it would be a betrayal of the Liberal Party ('Liberalism cannot put on the garb of Jingoism without suffering for it') and of his mentors – Peel, Aberdeen, Cobden (he was not ashamed to associate with the long-dead radical now) and Bright. As he reminded his colleagues

> I have come to be considered not only an English but a European statesman. My name stands in Europe as a symbol of a policy of peace, moderation and non-aggression. What would be said of my active participation in a policy that will be taken as plunging England into a whirlpool of militarism.

It was, he predicted, a policy that would 'end in a race towards bankruptcy by all the powers of Europe'.[18]

The cabinet, obviously very out of sympathy with him, followed Gladstone's presentation with a discussion, actually in his presence, of whether or not he should resign, but decided in the end he could go abroad and make a decision there himself. Gladstone left for Biarritz (in 'enemy' territory) once again and debated with his guests what he should do. He made clear in an outspokenly radical memorandum the one thing he would *not* do, agree to the navy estimates:

> The Plan
>
> I deem it to be in excess of public expectations
> I know it to be in excess of all precedent
> It entails unjust taxation
> It endangers sound finance
> I shall not minister to the alarming aggression of the professional elements
>   to the weakness of alarmism
>   to the unexampled narrowness of party
> Not lend a hand to dress Liberalism in Tory clothes
>
> I shall not break to pieces the continuous action of my political life, nor trample on the tradition from every colleague who has ever been my teacher. Above all I cannot & will not add to the perils & the coming calamities of Europe by an act of militarism which will be found to involve a policy, and which excuses thus the militarism of Germany, France or Russia. England's providential part is to help peace, and liberty of which peace is the nurse; this policy is the foe of both. I am ready to see England dare the world in arms: but not to see England help to set the world in arms.[19]

On his return to London, Gladstone was ready for action, but by this time the cabinet had clearly decided he should retire. When it met on 12 February, however, whatever his colleagues expected (or hoped), Gladstone chaired the meeting in the usual way. When the items on the agenda were completed and the time for the expected announcement of his resignation arrived, none was made and the ministers duly dispersed. Five days later a cabinet dinner was due to be held. Before then, Sir Algernon West had made it clear to the Grand Old Man that the cabinet believed he was surely going to announce his resignation at the dinner. Again, they were disappointed: 'Cabinet dinner. All. I believe it was expected I should say something. But from my point of view there is nothing to be said.'[20] It almost seems as if he was leading them on. On 27 February, however, he wrote to the Queen announcing to her his decision to retire, and the two met the next day. Gladstone wrote: 'I never saw her looking better. She was at the highest point of her cheerfulness. Her manner was personally kind throughout.' She was, no doubt, very pleased to be getting rid of the old man at last, for good. They could not find much to talk about, 'but fog, rain and the coming journey to Italy all did their duty and helped'. The only thing of any importance was Gladstone's 'impression, an impression only' of what the Queen intended to do as a result of his resignation:

> she has at present no idea of any thing but a simple and limited reconstruction, such as is necessarily consequent upon the retirement of a Prime Minister, and has no idea of resorting to the Tories or Opposition: further that she will not ask any advice from me as to the head; and further still that she will send for Rosebery.[21]

Gladstone's reflections on the Queen's reception show he was not very impressed with her actions. He commented that he received only one brief note from her

> in the process which has wound up an account reaching over 52 years from September 1[3] 1841 when I was sworn of the Privy Council ... the proceeding was brief through the interview ... The same brevity perhaps prevails in settling a tradesman's bill, when it reaches over many years ... Not one syllable proceeded from Her Majesty either as to the future or the past.[22]

Gladstone's final verdict was that his relations with the Queen had been rather like those he had enjoyed with a mule in Sicily in 1838: the animal had been efficient though unfriendly. It had been a long time since Gladstone and the Queen had been on anything approaching friendly terms.

Gladstone told his cabinet colleagues the next day, Thursday 1 March, and this, the 'blubbering Cabinet', was the last of the 556 he had chaired. The scene was 'really moving', according to Gladstone, but he was not over impressed by some of his colleagues. The Earl of Kimberley tried to speak first, but broke down. Harcourt read an enormously long prepared statement: 'nine-tenths buncrum', said the Premier. Morley and others were all in tears.[23] Gladstone then went to the Commons, announced the government's acceptance of amendments to the Local Government Bill and sat out Lord Randolph Churchill's tedious pronouncements on it. When he left the House of Commons, it was for the last time, sixty-one years after he first entered it.

Gladstone's fourth ministry cannot be seen as one of the high points of his career: he was defeated on all three of the issues that really mattered to him. It was no small achievement to see the Irish Home Rule Bill through the Commons, but he had no answer to the Lords' summary dismissal of the measure. In some ways, the cases of Uganda and naval expansion were worse. In both he was held off and effectively defeated by elements in his own party. Rosebery at the Foreign Office and Spencer at the Admiralty were more in sympathy with the age than Gladstone himself, and he found he simply could not prevail against them. The result of these disappointments was to highlight his increasing physical difficulties. An eighty-four year old prime minister who was going blind and increasingly deaf clearly could not last in the post. Even Gladstone, with his almost superhuman strength, found things were getting just too difficult for him: in the end, resignation was his only option.

The Liberal government did not outlast him for long. Rosebery, with the aid of Portal's report, was able to secure Uganda for the Empire. Spencer, helped by the Conservatives, was able to get agreement for his naval building programme. Paying for it would not be easy, but Harcourt managed to increase some taxes and introduce death duties and use the extra revenue raised to fund it. Rosebery was not, however, a successful prime minister. He offended the Irish Home Rulers by announcing that England, the 'predominant member' of the partnership, would have to be convinced of the justice of the Home Rulers' demands. He also upset some Liberals by having two horses in succession win the Derby. The government was suddenly defeated in the Commons on 21 June 1895 on a matter relating to War Office administration, at which Rosebery and several of his colleagues decided to dissolve Parliament. Most of the cabinet did not want to, and they would have been wise not to. Rosebery was no Gladstone, however, and in the July election the Liberals were heavily defeated. In total, when it was over, 177 Liberals and 82 Irish Nationalists faced 340 Conservatives and seventy-one Unionists – a Conservative majority of

152. Rosebery soon resigned and the Liberal Party was doomed to remain in opposition until December 1905.

RETIREMENT, 1894–1898

Gladstone announced on 7 July 1894 that he would not be seeking re-election to Parliament. This did not mean that in his last years he completely abandoned all involvement in politics. Rosebery did not treat him as a confidant, but Gladstone accepted he had not helped him become prime minister and was therefore not to expect any favours from him. Yet this did not prevent the former prime minister from intervening in those matters which he felt were a cause for public concern. Perhaps the most important of these were Gladstone's responses to massacres of Armenians in the Ottoman Empire. He was visited at Hawarden on 29 December 1894 (his eighty-fifth birthday) by a deputation of Armenian bishops. On 6 August the following year he addressed a large meeting at Chester, urging Salisbury's government to act against the Turks. Salisbury might have liked to do so, but, as he pointed out, with the French, German and Russian governments currently supporting Abdul Hamid, the Ottoman sultan, there was little Britain could do. (He might have added that Britain had her own interests to be concerned about, too, such as French advances on the Nile from West Africa.) On 24 September 1896, at Hengler's Circus in Liverpool, Gladstone addressed another large crowd on the wickedness of the Turks, a month later denouncing Abdul Hamid as the 'Great Assassin' and organiser of genocide. These were Gladstone's last major public appearances and the basis of his last major article in *The Nineteenth Century*: it was unfortunate neither had any real effect where it mattered.

Gladstone also spent time working on religious issues. His most substantial *The Works of Bishop Butler* appeared in February 1896. Aside from Gladstone's general feeling that Christianity was under fire in the modern world and needed defence, in September 1896 a new problem arose. In that year Pope Leo XIII published an Encyclical which stated that Anglican monastic orders were invalid. The Grand Old Man was furious: he had hoped, like most Anglican High Churchmen, that the Church of England and the Church of Rome might be getting closer, but now, it seemed, the Roman Church was continuing to pull away, as it had since 1870. When the Archbishop of Canterbury, Dr Edward Benson, and his wife visited Hawarden on their return from a visit to Ireland, Mrs Benson made an observation on the elderly statesman:

> I had never heard him so excited; what with Armenia, Lord Rosebery and most of all the Pope, all in one moment, the Archbishop sat with his teacup in his hand, I suppose for three quarters of an hour, waiting to drink.

It was the Pope's actions, she thought, which had particularly upset Gladstone.[24] Both of them were more upset the next day, however, when the unfortunate archbishop collapsed and died in the middle of a church service. Gladstone, who saw the funeral train off, was seen to be shocked and pale while waiting at the station.

Gladstone spent some time in these years continuing his travels to the continent. He did not take up the offer of a tour of the United States, as this was quite simply beyond his strength. He could still, however, travel to Europe, and on 8 January 1895 he and Catherine left for Cannes, reaching it after nearly thirty-five hours of non-stop travel. They then moved on to a grand hotel at Cap Martin, staying – although they probably did not realise it – in the same place at the same time as the Emperor Franz Josef of Austria-Hungary. The Gladstones returned to England in March, having benefited from the more genial climate of the Riviera. In the summer, he embarked on a two-week cruise around the Baltic, this time with his children Mary and Harry. Gladstone found this cruise beneficial, too, enjoying the weather and most, at least, of the sights. He did not, however, particularly appreciate the opening of the Kiel Canal by the Kaiser Wilhelm II of Germany. This canal, the construction of which had caused some concern in the Admiralty in London, connected the Baltic and North Seas, allowing Germany's new battle fleet to be moved against Russia and France (and Britain, too) as required. Gladstone saw the ceremonial attached to the event as another symbol of the dangerous militarism sweeping across Europe, and reportedly told those near him that the event 'meant war'.[25]

At the end of the year Gladstone and Catherine took another visit to Cannes, returning in March 1896, and they went there again between

January and March 1897. On the second of these occasions Gladstone made the acquaintance of the Queen's daughter, Princess Louise, Marchioness of Lorne. Much to Gladstone's surprise, he found that she shared his opinion that Britain should be giving her support to the Greeks in their war with the Ottoman Empire. He even had an audience with the Queen, who, with the Prince of Wales and party, was staying at a hotel near Nice. He thought the Queen seemed so old and frail that plans must be afoot to announce her abdication. Gladstone and Catherine's last visit to Cannes took place between the end of November 1897 and the middle of February 1898.

After his retirement, Gladstone was well aware that he could not expect to live very much longer, and, at about the time of Archbishop Benson's death, he began to prepare a final revision of his will. He made arrangements whereby on his death his three sons should each receive £27, 000 and holdings, while his three daughters were each to receive £15, 000. (In 1890 he had already divided £43, 000 between his surviving children.) On 7 December 1896 he drew up a 'Declaration', which he sealed in an envelope and gave to his son Stephen, to be opened after his death. This stated that Gladstone had 'at no period of my life … been guilty of the act which is known as that of infidelity to the marriage bed'. But this statement, Colin Matthew points out, is qualified and Gladstone's diary reinforces its qualifications.[26]

Just over three weeks later, on 29 December he made his last entry in his diary, which he had started seventy-one years before, on 16 July 1825 (he had stopped daily entries on 23 May 1894):

> In the last twelvemonth, eyes and ears have declined, but not materially. The occasional constriction of the chest is the only inconvenience that can be called new. I am not without hope that Cannes may have a mission to act upon it. Catherine is corporeally better than she was twelve months ago. ... The blessings of family life continue to be poured in the largest measure upon my unworthy head. Even my temporal affairs have thriven. ... As to politics I think the basis of my mind is laid principally in finance and philanthropy. The prospects of the first are darker than I have ever known them. Those of the second are black also; but with more hope of some early dawn. I do not enter on interior matters. It is so easy to write, but to write honestly nearly impossible.[27]

With the onset of severe facial pains in the autumn of 1897, his family doctor was summoned and he prescribed laudanum and suggested the Gladstones should visit the south of France, which had proved so beneficial before. Gladstone and Catherine left for Cannes in November. But this time it was not so rewarding. Gladstone found he could not work effectively any longer, and so in February 1898 he returned to London. He then went to Bournemouth, where he was at last persuaded to seek specialist medical advice. On 18 March 1898 inoperable cancer was diagnosed and Gladstone went home to Hawarden. He was strong enough to leave the house until 6 April, and to come down formally to dinner until 18 April, while he continued to get up most days until about 12 May. A week or so later, on Ascension Day, 19 May, he died.

***

The news reached a collection of newspaper reporters waiting downstairs, by inference, when they heard Stephen Gladstone's prayers for the dead. Special editions of London papers were issued. Herbert accepted the offer of a public funeral on behalf of the family and Gladstone's body was dressed in academic robes – he was a Doctor of Civil Law *honoris causa* of his beloved University of Oxford – and shipped by train to London. He lay in state in Westminster Hall – the first person to do so – on 26 and 27 May and the funeral itself was on Saturday, 28 May when he was buried in the north transept of Westminster Abbey.

Unlike Laura Thistlethwayte, Gladstone's great friend, who had died in May 1894, Catherine outlived him. She had spent many years at her husband's side, helping him, guiding him – usually away from resignation – calming him, when necessary or able. She seems to have been an effective head of the Gladstone household and, even if Gladstone thought she should not, she also played an important part in his political life. Her health, like his, had begun to give way in the 1890s, however. Even so, she had stood through her husband's funeral service until, at the end, sitting for a few minutes. After that, however, she stood and shook hands with and thanked the pallbearers. She managed to send the Queen an account of the service. Catherine survived her husband by only just over two years, and died in June 1900. She was buried next to her husband in Westminster Abbey on 19 June.

Gladstone's death made little difference to the world of politics. He himself thought that he had outlived his time and had been left behind by the political developments of the 1880s and 1890s. He certainly did not share the enthusiasm for imperialism so apparent in many circles, nor did he approve of the ever-increasing military spending that accompanied the expansion of the Empire. While some in the Liberal Party, such as Rosebery, disagreed with him, others did not. They also thought, however, that new social policies were an essential if the Liberals were to provide a viable alternative to the Conservatives and fight off a challenge from the newly-founded Independent Labour Party, established in Bradford in January 1893.

It might be said that Gladstone's death marks the end of an era. His fourth ministry had ended in disaster for the Liberal Party, but years in opposition did much to reinvigorate it, and many of the leading names of the great Liberal ministries from 1906 to 1914 had learned their trade while Gladstone led the Party, in and out of government. He had become widely known among the general public, too. Trainloads visited the Hawarden estate to see the Grand Old Man at work, chopping down trees – and he received numerous axes as gifts, to help him.

The last words can perhaps appropriately be left to Arthur Balfour, Prime Minister Salisbury's nephew and successor, and Conservative Leader of the House of Commons. As he told his fellow MPs:

> he added a dignity, as he added a weight, to the deliberations of this House by his genius, which I think it is impossible adequately to replace. It is not enough for us to keep up simply a level, though it be a high level, of probity and of patriotism. The mere average of civil virtue is not sufficient to preserve this Assembly from the fate that had overcome so many other Assemblies, products of democratic forces. More than this is required; more than this was given us by Mr. Gladstone.[28]

CONCLUSION

William Gladstone led a long and active life, in both the private and public sphere. It is not surprising that, even while he lived, considerable attention was paid to his private life. While he lived outwardly contentedly with his wife Catherine, he secretly spent hours in the company of London prostitutes and sometimes indulged in bouts of flagellation. After his death stories of this nature multiplied to the extent that in the 1920s the family took a member of the public to court for defamation of their late father's character. The publication of his diaries in more recent years has finally revealed, in stark detail, intimate facets of Gladstone's life. The reality, it appears, is not quite so salacious as the tales would have it.

Gladstone was born into a prosperous bourgeois family and most of his long-held beliefs were developed in the earliest years. Underpinning everything he believed and did was his unwavering faith in Christianity, inspired largely by two women in his life, his eldest sister, Anne, who died when Gladstone was eighteen years old, and his mother. Both of these women were low church evangelicals in their outlook, but Gladstone was a member of the high church wing of the Church of England at a time when it was gaining strength in the church community. His faith was reinforced during his years as an undergraduate at Oxford and fitted in well with that of many in the political party led by Sir Robert Peel. Gladstone's decision to enter politics rather than the Church was not an easy one for him to take, and his father had to help him to take it, and there were times, particularly earlier in his life, when he may have regretted it. But as time passed his belief that through politics he was carrying out God's will grew stronger and, to the end, never left him.

Gladstone was a strong-willed and, in many ways, larger-than-life character, who would nevertheless benefit from strong support to help him in life. He found it in a remarkable woman, Catherine Glynne. There were few people who could live contentedly with Gladstone for nearly fifty-nine years, but Catherine did. She shared many of his religious beliefs, listened to his outpourings on politics, and understood his involvement with ladies of the *demi-monde*. In the early days of their marriage it was clearly difficult for her to come to terms with his somewhat demanding and eccentric character, but as time passed she found ways to do so. Perhaps most importantly, she developed her own interests and commitments in charitable work. Visitors to the Gladstones' home would find Mrs G. circulating among the guests seeking donations of small change for her houses of refuge. Even if this meant she was sometimes away from Gladstone when he would have liked her around, he never interfered. When he really needed her – while touring Midlothian, for example – Catherine was always there: on the train, on the speech platform, in the houses of the great. Gladstone needed exceptional support throughout his life, and Catherine provided it.

Their children, too, played their part. Gladstone was no doubt a very dominant father, from whom it was not easy to get away. Of the sons, Henry fled to India, returning to help his father only much later in life, while the others stayed nearer home. If the eldest son, Willy, was something of a disappointment, he was forgiven, and after all he did provide a male heir. Herbert was much more like his father, a skilful and successful – and Liberal – politician. Stephen did what his father may have wanted to do himself at one time – he entered the Church of England. Until his father died, he remained stuck fast at Hawarden, despite his discontent. The daughters, too, struggled with mixed success to get away. Agnes managed to by marriage, but Mary, the Hawarden 'Chief of Staff,' remained in the family vicinity even when married, and continued to do some work for her father. Later, Helen had to return home to Hawarden and her father to succeed Mary and, like it or not, there she stayed while her father was alive. The Gladstones, then, if not a model family, were certainly a close one. It is not easy to judge by contemporary standards whether or not Gladstone was a 'good' father. To the extent that he did not alienate his children, it may safely be concluded he was a successful parent, but he was perhaps rather too domineering, and some discontent was certainly evident in his children's relations with him. For their part, they were prepared to remain closely associated with him, particularly, it may be said, after his death.

Gladstone left a memorandum to assure both his children and later generations that he was never unfaithful to Catherine, and there is no reason to disbelieve this assurance. But he did have a fascination for good-looking ladies, and this fascination may have had a sexual element. His friendship with Harriet, Duchess of Sutherland, and his years of meetings and correspondence with Laura Thistlethwayte figure prominently in his later life. He also spent much time patrolling the streets of London looking for prostitutes, even while prime minister – to the horror of his secretaries and of Lord Granville. It is clear that they did not see this as immoral in itself, but they were well aware of the damage it might cause if it was made public. The result was that some knowledge of these events reached the ears of the public, but the whole truth is less shocking than the partial truth and the additional tales that were known.

Much the same may be said of that other vice in which Gladstone at times indulged, self-flagellation. Once again, tales that Gladstone regularly beat himself, or was beaten by ladies of the night, circulated during his lifetime and continued after his death. However, the diaries have made it clear that again the full truth about this habit is less shocking than the partial truth previously reported. Gladstone was brought up to be well aware of his wickedness and his weakness, and sometimes he beat himself as a punishment for it. Beginning in 1849 he recorded using a whip to flagellate himself to curb lustful thoughts, and he did so on eight occasions that year. It was not unknown for others to do this (Newman was one of his contemporaries who did so), and to Gladstone it represented punishment for his unworthiness. But he never spent much time doing this, or continued with it over lengthy periods, and it does not really constitute an important element in his life story.

GLADSTONE THE POLITICIAN

Gladstone's private life does bear scrutiny, therefore, and it reflects the life of an extraordinary man: he would certainly have made an impression, whatever he did. But William Ewart Gladstone is most remembered as a politician, whose long life in the House of Commons witnessed a fundamental change in British politics. He was elected to Parliament in December 1832, just six months after the passage of the 'Great Reform Act' of that year and saw it through two other Reform Acts and radical changes in local government. When he was at school and when he entered university and politics, the political 'system' functioned much as it had done in the eighteenth century; when he retired, it had evolved into a recognisably modern one. Gladstone, too, was able to undergo a far-reaching change in his political outlook. When he entered Parliament he had come in on the right, reactionary, side of the political spectrum, on record as an opponent of Catholic emancipation and parliamentary reform; by the time he resigned he had become the 'People's William', the champion of popular Liberalism and Irish Home Rule. The extent of his political evolution and the length of his career make it one almost without parallel in British political history.

Britain's place in the world also changed in these years. The size of the British empire increased at unprecedented scale and speed, particularly from the 1880s onwards. Gladstone, despite his involvement in the process in 1882 with the occupation of Egypt, watched this development with dismay. As the world became a more militarised place, he became increasingly alienated from it.

In 1832 British politics was undergoing a radical change. Prior to that year the electoral system was shot through with anomalies: for example, in some constituencies there were no voters whatsoever; in others, a mass popular vote existed. Politics was something undertaken by people with money and spare time, and not all MPs, still less those peers who took the trouble to sit in the House of Lords, adopted an active role in the day-to-day affairs of Parliament when it was actually in session. Political parties were very underdeveloped. Cabinets did not meet regularly, and political decisions were made in clubs and over dinner. Few MPs, and certainly no elector, had an input into shaping party politics. Local government had similarly remained almost unchanged for centuries, and parish councils struggled with the impact of industrialisation and rapid population growth with little or no help from the centre.

By 1894 much of this had changed – the electoral system had been overhauled and the worst anomalies removed. Electors were chosen according to a national standard, and a majority of men, of whatever social class, had received the right to vote. MPs and peers, too, had organised themselves, or been organised, into political parties and all would identify with a party label – Liberal, Conservative, Liberal Unionist, Irish Nationalist or Ulster Unionist. They would regularly attend Parliament, voting on even minor issues. MPs, especially, now realised they had to be seen to be active since they had electors to report back to, via the daily newspapers. Although cabinets still met and shaped policy in secret, by 1894 there were annual party conferences made up of fee-paying party supporters, who expected the ministers, even the Prime Minister himself, to consider seriously and even adopt policies which they themselves suggested. Local government was also in the throes of reform, and here again the system that was emerging was recognisably modern. Local bodies were now to be largely elected, and among the electors were women. Britain, by 1894, had not yet become a parliamentary democracy, but it had clearly moved in that direction, and along with it, sometimes with reluctance, sometimes with ease, moved William Ewart Gladstone.

A recent study of Gladstone's life has suggested there were two sides to his personality. It might also be said that there were three 'political Gladstones': the young Tory zealot, the middle-aged ('Peelite') financier and the elderly, populist ('Palmerstonian') politician. If he never wavered in his Christian faith, his political evolution was profound.

In his first years in Parliament, young Gladstone was labelled a 'Tory', a 'rising hope' of those Tories whose philosophy was 'stern and unbending'. He spoke in defence of slavery; he wrote in defence of the established Anglican Church. But perhaps Gladstone was never quite as reactionary as he appeared, and if he was trying to become an ally of Peel he was going quite the wrong way about it. Ultra Tories were only one element in Sir Robert Peel's 'Conservative Party', as described in the 1834 Tamworth Manifesto, and Peel realised it was worth overlooking some of Gladstone's impetuosity, because he recognised ability when he saw it. Gladstone was not, and never had been, entirely opposed to all reforms, and Peel's awareness of this was enough for him to advance the young man's career.

The second phase of Gladstone's political career, that of the Peelite financier, actually lasted much longer, and outlived Peel himself by at least twenty years. It was Gladstone's time as vice-president and then president of the Board of Trade between 1841 and 1845 that brought to life his interest in finance. He sympathised with what Peel was trying to do: reform central government to make administration more efficient and ensure that public expenditure could be cut. Income tax, reintroduced in 1842 as a temporary measure, remained just that to Gladstone, who tried hard to see it abolished, although the outbreak of war with Russia in 1854 and the electors' rejection of the policy twenty years later made this impossible.

With Peel's resignation and death, Gladstone's career ran into problems. Personally, he would have been quite happy to ally with the Earl of Derby. But Derby's closest ally was Benjamin Disraeli, an individual with whom Gladstone found friendly relations impossible, while many of Derby's Tory followers were also objectionable to him, and they in any case certainly had no liking for him. This meant that Gladstone would have either had to remain an independent MP or else join the other, Liberal, side. At this stage, Gladstone had no particular regard for the Liberals' leader, Lord John Russell. But the rising power in Liberal circles was a man almost as odious to Gladstone as Disraeli, the flamboyant, ex-Tory, former foreign secretary, Lord Palmerston. Palmerston's views on politics and government spending ran almost directly counter to his own. Gladstone still believed the public should have little to do with the actual running of the country: Palmerston felt they should at least be encouraged to think they had a role to play in it. Gladstone remained convinced central government expenditure should be reduced: Palmerston thought there were more important things than that, things that governments should spend money on, such as ironclad warships and fortifications. It would have been difficult for these two men, with their apparently different policies and personalities to co-operate.

Gladstone's initial period in cabinet with Palmerston lasted for just over three years, refereed by the Earl of Aberdeen, and Gladstone found himself drafting a war budget in 1853 to finance a war with Russia, of which he approved. But the fall of Aberdeen's ministry brought Palmerston into office as prime minister and Gladstone's time in his cabinet lasted a mere three weeks. Once more, he was in opposition, and as time went by publishing increasingly hostile attacks on Palmerston's government. A dose of Tory rule, however, saw a reversal of this situation and made Gladstone decide to serve as Palmerston's Chancellor of the Exchequer. He spent the next six years fighting hard to keep expenditure down, but the result was uncertain. Palmerston forced through enormous loans for fortifications and estimates for warships. Gladstone had to choose: accept this policy or resign. But the elderly premier knew how to deal with the younger chancellor, realising that if Gladstone wanted to succeed him as Liberal leader, as he well knew he did, then he could not afford to resign. The policy worked and Palmerston remained prime minister until he died in October 1865. Gladstone, however, kept up the fight during the lifetime of the government. He encouraged the spread of international free trade, the Anglo-French Cobden–Chevalier Treaty of 1860 being a high point in this policy. At the same time as Palmerston was spending more money on defences against the French, Gladstone was able to see this treaty, which he viewed as a way of improving international relations, through the cabinet and Parliament. He also struggled, successfully, with the House of Lords and secured the abolition of duties on paper in 1861, against Palmerston's wishes, and he reduced income tax as best he could.

Gladstone's first premiership, from 1868 to 1874, saw him continue his drive for economy and he reduced government expenditure and the level of income tax. When the crisis over the level of defence spending came in 1874, Gladstone informed his colleagues, none of whom was really expecting it, that he intended to resign and to abolish income tax in the event of a Liberal victory. It came as a shock to him when, even with this promise, the Liberal Party lost the election. It seems no coincidence that in his last years, this disappointment meant that financial policy was no longer at the heart of Gladstone's political agenda. He stayed consistently loyal to Peel's legacy and always opposed increased government expenditure for any reason. But he realised, with increasing force over the years, that cutting taxes was only one of several things that would make him a popular politician, and it was this last consideration that came to dominate the final thirty or so years of his political life. With popular support he would be enabled to achieve his ambitions.

The development of Gladstone into a 'popular' politician only really began in the 1860s, and was seen in his speaking tours, especially to the north-east of England. The very success of this caused Palmerston increasing concern, but Gladstone was careful to reassure the elderly prime minister about his intentions. He had no reason to act too quickly; he could wait. Large audiences seemed to have appreciated what Gladstone had to say, if they could actually hear it, while Gladstone, on his part, seems to have appreciated large audiences. They reassured him about the 'character' of the British working classes, and convinced him they deserved to be included in the 'body politic' – they, at least the respectable men, should have the vote. His effective acquisition of the Hawarden estate helped him in this regard. He became an object of pilgrimage for more and more people, to see him at work in the woods, cutting down more and more trees. The high point of his career as a popular politician was doubtless his speaking tours of November 1879, the 'Midlothian campaign'. Here he seemed to have struck a genuine popular chord. It was wrong, he declared, for the British government to deploy ships and men in defence of a non-Christian empire that had massacred thousands of its Christian inhabitants. It was at last time, he said, for the Ottoman Empire to be expelled from Europe. The policy may not have been adopted, but Gladstone's attacks on the Conservative government, coupled with imperial disasters elsewhere in the world, did enough to bring him back to the leadership of the Liberal Party and back to the office of Prime Minister.

The story from then on, however, seems in some ways less successful. In the 1880s Gladstone adopted a policy that was not to the taste of some in his party, nor to the English electorate: Home Rule for Ireland. To Gladstone, justice demanded that the Irish people should have the political rights restored to them that had been unjustly taken away at the beginning of the century. But the attempts to secure the passage of Home Rule failed, while other policies that many felt the Liberal Party should have adopted, such as the inclusion of all men in the electorate or payment for MPs, were either lost altogether or relegated to second place. Nothing would divert Gladstone from Irish Home Rule: he knew what was right, he knew what had to be done, and others should – and surely would – see what he was doing was just.

Gladstone's political aims, therefore, varied over his lengthy career, and his success in achieving them also varied. What also needs to be considered is the effect of Gladstone's policies on the Liberal Party; to see how far they, and his determination to achieve them, damaged the party or perhaps even laid the foundations for its destruction.

GLADSTONE AND THE FUTURE OF LIBERALISM

Gladstone's own political career did not end on a particular high; he had not achieved Home Rule for Ireland and everything else mattered less to him. The effect of his career on the Liberal Party has been debated, and it may be that his longevity and obsessions did it a great deal of harm. The Liberal party was not Gladstone's own, and he had not been at the Willis's Room meeting in 1859 that is generally held to mark its birth. Indeed, in the 1840s and for most of the 1850s he had been on the opposite side of the House of Commons to those such as Russell, Bright and Palmerston who had got together to found it. He joined the party for a number of reasons. The one he most frequently gave was that it supported a policy he believed in – the unification of Italy. But he also joined it because the alternatives, political isolation and eventual obscurity or co-operation with the Conservatives, were unpalatable to him. However, the Liberal Party as it evolved after the older generation passed away was Gladstone's. The policies it stood for, like the disestablishment of the Church of Ireland, were Gladstone's, and those connected with the party who did not like the policies stayed fairly quiet. There was, however, a persistent drift of the 'Whig' aristocratic element away from the party throughout the later 1860s to the early 1880s, although when the public break came over Irish Home Rule, those who deserted the party at that point were not all Whigs. But those Liberals who chose not to support these 'Liberal Unionists' remained loyal to Gladstone, and it was the Unionists who became the outsiders, eventually submerged into the 'Conservative and Unionist Party', while the main body of the Liberal Party continued to carry the flag of Irish Home Rule well beyond Gladstone's death.

It is the years from 1886, when Gladstone was already seventy-six years of age, to his retirement that are seen as particularly detrimental to the Liberal Party and which ultimately compromised its future. His obsession with Home Rule and his dominance of the party prevented it from developing other policies to put to the electorate. The 1891 Newcastle Programme was the party's chance, and while the policies outlined in it were adopted, Gladstone did not prioritise them, telling the party faithful that Irish Home Rule was still the centre of their policies. When the party won the 1892 election, though not convincingly, Gladstone had his last try. His failure, and then the Government's adoption of naval and imperial policies directly opposed to his own, showed the world a defeated man.

The damage he had apparently caused the party became apparent in the brief premiership of his successor, Lord Rosebery. With the Grand Old Man safely out of the way, Rosebery was able to secure the policies his predecessor had stood out against for so long. But he did this with Conservative support, since many of his own party members were unhappy with this move and with him. His decision to dissolve Parliament and risk an election was a calamitous mistake, and after his defeat he did not stay as leader for long. The Liberal Party did not get back into office until December 1905, but it then remained there until a coalition government was formed with the Conservatives in 1915.

Although Gladstone's policies had lost the Liberal Party some members, enough remained for it to form one of the most effective governments of the twentieth century. It is doubtful whether he would have agreed with all of the policies of the Campbell Bannerman and Asquith ministries. These included the provision of state-funded old-age pensions and social security and increased defence expenditure, all involving higher taxes. But they also included, in 1914, Home Rule for Ireland (though the outbreak of war prevented this from coming into force). Even so, it was a Liberal Party that Gladstone would have recognised, and people undoubtedly remembered him when they voted for it.

The Liberal Party, however, has never been in office since 1915 as a majority party. In 1916 part of it, led by the former Chancellor of the Exchequer, David Lloyd George, formed a coalition with the Conservatives to fight and win the war, although some Liberals under Asquith's leadership refused to join. When the 'Coupon Election' was held in 1918, the candidates who held Lloyd George's endorsement or 'coupon', Liberals and Conservatives alike, won; and Asquith's Liberals were defeated. When Lloyd George himself was dropped by the Conservatives in 1922, his attempts to reunite the Liberal Party were rebuffed by those who had stood aside from the coalition. Faced by a united Conservative Party and an increasingly strong Labour Party, the Liberals had nothing, it seemed, to offer the electorate.

It would appear that Gladstone did not cripple the Liberal Party. Rosebery's defeat was not really Gladstone's responsibility, while the party's failure in the 1900 elections can be ascribed to the 'Boer War factor'. This election was called by the Conservatives to take advantage of what seemed to be imminent victory in the Boer War (although in fact it lasted for another two years). The Liberal ministry from 1905 to 1914 was one of the great reforming ministries. It was involvement in the First World War, and the split over its prosecution, that inflicted long-lasting injuries on the Liberal Party. It would be fairer to say that if anyone destroyed the Liberal Party, rather than Gladstone, it was either Lloyd George, for forming a coalition with the Conservatives, or Asquith, for not allowing him to reunite the party.

Gladstone was perceived by most of his contemporaries as a 'great' man. The quantity of work devoted to him even today is further evidence of his importance. By any standards, he was a man with extraordinary capacity for work, reading books, writing letters and papers of enormous volume. Even his diary, which for the most part simply notes what he did in the briefest form, is enormously long.

Gladstone's desire to do what was 'right', to bring 'justice' to those 'deserving' of it – in Britain and Ireland and further afield – cannot be questioned. But he would not be opposed when his mind was made up: the party, the public, everyone would have to go along with him. He did not help the Liberal Party but, as he saw it, the party was there to help him; and he was there to help carry out God's work for humanity.

Politicians have continued to see in Gladstone – as indeed many have in his arch-rival Disraeli – a figure to admire. His ideas and plans – of reducing government expenditure, of making central government more efficient and less oppressive – have been close to the heart of recent British leaders. Whether they have fully grasped his ideals remains an unanswered question. Gladstone helped Britain along the road to democracy, and his fights with Palmerston and especially with Disraeli showed the country how parliamentary government should be carried on. His orations and his writings, stirring battle-cries to any and every one, remain outstandingly forceful productions.

Was Gladstone's political career successful? There were various aims that he did not achieve. Home Rule for Ireland is the most obvious of these: he tried repeatedly to secure this, and did not live to see it passed. He did not prevent the annexation of Uganda, nor did he abolish income tax. Even so, it was a remarkable career by any standards. He served as prime minister four times for a total of fifteen and a half years, and was chancellor of the exchequer for sixteen and a half years. Perhaps the most important thing about his career was his emergence as a genuine popular politician, someone the masses could identify with. Gladstone became an iconic figure in his lifetime, and he remains so. He was, and still is, the archetypal 'Victorian', and, notwithstanding his 'failures', there can be no doubt that he was a great politician and a truly liberal statesman.

Notes

INTRODUCTION

1 Palmerston, in conversation with the Earl of Shaftesbury, 1864, in P. Guedalla, *Palmerston*, London, Benn, 1926, p. 401.

2 Gathorne Hardy, diary, 31 December 1898, in A.E. Gathorne Hardy (ed.) *Gathorne Hardy, First Earl of Cranbrook: a memoir with extracts from his diary and correspondence*, 2 vols, London, Longmans, 1910, II, pp. 364–5.

3 R.A. Cross, *A Political History*, [?London], privately printed, 1903, p. 103.

4 Disraeli, speech, 20 September 1876, quoted in R. Shannon, *Gladstone, II: Heroic Minister, 1868–1898*, London, Allen Lane, 1999, p. 183.

5 Beaconsfield to the Earl of Derby, letter, October 1876, quoted in P. Magnus, *Gladstone: A Biography*, London, John Murray, 1954, p. 245.

6 Queen Victoria to the Marquess of Lansdowne, letter, 12 August 1892, Lord Newton, *Lord Lansdowne: A Biography*, London, Macmillan, 1929.

7 Marquess of Salisbury to the Earl of Carnarvon, letter, 4 April 1867, Lady G. Cecil, *The Life of Robert, Marquess of Salisbury*, 4 vols, London, Hodder & Stoughton, 1921–31, I, p. 244.

8 W.V. Harcourt to Lord E. Fitzmaurice, letter, 6 January 1875, A.G. Gardiner, *The Life of Sir William Harcourt*, 2 vols, London, Constable, 1923, I, p. 285.

9 W.V. Harcourt to G.J. Goschen, letter, 7 January 1875, A.D. Elliot, *The Life of George Joachim Goschen, Viscount Goschen, 1831–1907*, 2 vols, London, Longman, 1911, I, p. 153.

10 Sir Charles Dilke, diary [1879], S. Gwynn and G.M. Tuckwell, *The Life of the Rt Hon. Sir Charles Wentworth Dilke*, 2 vols, London, John Murray, 1917, I, p. 279.

11 *Pall Mall Gazette*, 14 December 1883, quoted in J. Morley, *The Life of William Ewart Gladstone*, 3 vols, London, Macmillan, 1904, II, p. 415.

12 Quoted in D.A. Hamer, *John Morley: Liberal Intellectual in Politics*, Oxford, Oxford University Press, 1968, p. 45.

13 *The Spectator*, 29 October 1864, quoted in Morley, *Gladstone*, II, pp. 176–7.

14 F. Newman to Gladstone, letter, quoted in Morley, *Gladstone*, II, p. 177.

15 Morley, *Gladstone*, I, pp. 2–3.

16 Magnus, *Gladstone*, pp. xi–xii.

17 A.J.P. Taylor, *British Prime Ministers and Other Essays*, ed. C. Wrigley, London, Penguin, 2000, p. 33.

18 E.J. Feutchwanger, *Gladstone*, 2nd edn, Basingstoke, Macmillan, 1989, pp. xxii, xx.

19 H. Wilson, *A Prime Minister on Prime Ministers*, London, Weidenfeld & Nicolson, 1977, pp. 108–9.
20 P. Stansky, *Gladstone: A Progress in Politics*, New York and London, Norton, 1979, p. 26.
21 'Peter Stansky talks to Daniel Snowman', *History Today*, 52 (7, July 2002): 38.
22 A. Ramm, *William Ewart Gladstone*, Cardiff, G.P.C. Books, 1989, pp. 1; 118.
23 R. Shannon, *Gladstone, I: 1809–1865*, London, Hamish Hamilton, 1982.
24 Shannon, *Heroic Minister.*
25 Shannon, *Heroic Minister*, pp. xii, xiii–xvii.
26 H.C.G. Matthew, *Gladstone, 1809–1898*, Oxford, Oxford University Press, 1999, pp. 1–2.
27 R. Jenkins, *Gladstone*, Basingstoke, Macmillan, 1995.
28 T.L. Crosby, *The Two Mr. Gladstones: A Study in Psychology and History*, New Haven and London, Yale University Press, 1997, pp. 5–6.
29 E.F. Biagini, *Gladstone*, Basingstoke, Macmillan, 2000, p. 115.
30 F.W. Hirst, *Gladstone as Financier and Economist*, London, Benn, 1931; P. Knaplund, *Gladstone and Britain's Imperial Policy*, London, Cass, 1927; P. Knaplund, *Gladstone's Foreign Policy*, London, Cass, 1935; J.L. Hammond, *Gladstone and the Irish Nation*, London, 1938.
31 Matthew, *Gladstone*, p. vii.

1 EARLY LIFE AND CAREER, 1809–1834

1 Gladstone, memorandum, 'Private: recollections of the last hours of my mother. Fasque. September 23. 1835', B[ritish] L[ibrary] Add[itional] Ms 44752 f.174; J. Brooke and M. Sorensen, (eds), *The Prime Ministers' Papers: W.E. Gladstone, II: Autobiographical Memoranda, 1832–1845*, London, HMSO, 1972, pp. 60–1.
2 Gladstone, 'Beginnings or incunabula, 8 July 1892', BL Add. Ms 44790 ff.5–25; J. Brooke and M.Sorensen (eds), *The Prime Ministers' Papers: W.E.Gladstone, 1: Autobiographica*, London, HMSO, 1971, p.13.
3 J. Morley, *The Life of William Ewart Gladstone*, 3 vols, London, Macmillan, 1904, I, p.13.
4 Morley, *ibid.*, p.14.
5 Morley, *ibid.*, p. 15.
6 Morley, *ibid.*, p. 44.
7 Morley, *ibid.*, p. 36.
8 Diary, 6, 8, 12 July 1830; M.R.D. Foot (ed.), *The Gladstone Diaries, I: 1825–1832*, Oxford, Clarendon, 1968, pp. 311–12.
9 Gladstone to John Gladstone, letter, May 1831, quoted in Morley, *Gladstone*, I, p. 71.

10 Quoted in Morley, *ibid.*, p. 57.
11 Gladstone to John Gladstone, letter, 27 October 1830, Morley, *Gladstone*, I, p.59.
12 Diary, 14, 15, 25 June, 10 May 1830, Foot (ed.), *The Gladstone Diaries, I*, pp. 308; 310; 303.
13 Diary, 7–12 November, 13 November 1830, Foot (ed.), *The Gladstone Diaries, I*, pp. 391–2; Morley, *Gladstone*, I, pp. 77–80 and R. Shannon, *Gladstone: I: 1809–1865*, London, Methuen, 1982, pp. 32–4, tell the whole story of Gladstone's final examinations in detail.
14 At a speech delivered in Oxford, 5 February 1890, quoted in Morley, *Gladstone*, I, p. 80.
15 Diary, 4 August 1830, Foot (ed.), *The Gladstone Diaries, I*, p. 316; the whole letter, dated the same day, is in Morley, *Gladstone*, I, pp. 635–40.
16 John Gladstone to William Gladstone, letter, 10 August 1830. Extract quoted in *ibid.*, I, pp. 640–1.
17 Diary, 29 December 1830, Foot (ed.), *The Gladstone Diaries, I*, p. 336.
18 Gladstone to John Gladstone, letter, 8 July 1832, quoted in Morley, *Gladstone*, I, p. 88.
19 Quoted in Shannon, *Gladstone*, I, p. 40.
20 Memorandum. Private. 'A visit to Newark, September–October 1832', dated 17 Oct–27 November 1832. BL Add. Ms 44777, ff.1–12; Brooke and Sorensen (eds), *Autobiographical Memoranda, II*, pp. 3–20.
21 Brooke and Sorensen (eds), *Autobiographical Memoranda, II*, p.10.
22 *ibid.*, p.11.
23 *ibid.*, p. 14.
24 Memorandum, 9 and 10 October 1832, BL Add. Ms 44777 ff. 15–22; Brooke and Sorensen (eds), *Autobiographical Memoranda, II*, pp. 24–31.
25 Memorandum, 28 November 1832, BL Add. Ms 44777 ff.13–14; Brooke and Sorensen (eds), *Autobiographical Memoranda, II*, pp. 21–3.
26 Diary, 31 May 1833, M.R.D. Foot (ed.), *The Gladstone Diaries, II: 1833–1839*, Oxford, Clarendon, 1968, p. 32.
27 Diary, 6 October 1833, Foot (ed.), *The Gladstone Diaries, II*, p. 63.
28 Diary, 29 December 1833, Foot (ed.), *The Gladstone Diaries, II*, p. 78.
29 Quoted in Shannon, *Gladstone*, I, p. 43.

2 THE PEELITE, 1834–1852

1 Memorandum, 26 December 1834, B[ritish] L[ibrary] Add[itional] Ms 44819 ff.117–18; J. Brooke and M. Sorensen (eds), *The Prime Ministers' Papers: W.E. Gladstone, II: Autobiographical Memoranda, 1832–1845*, London, HMSO, 1972, pp. 39–40.
2 Quoted in N. Gash (ed.), *The Age of Peel*, London, Arnold, 1968, pp. 76–7.

3 Memorandum, 7 February 1835, BL Add. Ms 44819 ff. 9–11; Brooke and Sorensen (eds) *Autobiographical Memoranda, II*, pp. 41–3. Gladstone had discussed these events in a letter to his father on 26 January, quoted in J. Morley, *The Life of William Ewart Gladstone*, 3 vols, London, Macmillan, 1904, I, pp. 123–4.
4 Gladstone to John Gladstone, quoted in Morley, *Gladstone*, I, pp. 126–7.
5 Memorandum, 11 September 1897, quoted in Morley, *Gladstone*, I, p. 170.
6 The whole letter (and Catherine's reply) is printed in P. Magnus, *Gladstone: a Biography*, London, John Murray, 1954, pp. 38–40.
7 T.L. Crosby, *The Two Mr. Gladstones*, New Haven and London, Yale University Press, 1997, p. 33.
8 Quoted in R. Shannon, *Gladstone, I: 1809–1865*, London, Methuen, 1982, p. 107.
9 Memorandum, 16 September 1841, BL Add. Ms 44819 f. 73; Brooke and Sorensen (eds), *Autobiographical Memoranda, II*, pp. 162–3.
10 See Gladstone to Sir Thomas Fremantle, letter, 8 October 1841, and letter to the editor of the *Morning Herald* [8 October 1841], BL Add. Ms 44527 f. 37; Brooke and Sorensen (eds), *Autobiographical Memoranda, II*, pp. 165–6.
11 Memorandum, 5 February 1842, BL Add. Ms 44819 ff. 77–9; Brooke and Sorensen (eds), *Autobiographical Memoranda, II*, pp. 169–72.
12 Memorandum [11 April 1842], BL Add. Ms 44819 f. 82; Brooke and Sorensen (eds), *Autobiographical Memoranda, II*, pp. 175–6.
13 Peel to Gladstone, letter, 13 May 1843, BL Add. Ms 44275 ff. 140–1; Brooke and Sorensen (eds), *Autobiographical Memoranda, II*, pp. 196–7.
14 Memorandum, 13 May 1843, BL Add. Ms 44819 ff. 91–4; Brooke and Sorensen (eds), *Autobiographical Memoranda, II*, pp. 194–6.
15 Memorandum, 3 June [1843], BL Add. Ms 44819 ff. 98–9; Brooke and Sorensen (eds), *Autobiographical Memoranda, II*, pp. 203–4.
16 Memorandum, 11–13 February 1844, BL Add. Ms 44777 ff. 119–26; Brooke and Sorensen (eds), *Autobiographical Memoranda, II*, pp. 230–3.
17 Memorandum, 1 June 1844, BL Add. Ms 44777 ff. 186–7; Brooke and Sorensen (eds), *Autobiographical Memoranda, II*, p. 260.
18 Diary, 10 July 1845, M.R.D. Foot and H.C.G. Matthew (eds), *Gladstone Diaries, III, 1840–1847*, Oxford, Clarendon, 1974, p. 467.
19 Shannon, *Gladstone*, I, p. 181.
20 Memorandum, 6 December 1845, BL Add. Ms 44777 ff. 233–6; J. Brooke and M. Sorensen (eds), *The Prime Ministers' Papers: W.E. Gladstone, III: Autobiographical Memoranda, 1845–1866*, London, HMSO, 1978, pp. 11–13.
21 Diary, 22 December 1845, Foot and Matthew (eds), *Diaries, III*, pp. 506–7.
22 Memorandum, 9–10 July 1846, BL Add. Ms 44777 ff. 245–58; Brooke and Sorensen (eds), *Autobiographical Memoranda, III*, pp. 18–26.
23 Memorandum, 'Conversation with Lord Aberdeen ...', 19 October 1849, BL

Add. Ms 44777 ff. 298–300; Brooke and Sorensen (eds), *Autobiographical Memoranda, III*, pp. 46–7.

24 Memorandum, 'Conversations with Neapolitan political prisoners', 13 February 1851, BL Add. Ms 44739 ff. 1–4; Brooke and Sorensen (eds), *Autobiographical Memoranda, III*, pp. 66–70.

25 Memoranda, 'The Peelites and Party alignments', 25–6 March 1852, BL Add. Ms 44778 ff. 25–32; Brooke and Sorensen (eds), *Autobiographical Memoranda, III*, pp. 116–19.

3 THE RISE TO POWER, 1853–1868

1 Memorandum, 9 April 1853, B[ritish] L[ibrary] Add[itional] Ms 44741 f. 80; J. Brooke and M. Sorensen (eds), *The Prime Ministers' Papers: W.E. Gladstone, III: Autobiographical Memoranda, 1845–1866*, London, HMSO, 1978, pp. 131–2.

2 Memoranda, 11, 12 April 1853, BL Add. Ms 44778 ff. 84–97; ff. 98–105; Brooke and Sorensen (eds), *Autobiographical Memoranda, III*, pp. 132, 136–8.

3 Memorandum, 15 April 1853, BL Add. Ms 44778 ff. 112–7; Brooke and Sorensen (eds), *Autobiographical Memoranda, III*, pp. 141–2.

4 Diary, 18 April 1853, M.R.D. Foot and H.C.G. Matthew (eds), *The Gladstone Diaries, III: 1840–1847*, Oxford, Clarendon, 1974, p. 519.

5 Greville diary, 21 April 1853, H. Reeve (ed.), *The Greville Memoirs*, new edn, London, Longmans, 1888, VII, p. 59.

6 Memorandum, 'Conversation with Lord Aberdeen; the Reform Bill; the approaching war with Russia', 22 February 1854, BL Add. Ms 44778 ff. 167–74; Brooke and Sorensen (eds), *Autobiographical Memoranda, III*, pp. 147–9.

7 Memorandum, 9 March 1855, BL Add. Ms 44778 ff. 22–9; Brooke and Sorensen (eds), *Autobiographical Memoranda, III*, pp. 153–5.

8 Memorandum, 3 February [1855], BL Add. Ms 44745 ff. 97–106; Brooke and Sorensen (eds), *Autobiographical Memoranda, III*, pp. 161–3.

9 Memorandum, 'Peelite discussion on a juncture with Lord Palmerston. 5 February 1855', BL Add. Ms 44745, ff. 39–46; Brooke and Sorensen (eds), *Autobiographical Memoranda, III*, pp. 170–2.

10 'Conversations respecting Lord Palmerston's commission to form a ministry', 4 February 1855, BL Add. Ms 44745 ff. 108–19; Brooke and Sorensen (eds), *Autobiographical Memoranda, III*, 164–8.

11 Memorandum, 'Peelite discussion on a juncture with Lord Palmerston', 5 February 1855, BL Add. Ms 44745 ff. 39–46; Brooke and Sorensen (eds), *Autobiographical Memoranda, III*, pp. 170–2.

12 Memorandum, 28 February 1855, BL Add. Ms 44745 ff. 147–58; Brooke and Sorensen (eds), *Autobiographical Memoranda, III*, pp. 189–92.

13 Memorandum, February 1855, BL Add. Ms 44745 f. 159; Brooke and Sorensen (eds), *Autobiographical Memoranda, III*, p. 192.
14 Memorandum, 18 February 1855, BL Add. Ms 44745 ff. 71–8; Brooke and Sorensen (eds), *Autobiographical Memoranda, III*, pp. 177–9.
15 Gladstone to Aberdeen, letter, 13 October 1856, Aberdeen papers, BL Add. Ms 43071 ff. 321–2.
16 Stanley, journal, 4 June 1857, J.R. Vincent (ed.), *Disraeli, Derby and the Conservative Party*, Hassocks, Harvester, 1978, p. 151.
17 Gladstone to Derby, letter, 21 February 1858, quoted in J. Morley, *The Life of William Ewart Gladstone*, 3 vols, London, Macmillan, 1904, I, p. 57.
18 Gladstone to Derby, letter, 26 May 1858, quoted in Morley, *Gladstone*, I, p. 590.
19 *The Times*, 13 January 1859 in R. Shannon, *Gladstone, I: 1809–1865*, London, Methuen, 1982, p. 371.
20 Lucy Lyttelton, diary, quoted in R. Jenkins, *Gladstone*, London, Macmillan, 1995, p. 208; P. Guedalla (ed.), *Gladstone and Palmerston*, London, Gollancz, 1928, p. 55.
21 Memorandum, 1 September 1897, Brooke and Sorensen (eds), *The Prime Ministers' Papers: W.E. Gladstone, I: Autobiographica*, London, HMSO, 1970, p. 83.
22 Palmerston, diary, 5 June 1860, Broadlands papers, Southampton University, D20.
23 Memorandum, 26 May 1860, quoted in Morley, *Gladstone*, II, p. 32.
24 Phillimore, diary, 6 July 1860, quoted in Morley, *Gladstone*, II, pp. 35–6.
25 Diary, 30 May 1861, H.C.G. Matthew (ed.), *The Gladstone Diaries, VI: 1861–1868*, Oxford, Clarendon, 1978, p. 36.
26 Sir John Trelawney, diary, 8 July 1864, T.A. Jenkins (ed.), *The Parliamentary Diaries of Sir John Trelawney, 1858–1865*, London, Royal Historical Society, 1990, p. 133.

4 THE FIRST MINISTRY, 1868–1874

1 E. Ashley, in *National Review*, 1898, quoted in R. Shannon, *Gladstone: Heroic Minister, 1865–1898*, London, Allen Lane, 1999, p. 57.
2 Quoted in J. Morley, *The Life of William Ewart Gladstone*, 3 vols, London, Macmillan, 1904, II, p. 305.
3 Gladstone to Granville, letter, 17 July 1870, A. Ramm (ed.), *The Gladstone–Granville correspondence*, 2nd edn, Cambridge, Cambridge University Press, 1998, p. 112.
4 Gladstone to Coleridge (Solicitor General), 1870, quoted in Morley, *Gladstone*, II, pp. 313–14.
5 Memorandum, 25 December 1871, BL Add. Ms 44760 ff. 129–36; J. Brooke and M. Sorensen (eds), *The Prime Ministers' Papers: W.E. Gladstone, IV:*

Autobiographical Memoranda, 1868–1894, London, HMSO, 1981, pp. 22–5.

6 Speech, 21 December 1868, quoted in Morley, *Gladstone*, II, p. 368.

7 Gladstone to Bishop Moberley, letter, 1 July 1872; Gladstone to G.G. Glyn, letter, 3 July 1872, quoted in T.L. Crosby, *The Two Mr. Gladstones*, New Haven and London, Yale University Press, 1997, p. 137.

8 Quoted in E.J. Feutchwanger, *Gladstone*, 2nd edn, Basingstoke, Macmillan, 1989, p. 164.

9 Diary, 13, 24, 25, 26 December 1868, quoted in Morley, *Gladstone*, II, p. 259.

10 Diary, 13, 14, 15, 19, 20, 21, 23, 24 January, 4 February, 1869, quoted in Morley, *Gladstone*, II, p. 260.

11 Gladstone to Queen Victoria, letter, 13 February 1869, quoted in Morley, *Gladstone*, II, pp. 261–2.

12 Gladstone, memorandum, 14 August 1869, BL Add. Ms 44758 ff. 1–14; Brooke and Sorensen (eds), *Autobiographical Memoranda, IV*, pp. 6–16.

13 Diary, 20–25 July 1869, quoted in Morley, *Gladstone*, II, p. 279.

14 Speech in Wigan, 23 October 1868, quoted in *The Times*, 24 October 1868.

15 Gladstone to Granville, letters, 24 May, 8 September 1869, Ramm (ed.), *Gladstone–Granville*, pp. 22, 53.

16 Gladstone to Fortescue, letter, 15 September 1869, quoted in H.C.G. Matthew (ed.), *The Gladstone Diaries, VII: January 1869–June 1871*, Oxford, Clarendon, 1982, p. 129.

17 Granville to Gladstone, letter, private, 25 September 1869, Ramm (ed.), *Gladstone–Granville*, p. 59; diary, 3 November 1869, Matthew (ed.), *Diaries, VII*, p. 160.

18 Diary, 25 January 1870, Matthew (ed.), *Diaries, VII*, pp. 227–8.

19 Gladstone to Manning, letter [February 1870], quoted in Morley, *Gladstone*, II, p. 294.

20 Gladstone to Fortescue, letter, 3 September 1870, quoted in P. Bell, 'Gladstone, the Fenian prisoners and the failure of his first Irish mission', in P. Francis (ed.), *The Gladstone Umbrella*, St Deiniols Library, Monad Press, 2001, p. 107.

21 Diary, 16, 17, 20, 31 January, 2 February 1873, quoted in Morley, *Gladstone*, II, p. 437.

22 Gladstone to Queen Victoria, letter, 8 March 1873, quoted in Morley, *Gladstone*, II, p. 441.

23 Gladstone, Memorandum, 16 March 1873, BL Add. Ms 44761 ff. 100–1; Brooke and Sorensen (eds), *Autobiographical Memoranda, IV*, p. 26.

24 Gladstone to Granville, letter, 7 August 1870, Ramm (ed.), *Gladstone–Granville*, p. 121.

25 Gladstone to Bright, letter, September 1870, quoted in Morley, *Gladstone*, II, p. 347; Gladstone to Granville, letter, 10 December 1870, Ramm (ed.), *Gladstone–Granville*, p. 183.

26 Gladstone to Granville, letter, 14 January 1872, Ramm (ed.), *Gladstone–Granville*, p. 299.
27 Diary, 16, 18 March, 5, 27 April, 13 June 1872, quoted in Morley, *Gladstone*, II, pp. 410–11.
28 Memorandum, 13 March 1873, BL Add. Ms 44761 ff. 102–8; Brooke and Sorensen (eds), *Autobiographical Memoranda, IV*, p. 32.
29 Gladstone to Granville, letter, 'Private and Confidential', 8 January 1874, Ramm (ed.), *Gladstone–Granville*, p. 440.
30 Diary, 8 January 1874, quoted in Morley, *Gladstone*, II, p. 485.
31 Gladstone to Willy Gladstone, letter, 24 January 1874, quoted in Morley, *Gladstone*, II, p. 487.
32 Diary, 28 January 1874, H.C.G. Matthew (ed.), *The Gladstone Diaries, VII: July 1871–December 1874*, Oxford, Clarendon, 1986, p. 450.
33 Diary, 3 February 1874, quoted in Morley, *Gladstone*, II, p. 490.
34 Gladstone, Memorandum, 17 February 1874, BL Add. Ms 44762 f. 28; Brooke and Sorensen (eds), *Autobiographical Memoranda, IV*, pp. 34–5.

5 RETIREMENT AND MIDLOTHIAN, 1874–1880

1 Quoted in R. Shannon, *Gladstone, Heroic Minister, 1865–1898*, London, Allen Lane, 1999, p.138.
2 Memorandum, 1897, quoted in J. Morley, *The Life of William Ewart Gladstone*, 3 vols, London, Macmillan, 1904, II, p. 498.
3 Memorandum, 12 February [1874], quoted in Morley, *Gladstone*, II, p. 498.
4 Gladstone to Granville, letter, 12 March 1874, A. Ramm (ed.), *The Gladstone–Granville Correspondence*, 2nd edn, Cambridge, Cambridge University Press, 1998, pp. 449–50.
5 Gladstone to Granville, letter, 7 August 1874, Ramm (ed.), *Gladstone–Granville*, pp. 456–7.
6 Gladstone to Granville, letter, 13 January 1875, Ramm (ed.), *Gladstone–Granville*, pp. 464–5.
7 Gladstone to Catherine Gladstone, letter, 14 January 1875, quoted in Morley, *Gladstone*, II, p. 504.
8 Viscount Gladstone, *After Thirty Years*, London, 1928, pp. 6–7; L. Masterman (ed.), *Mary Gladstone (Mrs. Drew): Letters and Diaries*, London, 1930, p. 4, both quoted in T.L. Crosby, *The Two Mr. Gladstones*, New Haven and London, Yale University Press, 1997, pp. 95–6.
9 Quoted in Shannon, *Heroic Minister*, p. 158.
10 Gladstone to Granville, letters, 28 November 1875, 19 January 1876, Ramm (ed.), *Gladstone–Granville*, pp. 473–4, 479.
11 Quoted in Morley, *Gladstone*, II, pp. 553–4.
12 Diary, 31 May 1877, H.C.G. Matthew (ed.), *The Gladstone Diaries, IX: 1875–80*, Oxford, Clarendon, 1986, p. 223.

13 Speech, 30 July 1878, quoted in Morley, *Gladstone*, II, pp. 577–8.
14 Gladstone to Mme Novikoff, letter, 1 November 1878, quoted in Morley, *Gladstone*, II, pp. 582–3.
15 Memorandum, 11 December 1879, B[ritish] L[ibrary] Add[itional] Ms 44763 ff. 164–5; J. Brooke and M. Sorensen (eds), *The Prime Ministers' Papers: W.E. Gladstone: Autobiographical Memoranda, IV, 1868–1894*, London, HMSO, 1981, pp. 36–7.
16 Speech, December 1879, quoted in Morley, *Gladstone*, II, p. 596.
17 Diary, 28 December 1879, Matthew (ed.), *Diaries, IX*, pp. 470–1.
18 'Memorandum on the religious profession of my sister Helen Jane Gladstone', 8 February 1880, BL Add. Ms 44764 ff. 1–10; Brooke and Sorensen (eds), *Autobiographical Memoranda, IV*, pp. 37–44.
19 Speech, 22 March 1880, quoted in Morley, *Gladstone*, II, p. 610.
20 Diary, 5 April 1880, Matthew (ed.), *Diaries, IX*, p. 498.
21 Memorandum, 22 April 1880, BL Add. Ms 44764 ff. 43–7; Brooke and Sorensen (eds), *Autobiographical Memoranda, IV*, pp. 48–50.
22 Memorandum, 24 April 1880, BL Add. Ms 44764 ff. 50–5; Brooke and Sorensen (eds), *Autobiographical Memoranda, IV*, pp. 52–4.

6 THE SECOND AND THIRD MINISTRIES, 1880–1886

1 Memorandum, 23–25 April 1886, B[ritish] L[ibrary] Add[itional] Ms 44764 ff. 48–9; J. Brooke and M. Sorensen (eds), *The Prime Ministers' Papers: W.E. Gladstone, IV: Autobiographical Memoranda, 1868–1894*, London, HMSO, 1981, pp. 50–1.
2 Memorandum, quoted in R. Shannon, *Gladstone, II: Heroic Minister, 1865–1898*, London, Allen Lane, 1999, p. 251.
3 Letter quoted in Shannon, *Heroic Minister*, p. 251.
4 Memorandum, December 1883, BL Add. Ms 44767 ff. 131–33; Brooke and Sorensen (eds), *Autobiographical Memoranda, IV*, pp. 64–5.
5 Gladstone to Queen Victoria, letter, 29 July 1880, quoted in Morley, *Gladstone*, III, p. 24.
6 Speech, 25 July 1881, quoted in Morley, *Gladstone*, III, p. 42.
7 Granville to Hartington, letter, 8 July 1882, quoted in Shannon, *Heroic Minister*, p. 302.
8 Speech, 2 November 1882, quoted in Morley, *Gladstone*, III, p. 146.
9 Dilke, diary, 21 April 1882, quoted in Shannon, *Heroic Minister*, p. 331.
10 Quoted in Morley, *Gladstone*, III, p. 166.
11 Queen Victoria to Gladstone, telegram, 5 February 1885, P. Guedalla (ed.), *The Queen and Mr. Gladstone*, 2 vols, London, Hodder & Stoughton, 1933, II, p. 326.
12 Gladstone to Queen Victoria, 5 February 1885, quoted in Morley, *Gladstone*, III, pp. 167–8.

13 Speech, [1885], quoted in Morley, *Gladstone*, III, p. 184.
14 Gladstone, letter, 10 June 1890, quoted in Morley, *Gladstone*, III, p. 169.
15 C.S. Parnell, speeches, 21 September, 24 November 1879, quoted in D.G. Boyce, *Nineteenth-century Ireland: The Search for Stability*, Dublin, Gill and Macmillan, 1990, pp. 164, 165.
16 Memorandum, [25 September 1897], quoted in Shannon, *Heroic Minister*, p. 268.
17 Gladstone to Hartington, letter, 22 October 1883, quoted in H.C.G. Matthew, *Gladstone, 1809–1898*, Oxford, Oxford University Press, 1999, p. 426.
18 Gladstone to Earl Spencer, letter, 9 May 1885, quoted Matthew, *Gladstone*, p. 460.
19 Queen Victoria to Gladstone, letter, 13 June 1885; Gladstone to Queen Victoria, letter, 14 June 1885, both quoted in Morley, *Gladstone*, III, pp. 209–10.
20 Memorandum, 'Sketch' of a Home Rule Bill, 14 November 1885, quoted in Matthew, *Gladstone*, p. 463.
21 E.W. Hamilton, diary, 29 June [1886], BL Add. Ms 48642 f. 113, quoted in Brooke and Sorensen (eds), *Autobiographical Memoranda, IV*, p. 105.
22 Hamilton, diary, 9 April 1886, quoted in Shannon, *Heroic Minister*, p. 425.
23 Speech, 7–8 June 1886, quoted in Shannon, *Heroic Minister*, p. 439.

7 OPPOSITION, THE FOURTH MINISTRY AND RETIREMENT, 1886–1895

1 Letter, 28 June 1886, quoted in J. Morley, *The Life of William Ewart Gladstone*, 3 vols, London, Macmillan, 1904, III, p. 343.
2 Speech, 28 June 1886, quoted in H.C.G. Matthew, *Gladstone, 1809–1898*, Oxford, Oxford University Press, 1999, pp. 348–9.
3 Diary, 8 July 1886, H.C.G. Matthew (ed.), *The Gladstone Diaries, with Cabinet Minutes and Prime Ministerial Correspondence, XI: July 1883–December 1886*, Oxford, Clarendon, 1990, p. 585.
4 Diary, 7 June 1887, H.C.G. Matthew (ed.), *Gladstone Diaries, XII: 1887–1891*, Oxford, Clarendon, 1994, p. 40.
5 Speech, June 1888, quoted in T.L. Crosby, *The Two Mr. Gladstones*, New Haven and London, Yale University Press, 1997, p. 212.
6 Speech, 7 November 1888, quoted in Crosby, *Two Mr. Gladstones*, p. 212.
7 Memorandum, 21 November 1890, Matthew (ed.), *Diaries, XII*, p. 338.
8 The article, and Gladstone's views, are fully discussed in Matthew, *Gladstone*, pp. 569–71.
9 Gladstone to Mrs Laura Thistlethwayte, letter, 6 April 1891, Matthew (ed.), *Diaries, XII*, pp. 526–7.
10 Diary, 15 July 1892, Matthew (ed.), *Gladstone Diaries, XIII: 1892–1896*, Oxford, Clarendon, 1994, p. 43.

11 Gladstone to Queen Victoria, letter, [2] March 1894, quoted in Morley, *Gladstone*, III, p. 515.
12 Matthew, *Gladstone*, p. 588.
13 Comments, dated 11 May 1893, quoted in Morley, *Gladstone*, III, p. 499.
14 Rosebery to Gladstone, letter, 29 September 1892, quoted in Matthew, *Gladstone*, p. 596.
15 Gladstone to Spencer, letter, 26 September 1892, quoted in R. Shannon, *Gladstone: Heroic Minister, 1865–1898*, London, Allen Lane, 1999, p. 529.
16 Speech, 17 November 1893, quoted Shannon, *Heroic Minister*, p. 551.
17 Diary, 19 December 1893, Matthew (ed.), *Diaries, XIII*, p. 342.
18 Undated remarks quoted in Morley, *Gladstone*, III, pp. 507–8.
19 Memorandum, 20 January 1894, in Matthew, *Gladstone*, pp. 603–4.
20 Diary, 17 February 1894, Matthew (ed.), *Diaries, XIII*, p. 378.
21 Memorandum, 28 February 1894, BL Add. Ms 44776,ff. 57–8; J. Brooke and M. Sorensen (eds), *The Prime Ministers' Papers: W.E. Gladstone, IV: Autobiographical Memoranda, 1868–1894*, London, HMSO, 1981, pp. 93–4.
22 Memorandum, 10 March 1894, BL Add. Ms 44776 ff. 61–2; Brooke and Sorensen (eds), *Autobiographical Memoranda, IV*, pp. 96–7.
23 Shannon, *Heroic Minister*, p. 562.
24 Mrs. E.W. Benson, journal, 10 October 1896, quoted in Shannon, *Heroic Minister*, p. 583.
25 A story told in P. Magnus, *Gladstone: A Biography*, London, John Murray, 1954, p. 429.
26 The 'Declaration', dated 7 December 1896, is printed in Matthew, *Diaries, XIII*, p. 429. Matthew discusses the question in detail in *Gladstone*, pp. 629–30.
27 Diary, 29 December 1896, Matthew (ed.), *Diaries, XIII*, p. 428.
28 A.J. Balfour, speech, 20 May 1898, quoted in Morley, *Gladstone*, III, p. 530.

SELECT BIBLIOGRAPHY

There have been a considerable number of books and articles about Gladstone and this is a very select introduction to them.

UNPUBLISHED PAPERS

Gladstone papers

Gladstone met or corresponded with some 22,000 people during his long life. He accordingly left a huge collection of manuscripts relating to his life, some of which have been printed. The Gladstone papers at the British Library and St Deiniols Library have been published in microfilm by Research Publication International, Reading.

British Library

Additional Manuscripts 44086–44835
750 volumes dating from 1818 to 1898 of general and political correspondence and papers, autobiographical and literary papers, and notes for speeches.
Additional Manuscripts 56444–56453
Papers removed from Hawarden to help Morley write Gladstone's Life.
MS Loan 78
Twenty-eight packets of correspondence with the Queen, Prince Consort and other members of the royal family, dating from 1845 to 1897.

Lambeth Palace Library

Ms 1416–1455; 2758–2774
Journals and related papers, 1825–1936.

St Deiniols Library, Hawarden

Some 50,000 items, dating from 1806 to 1898 of personal, family, business and miscellaneous papers on a wide variety of subjects, including correspondence between Gladstone and his wife, papers on the Newark elections, and on the future of the archive.

PRINTED PAPERS

Included are some of the more important published manuscript collections.

Bahlman, D.R., ed., *The Diary of Sir Edward Walter Hamilton, 1880–1885*, 2 vols, Oxford, Clarendon, 1972, *1885–1906*, Hull, Hull University Press, 1997.
A detailed journal kept by Hamilton, who was a secretary in Gladstone's last three ministries and a personal friend of the Earl of Rosebery. Especially useful on the Egyptian crisis of 1882 and the Home Rule crisis of 1885–6.

Bassett, A.T., ed., *Gladstone to his Wife*, London, Methuen, 1936.
A collection of private letters from Gladstone, taken from the family papers held at Hawarden, covering the whole of their married life.

Benson A.C. and Buckle, G.E., eds, *The Letters of Queen Victoria*, 9 vols, London, John Murray, 1907–32.
Includes some of the correspondence between Gladstone and the Queen, as well as that of other politicians. The documents themselves are edited and the full extent Gladstone's alienation from the Queen is not brought out.

Brooke, J. and Sorensen, M., eds, *The Prime Ministers' Papers Series: W.E. Gladstone*, 4 vols, London, HMSO, 1971–84.

Volume I	*Autobiographia*
Volume II	*Autobiographical Memoranda, 1832–1845*
Volume III	*Autobiographical Memoranda, 1845–1866*
Volume IV	*Autobiographical Memoranda, 1868–1894*

A scholarly edition of papers from Gladstone's papers and the Royal Archives, prepared and edited by the Royal Commission on Historical Manuscripts. These volumes offer very useful insights into Gladstone's thoughts at critical moments in his life and career.

Gladstone, W.E., *Gleanings of Past Years*, 7 vols, London, John Murray, 1879.
A collection by Gladstone himself of what he considered to be the most important of his earlier reviews, pamphlets and articles.

Gladstone, W.E., *Midlothian Speeches, 1879*, ed. M.R.D. Foot, Leicester, Leicester University Press, 1971.
A collection of speeches delivered by Gladstone during his first Midlothian campaign, edited by a modern authority.

Gladstone, W.E., *Later Gleanings*, London, John Murray, 1897.
A further selection by the Grand Old Man of some of his later works, continuation of his earlier book.

Guedalla, P., ed., *The Palmerston papers: Gladstone and Palmerston, being the correspondence of Lord Palmerston and Mr. Gladstone, 1851–1865*, London, Victor Gollancz, 1928.
Letters from these two politicians, taken from the Gladstone papers at the British Library and the Broadlands papers.

Guedalla, P., ed., *The Queen and Mr. Gladstone*, 2 vols, London, Hodder & Stoughton, 1933.
A collection of the correspondence between the Queen and Gladstone, drawn from both the Gladstone papers and the Royal Archives, supplementing the Benson and Buckle edition. Scholarly apparatus is not included in this or in the Palmerston collection, but both remain very useful documentary sources.

Matthew, H.C.G. and Foot, M.R.D., eds, *The Gladstone Diaries: With Cabinet Papers and Prime Ministerial Correspondence*, 14 volumes, Oxford, Clarendon, 1969–94.

Volumes 1–2	ed. Foot, M.R.D.
Volumes 3–4	ed. Foot, M.R.D. and Matthew, H.C.G.
Volumes 5–14	ed. Matthew, H.C.G.

A major publication project, reproducing in full Gladstone's diary and including in the later volumes, memoranda and other papers at critical moments. Full scholarly apparatus is provided. The diaries themselves, however, sometimes offer only limited insights into Gladstone's thoughts.

Ramm, A., *The Political Correspondence of Mr. Gladstone and Lord Granville, 1868–1876* 2nd edn, Cambridge, Cambridge University Press, 1998, *1876–1886*, 2 vols, Oxford, Clarendon, 1962.
A scholarly edition of most of Gladstone's and Granville's correspondence, including full editorial apparatus. A very valuable collection of material dealing with all aspects of government policy.

GENERAL BIOGRAPHIES

Biagini, E.F., *Gladstone*, Basingstoke, Macmillan, 2000.
A concise biography, stressing Gladstone's contribution to the contemporary British political agenda, and stressing the influences, both domestic and foreign, on his policies.

Crosby, T.L., *The Two Mr. Gladstones: A Study in Psychology and History*, New Haven and London, Yale University Press, 1997.
A survey of Gladstone's life and career, bringing out his psychological responses to political stress and his need for control over all aspects of his life, explaining how he achieved this.

Feuchtwanger, E.J., *Gladstone*, 2nd edn, Basingstoke, Macmillan, 1989.
An updated version of a biography first published in 1975, with an introductory essay reflecting more on his private life. A chronological account of Gladstone's life.

Jenkins, R., *Gladstone*, Basingstoke, Macmillan, 1995.
A detailed and lively biography by a Social Democrat politician, based on printed primary sources. A sympathetic portrait of Gladstone, portraying him as an ancestor of modern social democracy.

Kelly, R. and Cantrell, J., eds, *Modern British Statesmen, 1867–1945*, Manchester, Manchester University Press, 1997.
Includes an essay by Michael Lynch surveying Gladstone's career, placing him in context and stressing some of his similarities with his great opponent, Disraeli. Lynch also contributes an essay on Disraeli and other figures dealt with include Parnell, Salisbury, Joseph Chamberlain and A.J. Balfour.

Machin, H., 'Profile: Gladstone', *Historian* 48 (1995): 16–19.
A brief, introductory survey of Gladstone's life and career.

Matthew, H.C.G., *Gladstone, 1809–1898*, Oxford, Oxford University Press, 1999.
A one-volume combined edition of two volumes, first published in 1986 and 1995, by the main editor of Gladstone's diaries. Detailed and analytical and studying his career from a basically narrative perspective, although chapters are often arranged thematically to deal with different aspects of it.

Matthew, H.C.G., 'Gladstone's death and funeral', *Historian* 57 (1998): 20–4.
A brief look at the end of Gladstone's life, by a leading authority.

Morley, J., *The Life of William Ewart Gladstone*, 3 vols, London, Macmillan, 1904.
A very detailed biography of Gladstone, concentrating almost solely on his political life. Prepared by a leading Liberal admirer of Gladstone at the request of his family, this offers the starting point for all other works on the 'Grand Old Man' and is designed to show him as the model for Liberals of later generations.

Ramm, A., *William Ewart Gladstone*, Cardiff, GPC Books, 1989.
A concise 'Political Portrait', but dealing nevertheless with Gladstone's intellectual and religious development, as well as his political career.

Shannon, R., *Gladstone*, Volume 1 *1809–1865*, London, Hamish Hamilton, 1982, Volume 2 *Heroic Minister, 1865–1898*, London, Allen Lane, 1999.
Two extremely detailed volumes, chronological in arrangement and largely based on Gladstone's diaries. Most information on Gladstone's life is to be found in these volumes, which extend to over 1,800 pages of text.

Stansky, P., *Gladstone: A Progress in Politics*, New York and London, Norton, 1979.
Deals with the evolution of Gladstone's ideas by looking at fourteen of his speeches on different subjects, such as foreign policy, finance, Irish Home Rule and religion.

COLLECTIONS OF ESSAYS

Bebbington, D. and Swift, R., eds, *Gladstone, Centenary Essay*, Liverpool, Liverpool University Press, 2000.
A collection of longer essays, based on lectures from the 1998 Gladstone Centenary Conference. It includes a study of Gladstone's first administration, his relations with Peel and his work on Homer.

Francis, P., ed., *The Gladstone Umbrella: Papers Delivered at the Gladstone Centenary Conference, 1998*, Hawarden, Monad Press, 2001.
Subjects dealt with in this collection of shorter papers from the 1998 conference include Gladstone's views of France and aspects of his Irish and Ugandan policies, his relations with Lord Palmerston, and one on Catherine Gladstone and Victorian philanthropy.

Jagger, P.J., ed., *Gladstone*, London, Hambledon, 1998.
Aspects of Gladstone's life and career covered in these thirteen essays on a wide variety of subjects, including his relations with Disraeli, Garibaldi and John Ruskin and the working classes, as well as his policy towards Ireland and the railways.

Jagger, P.J., ed., *Gladstone, Politics and Religion: A Collection of Founder's Day Lectures at St Deiniol's Library, Hawarden, 1967–83*, London, Macmillan, 1985.
A collection of essays dealing with aspects of Gladstone's life and career. This includes material on Gladstone's spiritual relations, his relationships with Palmerston and Morley, and the Midlothian campaign.

Kinzer, B., ed., *The Gladstonian Turn of Mind*, Toronto, Toronto University Press, 1985.
A further collection of essays covering different aspects of Gladstone's life and career. This volume includes a study of his relationship with his daughters and his sisters Anne and Helen, the House of Lords and his views on Europe.

GLADSTONE'S FAMILY

Checkland, S.G., *The Gladstones: A Family Biography, 1764–1851*, Cambridge, Cambridge University Press, 1971.

A scholarly appraisal, dealing mostly with William's father, John, and including material on their relationship, as well as on William's education and career until his father's death.

Marlow, J., *Mr. and Mrs. Gladstone: An Intimate Biography*, London, Weidenfeld and Nicolson, 1977.
A study of a private side of Gladstone's life, his relationship with his wife and family.

GLADSTONE'S RELIGION

Butler, P.J., *Gladstone, Church, State and Tractarianism: A Study of his Religious Ideas and Attitudes, 1809–1859*, Oxford, Oxford University Press, 1982.
A monograph based on a doctoral thesis, which argues that the best way to see Gladstone's political development lies in his synthesis of two rival impulses, Liberalism and Catholicism.

Jagger, P.J., *Gladstone: The Making of a Christian Politician: The Personal and Religious Life of William Ewart Gladstone, 1809–1832*, Addison Park, Pa., Pickwick Publications, 1991.
A detailed study of Gladstone's religious development at a crucial time in his personal life.

ASPECTS OF GLADSTONE'S CAREER

Blake, R., *Gladstone, Disraeli and Queen Victoria*, Oxford, Clarendon, 1993.
A brief study of Gladstone's relations with two other leading figures of the day, by a leading authority on Disraeli.

Gardiner, J.P., 'Gladstone, gossip and the post-war generation', *Historical Research* 74 (2001): 409–24.
A survey of Gladstone's reputation at a time, between 1918 and 1939, when the Victorians were subject to denigration. It concludes that Gladstone's reputation was not diminished, despite the gossip-mongering to which he was subject.

Goodlad, G.D., 'The Liberal Party and Gladstone's Land Purchase Bill of 1886', *Historical Journal* 32 (1989): 627–41.
Stresses the importance of this Bill, despite its failure on its first reading, and its contribution to arousing opposition to Gladstone and to the split in the Liberal Party.

Gunter, C. and Maloney, J., 'Did Gladstone make a difference? Rhetoric and reality in mid-Victorian finance', *Accounting, Business, and Financial History* 9 (1999): 325–47.

Assesses Gladstone's fiscal policy and uses statistical calculation to show that he did not make a significant difference to trends in public spending, taxation, the balance of the budget and size of national debt.

Harrison, R., *Gladstone's Imperialism in Egypt*, Westport, Ct., Greenwood, 1995.
A detailed survey of the Gladstone governments' relations with Egypt, the crisis of 1882, the decision to occupy the country and its effects.

Jenkins, T.A., *Gladstone, Whiggery and the Liberal Party, 1874–1886*, Oxford, Clarendon, 1988.
A monograph detailing Gladstone's relationship with the Whig and radical elements in the Liberal Party and the strains in his second and third ministries and over Ireland which led to the party split.

Meisel, J.S., 'The importance of being serious: the unexplored connection between Gladstone and humour', *History* 84 (1999): 278–300.
A study of Gladstone's 'real or perceived' humourlessness and how it functioned in his public life, based on printed sources. This concludes Gladstone's 'seriousness' helped him withstand the attacks of his enemies and advance his position.

Parry, J.P. *Democracy and Religion: Gladstone and the Liberal Party, 1867–1875*, Cambridge, Cambridge University Press, 1986.
A long study, stressing the connection between ecclesiastical and political history. Deals with the aspirations of different members of the Liberal Party and the impact of the policies of Gladstone's first ministry on them.

Saab, A.P., *Reluctant Icon: Gladstone, Bulgaria and the Working Classes, 1856–1878*, London, Harvard University Press, 1989.
A detailed investigation of Gladstone's Near Eastern policy, exploring the background to and impact of his *Bulgarian Horrors* pamphlet.

Winstanley, M.J., *Gladstone and the Liberal Party*, London, Routledge, 1990.
A Lancaster Pamphlet offering an introduction to the history of the nineteenth-century Liberal Party and Gladstone's place in it.

POLITICAL SURVEYS

Adelman, P., *Gladstone, Disraeli and Later Victorian Politics*, Harlow, Longman, 1997.
A concise review of politics in the later part of Gladstone's career.

Bentley, M., *Politics Without Democracy, 1815–1914: Perception and Preoccupation in British Government*, London, Fontana, 1984.

A lively survey of 'high politics' over these years, in which Gladstone plays more than a 'walk on' part.

Biagini, E.F., *Liberalism, Retrenchment and Reform: Popular Politics in the Age of Gladstone, 1860–1880*, Cambridge, Cambridge University Press, 1992.
A detailed study of popular liberalism in the twenty years which witnessed Gladstone's rise to pre-eminence.

Boyce, D.G., *Nineteenth-century Ireland: The Search for Stability*, Dublin, Gill and Macmillan, 1990.
A general survey of Irish history, placing Gladstone's policy into context, from an Irish perspective.

Jenkins, T.A., *Parliament, Party and Politics in Victorian Britain*, Manchester, Manchester University Press, 1996.
A study focusing on the period from the mid-1850s to Palmerston's death in 1865 which centres on Palmerston's ministries and Gladstone's relationship with them.

Jenkins, T.A., *The Liberal Ascendancy, 1830–1886*, Basingstoke, Macmillan, 1994.
A survey of the growth of Liberal power and the strains put upon it, climaxing in the split over Irish Home Rule. It assesses Gladstone's contribution in a more general context, as well as those of older leading Liberal figures such as Russell and Palmerston.

Parry, J.P., *The rise and fall of Liberal Government in Victorian Britain*, New Haven and London, Yale University Press, 1993.
A study reviewing the evolution of the Liberal Party and Gladstone's role in it.

Searle, G.R., *The Liberal Party: Triumph and Disintegration, 1886–1929*, Basingstoke, Macmillan, 1992.
A survey of the later years of the Victorian Liberal Party, from the split in 1886 and including Gladstone's last ministry, which assesses their roles in its eventual collapse.

Steele, E.D., *Palmerston and Liberalism, 1855–1865*, Cambridge, Cambridge University Press, 1991.
A detailed study of Palmerston's later political career, but very helpful to an understanding of his relationship with Gladstone and to the development of the Liberal Party.

Index